MARCHING
THROUGH GEORGIA

MARCHING THROUGH GEORGIA

WILLIAM T. SHERMAN'S
PERSONAL NARRATIVE OF
HIS MARCH THROUGH GEORGIA

EDITED BY MILLS LANE

A BEEHIVE PRESS BOOK
ARNO PRESS · New York · 1978

Reprint edition 1978 by Arno Press Inc.

Originally published as "War Is Hell!"
Copyright © 1974 by The Beehive Press, Savannah,
   Georgia.

This volume is based on the second volume of
Memoirs of General William T. Sherman by Himself,
published by D. Appleton and Company,
New York, in 1875.

Library of Congress Cataloging in Publication Data

Sherman, William Tecumseh, 1820-1891.
   Marching through Georgia.

   Reprint of the ed. published by Beehive Press,
Savannah, under title: War is hell.
   Based on the 2nd vol. of Memoirs of General
William T. Sherman by himself.
   Includes bibliographical references.
   1. Sherman's March to the Sea.   2.   Sherman,
William Tecumseh, 1820-1891.   3.   United States—
History—Civil War, 1861-1865—Personal narratives.
4.   Generals—United States—Biography.   I.   Lane,
Mills, II.   Title.
E476.69.S57   1978   973.7'37   78-8731
ISBN 0-405-11411-7

Manufactured in the United States of America.

CONTENTS

ILLUSTRATIONS

INTRODUCTION

By the end of 1864, the Civil War was rushing to a conclusion and the Confederacy was disintegrating. During the autumn, General William T. Sherman with sixty-two thousand men, thirty-five thousand horses, mules and cattle, twenty-five hundred wagons, six hundred ambulances and a horde of stragglers marched across the heart of Georgia. His purpose was to destroy the enemy's economic system and to demoralize the civilians. Already Union forces held the Mississippi River and territory north of Vicksburg and St. Louis in the West and everything north of the Tennessee River and most of Tennessee and Virginia in the East. All the Confederate seaports had been blockaded and outside Atlanta Sherman heard the first news that Farragut had entered Mobile Bay. While Sherman was penetrating Georgia, Grant was advancing on Richmond. In the North, Sherman's triumphant procession through Georgia in the bosom of the South strengthened the war party at a critical time and insured President Lincoln's reelection in November. To the southerners, the march brought an apocalyptic revelation that the war had been lost. For Georgians, the march was the most famous and terrible event of their state's history, the last great act of war, the first act of Reconstruction and the symbol of more than a decade of human distress.

But Sherman's "march from Atlanta to the sea" was really only one part of a more important expedition which began at Chattanooga, Tennessee, in May, 1864, and which ended near Durham, North Carolina, in April, 1865. Indeed, Sherman's army faced sustained resistance only in the mountains of north Georgia before it reached Atlanta, and Sherman's men were able to march beyond Atlanta to the coast without opposition. Despite the celebrated destruction of Georgia, the Federal force inflicted greater damage, with far greater personal vengeance, in South Carolina, the hated birthplace of secession. In fact, the damage done by Sherman's army extended only over a small part of Georgia, and most of the state remained untouched by actual war. The march was most important as a political triumph, conceived by a military man who distrusted politicians all his life, and as a glimpse of ruthless twentieth-century total war, directed by a man who was himself fatalistic, insecure and plagued with failure. Though the effects of Sherman's march were computed in terms of miles and tons of physical destruction, the greatest effect of the march was upon the people of the South and Georgia in particular. Though the march caused Georgians to remember the years of Civil War and Reconstruction as a depressing, destructive time, Sherman's march was really the pivot point for an era which brought the industrial revolution to Georgia and which gave political power to the middle class for the first time, two exhilarating, constructive social developments.

In 1860 no Republican electors appeared on the ballot in Georgia and no votes were cast for the Republican candidate. But even before the news reached the South, people were sure that Abraham Lincoln had been elected President. Political frustrations and social fears had been fermenting for a generation. Now, in November the state legislature appropriated one million dollars for military purposes, authorized a small army of ten thousand troops and called a convention of the people's representatives to decide what response Georgia should make to the unwanted but inevitable election results. By the time the convention assembled at Milledgeville in January, 1861, four states—South Carolina, Mississippi, Florida and Alabama—had already seceded. The Governor, two of the three Justices of the state Supreme Court, the two Senators and six Congressmen from the state and four of the five living former Governors favored immediate secession. On January 19, 1861, Georgia became the fifth state to secede from the United States. In February, the state sent delegates to form a provisional regional government at Montgomery in Alabama. Alexander Stephens of Georgia became Vice President of the new Confederacy, and Robert Toombs of Georgia, who had expected to become its President, was made Secretary of State.

In January, 1861, a cheerful band of Georgia volunteers sailed down the Savannah River to

capture Fort Pulaski, on Cockspur Island at the mouth of the river, before the Federal government could fortify it, and their happy, holiday mood demonstrated sadly that they did not foresee the bitter, bloody war ahead. The people of Georgia embraced secession hastily and without preparation, because they did not expect any war. Georgia simply lacked the population, capital and experience of manufacturing industry necessary to wage a war. Three generations of Georgians had invested almost everything in land, slaves and cotton. Georgia was the largest state east of the Mississippi, but its population was small and sparsely settled. Agriculture meant a static economic tradition. The undeveloped industrial economy, the region's reputation for slavery and the few job opportunities all discouraged the migration of skilled artisans and workers to Georgia, another element of a cycle of limited growth and opportunity. The cheapness of labor made inventiveness and machinery unnecessary. In 1860 there were only four cities in Georgia with more than 5,000 people, and only 4.9 per cent of the people of Georgia lived in them. Only 11,575 of the population, or 1.09 per cent of Georgians, worked at manufacturing jobs. In 1860, only $10,890,975 was invested in industry, while $202,694,855 was invested in slaves.[1]

During the 1820's the state legislature had laid out inland towns at the headwaters of the major rivers, the most interior places where ships from the coast could navigate. The first steamers did not travel to Macon until 1829 and regular service did not commence until the early 1830's. These new cities, Columbus and Macon, with older Augusta, became centers for local cotton markets. Only incidentally they became manufacturing towns, putting to good use the water power and cotton supplies at hand. The major railroads in Georgia were chartered in the 1830's, their main routes completed in the 1840's and short routes added in the 1850's. But these railroads merely replaced the steamboats, serving the needs of agriculture and not mercantile commerce. The rapid economic expansion of Georgia during the 1850's was limited to grain milling, lumbering and cotton manufacturing. At the war's outbreak there was no heavy industry in Georgia, except foundries in Macon which made railroad supplies, so the state found herself engaged in a war without the means to wage it. Governor Brown appealed to the people to turn in their firearms for the state's defense. The difficulty of securing guns was so great that the Governor raised a battalion of troops armed only with wooden pikes. Because they were so poorly equipped, many of Georgia's first volunteers were not accepted by the Confederate government. At Savannah Josiah Tattnall took command of a "mosquito fleet" of four ships—an old paddle-wheeled passenger steamer and three remodelled tug boats—Georgia's entire "navy" in 1861 and a further reflection of the state's economic situation.

The self-imposed isolation of secession compelled Georgia to become more self-sufficient. All kinds of miscellaneous products which had been imported—furniture, coffins, matches, ink, paper, glass, medicines and farm machinery—now had to be produced within the state. The tremendous public spending of the war stimulated Georgia's economy. Mechanics and factory workers were exempt from the Confederate draft. The state government established a powder mill and gunshop at Augusta, a cannon factory at Rome, others at Athens, Milledgeville, Columbus and Macon. In 1861 the legislature offered ten thousand dollars to anyone who would build a cannon factory. Arsenals were set up in Atlanta, Savannah, Macon, Augusta and Columbus, and the state penitentiary at Milledgeville was converted into a rifle factory in 1862. Confederate quartermasters built garment shops at Augusta, Atlanta and Columbus. There was not only more economic development during the war but also a different quality of growth. Significantly, while no new cotton mills were opened in Georgia, eight new iron mining companies were chartered during 1861–63. True industrial products were made in Georgia for the first time. Factories which had made only limited railroad supplies before 1861 now produced other machinery and equipment. Atlanta's rolling mill, no longer just reworking railroad iron, began making heavy plate for gunboats. The Athens Foundry became a cannon factory. The static pattern of agrarian life close to the land was disrupted by the war, as people moved to the cities and turned to factory work. Georgia society became more specialized with professionals, producers and consumers.[2]

The war stimulated production of farm products across the Georgia countryside, and wartime restrictions on cotton planting prodded reluctant farmers to diversify their crops. From the mountains to the coast, Georgia became a vast harvest land of corn, wheat, sugar, lumber, rice and livestock. The well-filled corn, wheat and oat cribs which Sherman's army found proved Georgia's agricultural productivity, even while distant Virginia was suffering. Fenwick Hedley, who marched with Sherman, called Georgia "literally a land overflowing with milk and honey." Nineteen-year-old Jezze Dozer of Illinois wrote from Big Shanty in Georgia: "I went and got some apples and kooked them for supper. The wheat is getting nearly ripe. Corn knee high. Our teemsters are reeping the wheat and feeding it to their teems. The Citizens here think the yankees are harvesting their wheat too soon." Dolly Lunt Burge faced the bluecoat invasion at Covington:

"Like demons they rush in! To my smoke-house, my dairy, pantry, kitchen, and cellar, like famished wolves they come, breaking locks and whatever is in their way. The thousand pounds of meat in my smoke-house is gone in a twinkling, my flour, my meat, my lard, butter, eggs, pickles, wine are all gone. My eighteen fat turkies, my hens, chickens, and fowls, my young pigs are shot down in my yard." John Van Duser, a Union officer, recorded: "I have never seen a country better supplied than this—Turkeys Chickens Geese beef Cattle Sheep & swine in abundance. The story of starvation in the South is played out." From Savannah George Hanger wrote his family in Ohio: "Does every body talk of starving out the rebel army? If so, I think that if they had of been on this trip it would make converts of them. Of all the sweet potatoes and molasses that I ever saw, this state beats them all."[3]

The future site of Atlanta had been uninhabited Indian territory until 1821, but the economic impact of the war transformed the place into a boom town with the prospect of future greatness. During the early 1840's three converging railroads—the Western and Atlantic to Chattanooga and the Midwest, the Georgia Railroad to Augusta and South Carolina, the Macon and Western Railroad south toward the coast—came together at a village first called "Terminus." Robert Somers, who came to Atlanta in 1870, caught the spirit of the city's birth: "The various railroads which meet at this crowded point do not go to the town; the town is gathering in thick and hot haste about the railways." One local citizen boasted, "I guess the railways were here before the people came to Atlanta . . . the new city rising up around the place where it was convenient for the locomotives to be fed with wood and water." In 1847 Atlanta was still a shanty town of twenty-five hundred inhabitants, thirty stores, two hotels, surrounded by woods, the streets filled with stumps but alive with people and progress. There were no churches then and preaching was held, prophetically, in the railroad depot. Charles Olmsted remembered Atlanta in the 1850's as "a sorry looking place, always associated in my mind with rain and a super abundance of red-clay mud." Felix DeFontaine, war correspondent of the Charleston *Courier*, complained in March, 1862, that Atlanta's mud was "six inches deep and rising." Pedestrians were cautioned to cross streets only on stepping-stones which rose above a sea of mud. In 1861, Atlanta's promoters made a determined, though unsuccessful, effort to make their city the capital of the new Confederacy. There were so many strangers coming to Atlanta during the busy war years that street signs had to be put up for the first time. Atlanta's population increased from 11,468 in 1860 to more than

16,000 before the war's end. In a new era of interstate commerce inaugurated by the Civil War, Atlanta would become a great regional distribution center. Significantly, railroad mileage in Georgia increased thirty per cent during the decade of the Civil War, despite considerable destruction at the close of the struggle. Sherman's burning of Atlanta in 1864 was the most dramatic possible recognition of the city's growing importance.[4]

There was no sustained military action in Georgia until Sherman entered the state in May, 1864, though the war had raged in Virginia, Tennessee and Mississippi for three destructive years. In October, 1861, a fleet of forty-one Federal ships had sailed to Port Royal in South Carolina and, after forcing the Confederates to a hasty retreat, the invaders landed just twenty-five miles from Savannah. By December the Federal force had surrounded the mouth of the Savannah River and enemy gunboats were cruising around the coastal islands. In April, 1862, Fort Pulaski was captured, sealing the blockade of the port of Savannah. But the Federals never tried to attack the city from the sea. There were minor military episodes along the coast. In April, 1862, Federals and Confederates tangled at Whitemarsh Island; in March, 1863, Northern troops tried without success to dislodge the Confederates at Fort McAllister, an earthenwork fortification on the Ogeechee River outside Savannah; in June, 1863, the Federals destroyed a bridge over the Turtle River near Brunswick; and in July, 1863, the coastal town of Darien was burned. In north Georgia there were two attempts to cut the Western and Atlantic Railroad. In April, 1862, Captain James Andrews led twenty soldiers disguised as civilians in the daring theft of a train parked outside Marietta. The raiders fled toward Tennessee, destroying bridges and tracks behind them, until their engine ran out of fuel and they were captured. In April, 1863, Abel D. Streight and his cavalry of sixteen hundred men were repulsed near Rome and captured just across the Alabama line by Nathan Bedford Forrest. In September, 1863, a terrible battle was fought at Chickamauga Creek, but it was part of the Tennessee campaign around Chattanooga and took place only incidentally in Georgia. In the early spring of 1865, months after Sherman had left Georgia and a week after Lee's surrender, General James M. Wilson made a cavalry raid from Columbus to Macon.

In May, 1864, General Sherman's army left Tennessee and crossed into Georgia. Chauncey Cook, a seventeen-year-old soldier from Wisconsin, wrote from north Georgia, explaining the situation to his parents: "If we can take Atlanta, now the strongest fortified city in the South, we can march to the sea, and then good-bye to the rebellion." The march would follow the Western and Atlantic Railroad from Chattanooga to Atlanta, the Macon and Western Railroad from Atlanta toward Macon and the Central Railroad to Savannah. In the north Georgia mountains, the Union army of ninety-nine thousand faced an inferior Confederate force of forty-four thousand. The Confederate commander, Joseph E. Johnston, tried to avoid a direct test of strength, carefully choosing well-defended ground, fading and dodging back behind destroyed bridges and railroads, while Sherman's greater force was able to outflank the rebels and push them back relentlessly toward Atlanta. On June 27 Sherman launched a costly and unsuccessful direct assault on Kennesaw Mountain, which was held by the Confederates, but by again outflanking them he forced Johnston's men into Atlanta's trenches, the final retreat. On July 17 Johnston was relieved of command by President Jefferson Davis. The new commander, John B. Hood, attempted to regain the initiative with two disastrous offensives at Peachtree Creek and Ezra Church during the last days of July. After Sherman had bombarded Atlanta for forty days, part of the Federal force swung around south of the city, threatening the Confederate supply routes leading to Macon. When Hood found he could not check this Union force at Jonesboro, he was compelled to evacuate Atlanta on September 1.[5]

These mountain campaigns brought the terrible horror of the Civil War home to Georgia for the first time. The soldiers faced wild, desperate dashes across picket lines, under screaming artillery shells and shrapnel, struggling through obstructions, tripping, falling, rising to fall again, rushing on toward more intense gunfire and the probability of death. Theodore Upson, a nineteen-year-old Indiana volunteer, recorded the action in mid-August: "Yesterday the Johnnies attacked us with a heavy force. They charged our works. We could see them plainly. Orders were given to hold our fire till they got close. When we did open up their lines seemed to melt away. Time after time those brave desperate men tried to advance their line, but it was of no use." The troops, many of them boys, were offered liquor to stiffen their courage before battle. Union veterans remembered how the Confederates would charge with their hats pulled down low over their eyes, like men who knew they were throwing away their lives, so they could not see the certain destruction awaiting them. At Dalton in April, Benjamin Smith of Illinois found unburied Union dead, lying naked in the hot blistering sun, stripped of clothing by the retreating rebels. Near Marietta, Sherman wrote his wife at the end of the brutal summer: "It is enough to make the whole world start at the awful amount of death and destruction that now stalks abroad. I begin to regard death and mangling of a couple of thousand men as a small affair, a kind of morning dash—and it may be well that we become so hardened." From May to September, 4,988 Union soldiers and 3,044 Confederates were killed in Georgia. In July and August, 46,332 Southern and 62,750 Northern soldiers were hospitalized—one in every two Confederates and one in every three Federals each month. Malaria, typhoid fever, diarrhea, dysentery, exposure, measles, chicken pox did the work which battle wounds could not accomplish.[6]

As Sherman's army advanced, the Georgians fell back in dismay. From Marietta Sherman wrote his wife: "We have devoured the land. All the people retire before us and desolation is behind. To realize what war is one should follow our tracks." In Marietta there was confusion and panic, the Sisters of Charity loading hospital bedsteads and mattresses into wagons, slaves staggering under burdens of hastily assembled belongings and locomotives steaming up and down the tracks. Minerva McClatchey, who chose to remain at Marietta while her husband fled to south Georgia, saw alarmed citizens with slaves, horses, cows, hogs and sheep racing ahead of Sherman, heard picket guns and skirmishing and the shrieks and cries of wounded soldiers passing in ambulances and finally faced an invasion of rough, strange men. The roads into Atlanta were lined with carcasses of horses, hogs and cattle, and the air was heavy with the stench of death and gunpowder. As Sherman's triumphant army passed, the sallow, defeated poor whites watched from the sides of the roads. When Chauncey Cook of Wisconsin tried to offer people Confederate money, they merely smiled sadly and shook their heads. James Patton, an Indiana doctor who had joined Sherman at Chattanooga, saw a young woman on the roadside before Atlanta, skinning a dead cow, while her starving little girl tore at the raw, bloody meat with both hands. Jezze Dozer, that Illinois boy, wrote from outside Atlanta in July: "I could see a sad heart in every man's face."[7]

As refugees and soldiers began to fall back into beleaguered Atlanta, emergency hospitals were set up in the streets. Kate Cumming, a Confederate nurse, found herself surrounded by hundreds of dirty, bleeding and weary soldiers. At times physicians had only old tent cloth to bandage wounds, and the soldiers were eating with their fingers because there were no dishes, knives or forks. Rufus Mead of Connecticut described such a frantic hospital scene on the Union side after the battles for Atlanta: "The poor fellows lay there wounded in every part of the body, some crazy & raving and others suffering all that mortals can. Doctors were busy cutting off limbs which were piled up in heaps to be carried off and buried, while the stench even then was horrible. Flies were flying around in swarms and maggots were crawling in wounds before the Drs could get time to dress them." In Atlanta, ten-year-old Carrie Berry huddled in her basement, while exploding shells fell in the garden outside. As trainloads of wounded soldiers fled Atlanta, the Female College and most of the churches in Macon were turned into hospitals, and when there was no more shelter in Macon, more hospitals were established at Milledgeville. When Macon was evacuated a few weeks later, Eliza Andrews would see houses boarded up, ragged foot soldiers ready to march but not knowing where, liquor emptied into gutters by fearful civil authorities.[8]

General Hood abandoned Atlanta on September 1, after destroying eighty-one carloads of ammunition. Outside the city, Sherman's soldiers could hear the blasts and see the red glow of fire from these explosions. In a few weeks the city's population had dropped from more than sixteen thousand to less than three thousand. General W. P. Howard reported to Governor Brown how he had discovered two hundred fifty wagons of deserters, stragglers and country people plundering Atlanta during that quiet interlude, like the eye of a hurricane, between the Confederate retreat and the Federal advance. Sherman's army found the houses perforated with shells and the trees splintered with cannonballs. Sherman ordered the civilians to leave the city, offering them transportation to the North or to a neutral camp, called Rough-and-Ready, if they were determined to flee farther south. On November 15, as his army was preparing to leave the city, Sherman ordered his chief engineer to destroy by powder and fire the depot, storehouses and machine shops of Atlanta. Buildings which could not burn were demolished with battering rams. Drunken soldiers, flanked on both sides by burning buildings, raced up and down the streets on foot or horseback. Sherman's aide George Nichols recorded the scene: "The heaven is one expanse of lurid fire; the air is filled with flying, burning cinders; buildings covering two hundred acres are in ruins or in flames; every instant there is the sharp detonation or smothered burning sound of exploding shells and powder concealed in the buildings, and then the sparks and flame shoot away up into the black and red roof, scattering the cinders far and wide." Henry Hitchcock, Sherman's adjutant, saw: "The grandest and most awful scene . . . immense and raging fires, lighting up the whole heavens. First bursts of smoke, dense, black volumes, then tongues of flame, then huge waves of fire roll up into the sky; presently the skeletons of great warehouses stand out in relief against and amidst sheets of roaring, blazing, furious flames. Now and then there are heavy explosions; it is a line of fire and smoke, lurid, angry, dreadful to look upon." Most of the central part of the city, but not all of Atlanta, was burned. James Patton glanced back toward the city as the Yankees departed on November 15: "We could see Atlanta burning. I looked at my watch and could see the time very plainly at a distance of ten miles."[9]

Sherman abandoned his supply lines in Tennessee, cut the telegraph wires and moved boldly into the interior of Georgia. For nearly a month the people of the North knew what his army was doing only from reports in Confederate newspapers. From Atlanta the Union army marched in three parallel columns, five to fifteen miles apart, forming a thirty- to sixty-mile front, making good ten to fifteen miles each day across country. The right wing, commanded by Major-General Oliver Howard, moved through Jonesboro, Monticello, Gordon, Irwinton. The left wing under Major-General H. W. Slocum headed to Covington, Madison, Eatonton, Milledgeville. Brigadier-General Judson Kilpatrick led a cavalry which struck toward Macon, fell back to Gordon and rejoined Sherman at Milledgeville. The Governor and legislature, then in session, hastily abandoned the state capital. The Governor pardoned all prisoners in the penitentiary who would join the militia. Sherman's army entered Milledgeville on November 22, burning the depot, arsenal and penitentiary and blowing up the magazine but not destroying the Capitol or Governor's Mansion. Federal soldiers held a mock session of the legislature and repealed the secession ordinance. The army marched to Sandersville, Louisville and Millen, where the railroad depot was burned on December 3. On December 13, Federal forces under General W. B. Hazen attacked and captured Fort McAllister, which separated Sherman's army from the Federal fleet off the Georgia coast. During the dark night of December 20, the Confederates abandoned Savannah, retreating silently across the river on pontoon bridges which had been strewn with rice straw to muffle the sound of horses and wagons. Early the next morning the citizens of Savannah surrendered their city without vain resistance, and Sherman dispatched his famous wire to President Lincoln: "I beg to present to you as a Christmas gift the city of Savannah, with one hundred and fifty heavy guns and plenty of ammunition, also about twenty-five thousand bales of cotton."

For the Federal army, the march through Georgia was, as one soldier described it, "one big picnic." Sherman's men had tramped from Atlanta to the sea without opposition. There had been only women and children, most of them hiding. There had been plenty of food, the war seemed to be ending and the mood of the victorious army was jubilant. George Bradley, a Wisconsin chaplain, wrote from the outskirts of Milledgeville in late November: "The soldiers seem cheerful and happy, and all, or nearly all, are pleased to have a part in this, the *grandest affair* of the whole war. I heard one say, a day or two since, that he would not have missed it for fifty dollars." George Sharland, an Illinois private, saw his comrades burden themselves with reckless bounty, unskinned pork meat speared on the points of their bayonets, meal and flour filling their haversacks, and frying pans, coffee pots and kettles tied to their knapsacks. From Savannah in December, Rufus Mead of Connecticut summed up the march: "We had a glorious old tramp right through the heart of the state, rioted and feasted on the country, destroyed all the RR, in short found a rich and overflowing country filled with cattle hogs sheep & fowls, corn sweet potatoes & syrup, but left a barren waste for miles on either side of the road, burnt millions of dollars worth of property, wasted & destroyed all the eatables we couldn't carry off and brought the war to the doors of Georgians so effectively, I guess they will long remember the Yankees. I enjoyed it all the time we had pleasant weather & good roads, & easy times generally."[10]

For Georgians, the march brought disaster and the profound sorrow of defeat. Civilians saw their own troops steal and plunder. Condeferate deserters and stragglers preceded and followed Sherman's army. The newspapers of Georgia and Confederate leaders called upon the people to destroy their supplies and stock to keep them from the invaders. Sherman estimated the destruction in Georgia at $100,000,000, of which $80,000,000 was mere waste. General Howard estimated that his wing of the army had burned 3,523 bales of cotton, carried off 9,000 head of cattle, 931 horses and 1,850 mules, consumed or destroyed 9,000,000 pounds of corn and fodder, taken up 191 miles of railroad. General Slocum estimated his wing of the army had captured or consumed 919,000 rations of bread, 1,217,527 rations of meat, 483,000 rations of coffee, 581,534 rations of sugar, 1,146,500 rations of soap, 137,000 rations of salt, 4,090 horses and mules, 11,000,000 pounds of grain and fodder, 119 miles of railroad, 17,000 bales of cotton. General Kilpatrick added 14,000 bales of cotton, 12,900 bushels of corn and 160,000 pounds of fodder. Mary Jones and her pregnant daughter faced invading bluecoats in Liberty County for a month, at times barricading themselves inside the house while strangers killed sheep, hogs and cattle outside. "Clouds and darkness are around us. The hand of the Almighty is laid in sore judgement upon us," she wrote. "We are a desolated & smitten people."[11]

On January 21, 1865, General Sherman's army crossed the Savannah River into South Carolina and left Georgia in a sea of confusion. After the fall of Richmond, the Confederate government fled south, held its final meeting at Washington, Georgia, and Jefferson Davis was arrested near Irwinville on May 10. Governor Brown, Vice President Stephens, Senator Benjamin Hill, General Howell Cobb were also arrested. Major Henry Wirz, commander of Andersonville Prison, was hanged at Washington. Robert Toombs fled to Europe until it was safe to return. Defeated soldiers were straggling home on foot, eating raw turnips, meat skins, parched corn, anything they could find. About one hundred twenty-five thousand Georgians fought in the Civil War, and about twenty-five thousand were killed. In 1870 there would be ten thousand *fewer* young white men in Georgia, twenty to twenty-nine years of age, than there had been in 1860. John Kennaway, who followed Sherman's track in 1865, found ruins of homes at Calhoun, blank walls and skeleton houses at Marietta, a landscape littered with broken wagons, spent ammunition, abandoned breastworks, graves and skeletons of horses. But he reflected that the greatest evidence of disaster was not the ruined property or ravaged countryside, but the faces of the ruined, ravaged people of Georgia: "I do not remember to have seen a smile upon a single human face."[12]

On April 30, General Johnston telegraphed Governor Brown that hostilities with the United States had ceased, and Federal authority, already established at Macon and Savannah, was extended over the whole state in April, May and June. In May, President Johnson proclaimed James Johnson, a Columbus lawyer, the Provisional Governor and instructed him to call a convention of "loyal Georgians" to form a new government. In October the convention repealed the secession ordinance, abolished slavery and repudiated the Confederate war debt. In November Charles Jenkins, a judge who had been a Unionist before the war, was elected Governor, and a new state legislature ratified the Thirteenth Amendment and passed laws which guaranteed the civil equality of freedmen. In March, 1867, Congress passed, over the President's veto, the military reconstruction act. Georgia's first government was abolished and the state was returned to military rule. Again the state government was reorganized, with more blacks included and more whites excluded. In April, 1868, Rufus Bullock was elected Governor, and in July the new legislature ratified the Fourteenth Amendment. In 1869 the Republican Governor quarreled with the conservative legislature. In December, 1869, the United States Congress again imposed military control over Georgia and the state government was reconstructed for a third time. The new legislature, which included many Negroes and Republicans who had been excluded formerly, finally ratified the Fifteenth Amendment, which guaranteed Negro suffrage. Georgia was formally readmitted to the United States in July, 1870.

Though it took more than five years for Georgia to return to the Union, Georgians had quickly regained control of their own affairs. Georgia was reconstructed three times precisely because the conservatives in the state were so powerful. The very first legislature in 1865, in a daring demonstration of strength, elected Alexander Stephens, former Vice President of the Confederacy, and Herschel V. Johnson, former Confederate Senator, to the the United States Senate and seven former Confederate officers to the House of Representatives. In October, 1866, the legislature refused to ratify the Fourteenth Amendment, which would have secured Negro civil rights. In the April, 1868, legislature radicals and Democrats were about equally represented, and relatively few white voters had been disfranchised at this time. In September the legislature expelled its Negro members, three state senators and twenty-five representatives. In November, the Republicans were not able to carry Georgia for Grant. In March, 1869, the state Senate rejected the Fifteenth Amendment, although the House narrowly ratified it. Then Congressional Reconstruction, twice imposed, seemed to take government from the whites and turn it over to the Republicans and Negroes. So white Georgians turned from government to informal means to control their political life. Though the freedmen exercised a political voice briefly in 1867 and 1868, the vigilante activities of the Ku Klux Klan quieted political revolution by Negroes in Georgia. Freedmen wandered to the cities to test freedom in 1866 and 1867, but they returned to plantations as renters and croppers, and social life resumed its accustomed pace and place. In the December, 1870, election the Democrats won overwhelming control of the state legislature. Faced with probable impeachment by an angry conservative legislature, Governor Bullock resigned his office and fled from Georgia in October, 1871.[13]

Nevertheless, there was a real social and political revolution taking place in Georgia during these years. The Civil War had brought the industrial revolution to Georgia, and Reconstruction would bring power to the middle class. In 1857 Joseph E. Brown, a pugnacious lawyer, had been elected governor and was subsequently reelected three times during the war, an achievement unprecedented in the state's history. A self-made, professional man from north Georgia who appealed to the common people for support, Brown's political success represented a shift of power from the old planters of middle Georgia. The reorganization of state government after 1865 effectively eliminated most of the old leading class—military officers above the rank of colonel, Confederate officials and men whose worth exceeded twenty thousand dollars.[14] The course of events during the war strengthened this new middle class at the expense of the planter class. The rapid inflation and depreciation of the currency benefitted people with debts and penalized people with money in the bank. The war destroyed the value of bank stock, railroad shares, land, slaves and Confederate currency, the wealth of rich men during the war. In the aftermath of Sherman's march, the planters were left without liquid capital or available labor. During the late 1860's the acreage under cultivation, the size of farm units, the value of land and crop production all declined in Georgia. At the same time, the value of taxable property in towns and cities increased from $38,000,000 to $55,000,000 between 1867 and 1872. Between 1860 and 1870 the value of farms in Georgia decreased from $157,072,803 to $94,559,468 and the value of farm machinery and equipment decreased from $6,844,387 to $4,614,701. During the same interval, the number of industrial establishments increased from 1890 to 3836, invested capital rose from $10,890,875 to $13,930,125, yearly industrial production expanded from $16,925,564 to $31,196,115. While the planters had been weakened, a new class of rich men whose wealth did not rest on land and slaves was strengthened.[15]

Atlanta, which had been created and then destroyed by the war, was a scene of amazing recovery. In the midst of crumbling walls, solitary chimneys and charred timbers, the city was fast rebuilding. Sidney Andrews described the scene in November, 1865: "From all this ruin and devastation a new city is springing up with marvellous rapidity. The streets are alive from morning till night with drays and carts and hand-barrows and wagons, hauling teams and shouting men, with loads of lumber and loads of brick and loads of sand, with piles of furniture and hundreds of packed boxes, with mortar-makers and carpenters and masons, with rubbish removers and house-builders, with a never-ending throng of pushing and crowding and scrambling and eager and excited and enterprising men, all bent on building and trading and swift fortune-making." People were living in shacks and tents, establishing stores in half-roofed houses. In 1867 a Milledgeville newspaper complained, "Atlanta is certainly a fast place in every sense of the word, and our friends in Atlanta are a fast people. They live fast, and they die fast. They make money fast, and they spend it fast. They build houses fast, and then burn them down fast. To a stranger, the whole city seems to be running on wheels, and all of the inhabitants continually blowing off

steam." In 1868 Elizabeth Sterchi, a middle-aged Swiss school teacher, called Atlanta "the great Babylon," overrun at night with drunken, rowdy men and wicked women. "Atlanta is crowded with poor people piled one upon the other, perfect heathen in a civilized country, with the most savage tastes, fighting, murdering, stealing, quarreling, begging, swearing, drinking, and possessing the most abject ideas of life." "The god of Atlanta," she wrote, "is money."[16]

The lesson of defeat seemed to be that tangible success mattered more than philosophical principles. "Now that money is acknowledged to be the ruling power in the country," a Savannah man wrote, "it is clear that so long as the South remains under the ban of poverty, so long will she remain in the minority of the government. The answer: Get rich!" Georgia's leaders after the war were tough, realistic, pragmatic, opportunistic men. Atlanta was advertised as "a new place—modern, democratic—a fresh production, wholly practical, without antiquities or prejudices." Joseph E. Brown urged the people to accept each new plan of Congressional Reconstruction, no matter how severe the terms or how expedient the cooperation, because recovery in the future was more important than loyalty to a lost past. The new promoters conspired with the Reconstructionists, who brought power with them to Atlanta. In 1867 the Governor of the Third Military District moved his headquarters from Montgomery to Atlanta. In 1868 the Republican administration moved the state capital from Milledgeville to Atlanta. The city's industrialists were financial partners of political leaders who were hated by most Georgians. Hannibal Kimball, who came to Georgia from Chicago in 1866, became the city's most famous local tycoon, constructing the new state capitol and a palatial hotel in Atlanta. Republican Governor Bullock issued state bonds worth more than thirty million dollars to finance Kimball's railroads. The new leaders of Atlanta welcomed the return of Republicans to their city after the end of Reconstruction. Bullock was able to return to Atlanta and resume his business career, despite charges of corruption which had forced him to flee Georgia in 1871. Joe Brown announced in the North that his state wanted a great importation of "Yankee energy, Yankee enterprise, Yankee education, and Yankee business sense." In 1881 Atlanta became the scene of an International Cotton Exposition, designed to promote industry and investments in Georgia. The most famous stockholder of that enterprise, the man most celebrated and lionized when he came to Atlanta, was former General William T. Sherman. At last, the forces of economic and social change which came to Georgia during Civil War and Reconstruction had produced this happy, if ironic, reconciliation.[17]

NOTES TO THE INTRODUCTION

1. Broadus Mitchell, *The Rise of Cotton Mills in the South* (Baltimore, 1921), pp. 10, 27; McWhorter S. Cooley, "Manufacturing in Georgia during the Civil War Period, 1860–70" (MA Thesis, University of Georgia, 1929), pp. 4, 5, 6.

2. T. Conn Bryan, *Confederate Georgia* (Athens, 1953), p. 106.

3. F. Y. Hedley, *Marching Through Georgia* (Chicago, 1885); Wilfred W. Black, "Marching with Sherman through Georgia and the Carolinas," *Georgia Historical Quarterly*, 52 (1968), 317; Dolly Lunt Burge, *A Woman's Wartime Journal* (New York, 1918), p. 22; Charles J. Brockman, Jr., "The John Van Duser Diary of Sherman's March from Atlanta to Hilton Head," *GHQ*, 53 (1969), 223; F. B. Joyner, "With Sherman in Georgia— A Letter from the Coast," *GHQ*, 42 (1958), 441.

4. Robert Somers, *The Southern States Since the War* (London, 1871), pp. 93, 95; William Irvine, "Diary and Letters of William N. White," *Atlanta Historical Bulletin*, 10 (1937), 39; Clyde C. Walton, *Private Smith's Journal* (Chicago, 1963), p. 47; James M. Merrill, "Personne Goes to Georgia: Five Civil War Letters," *GHQ*, 43 (1959), 209.

5. Chauncey Cook, "Letters of a Badger Boy in Blue," *Wisconsin Magazine of History*, v (1921–22), 93.

6. Oscar Osburn Winther, *With Sherman to the Sea* (Baton Rouge, 1943), p. 122; Athearn, "An Indiana Doctor Marches with Sherman," *Indiana Magazine of History*, XLIX (1953), 410; Walton, *op. cit.*, p. 148; M. A. DeWolfe Howe, *Home Letters of General Sherman* (New York, 1909), p. 299; James O. Breeden, "A Medical History of the Later Stages of the Atlanta Campaign," *Journal of Southern History*, 35 (1969), 54, 56.

7. Howe, *op. cit.*, p. 298; F. Jay Taylor, *Reluctant Rebel* (Baton Rouge, 1959), pp. 169, 172; T. Conn Bryan, "A Georgia Woman's Civil War Diary: The Journal of Minerva Leah Rowles McClatchey, 1864–1865," *GHQ*, 51 (1967), 200; Spencer B. King, *The War-Time Journal of a Georgia Girl* (Macon, 1960), p. 32; Cook, *op. cit.*, p. 97; Athearn, *op. cit.*, p. 409; Wilfred W. Black,
"Marching with Sherman through Georgia and the Carolinas," *GHQ*, 52 (1968), 324.

8. Kate Cumming, *A Journal of the Hospital Life in the Confederate Army* (Louisville, 1866), p. 127; James A. Padgett, "With Sherman through Georgia and the Carolinas: Letters of a Federal Soldier," *GHQ*, 32 (1948), 302; Earl Schenck Miers, *The General Who Marched to Hell* (New York, 1951), p. 156; New York *Tribune*, October 5, 1864; King, *op. cit.*, pp. 154–5.

9. Ralph B. Singer, "Confederate Atlanta" (PhD Thesis, University of Georgia, 1973), p. 264; Miers, *op. cit.*, p. 221; New York *Tribune*, November 15, 1864; Henry Russell Hitchcock, *Marching With Sherman* (New Haven, 1927), p. 57; Athearn, *op. cit.*, p. 417.

10. George C. Osborn, "Sherman's March through Georgia: Letters from Charles Ewing to His Father Thomas Ewing," *GHQ*, 42 (1958), 326; G. S. Bradley, *The Star Corps; or Notes of an Army Chaplain* (Milwaukee, 1865), p. 190; George Sharland, *Knapsack Notes of Sherman's Campaign through the State of Georgia* (Springfield, 1865), p. 39.

11. Alan Conway, *The Reconstruction of Georgia* (Minneapolis, 1966), p. 14; Haskell Monroe, *Yankees A'Coming* (Tuscaloosa, 1959), p. 76.

12. King, *op. cit.*, pp. 32–3; C. Mildred Thompson, *Reconstruction in Georgia* (Savannah, 1972), p. 329; John H. Kennaway, *On Sherman's Track* (London, 1867), p. 106.

13. Conway, *op. cit.*, pp. 145–6, 161.

14. Ellen Louise Sumner, "Unionism in Georgia 1860–1861" (MA Thesis, University of Georgia, 1960), p. 175.

15. Thompson, *op. cit.*, p. 306; Bryan, *Confederate Georgia*, pp. 117, 136.

16. Sidney Andrews, *The South Since the War* (Boston, 1866), p. 340; Whitelaw Reid, *After the War* (New York, 1866), p. 355; Milledgeville paper quoted in Thompson, *op. cit.*, p. 310; Adelaide L. Fries, "The Elizabeth Sterchi Letters," *AHB*, v (1940), 123, 198, 200.

17. Savannah *Morning News*, November 5, 1880; Atlanta *Constitution*, January 25, 1881.

MARCHING THROUGH GEORGIA

THE END OF THE WAR

THE grand review of the army was a splendid success, and was a fitting conclusion to the campaign and the war. On the 19th of May, 1865, I received a copy of War Department Special Order 239, ordering a grand review, by the President and cabinet, of all the armies then near Washington; General Meade's to occur on Tuesday, May 23d, mine on Wednesday, the 24th. The morning of the 24th was extremely beautiful, and the ground was in splendid order for our review. Washington was full of strangers, who filled the streets in holiday-dress, and every house was decorated with flags. The streets were filled with people to see the pageant, armed with bouquets of flowers for their favorite regiments or heroes, and every thing was propitious.

Punctually at 9 a.m. the signal-gun was fired, when in person, attended by General Howard and all my staff, I rode slowly down Pennsylvania Avenue, the crowds of men, women, and children, densely lining the sidewalks, and almost obstructing the way. We were followed close by General Logan and the head of the Fifteenth Corps. When I reached the Treasury-building and looked back, the sight was simply magnificent. The column was compact, and the glittering muskets looked like a solid mass of steel, moving with the regularity of a pendulum. We passed the Treasury-building, in front of which and of the White House was an immense throng of people, for whom extensive stands had been prepared on both sides of the avenue. As I neared the brick-house opposite the lower corner of Lafayette Square, some one asked me to notice Mr. Seward, who, still feeble and bandaged from his wounds, had been removed there that he might

1

behold the troops. I moved in that direction and took off my hat to Mr. Seward, who sat at an upper window. He recognized the salute, returned it, and then we rode on steadily past the President, saluting with our swords. All on his stand arose and acknowledged the salute. Then, turning into the gate of the presidential grounds, we left our horses with orderlies and went upon the stand, where I found my wife Ellen and son Tom. Passing them, I shook hands with the President, General Grant, and each member of the cabinet. I then took my post on the left of the President, while the army passed.

It was, in my judgment, the most magnificent army in existence—sixty-five thousand men, in splendid *physique*, who had just completed a march of nearly two thousand miles in a hostile country, in good drill, and who realized that they were being closely scrutinized by thousands of their fellow-countrymen and by foreigners. Division after division passed, each commander of an army corps or division coming on the stand during the passage of his command, to be presented to the President, cabinet, and spectators. The steadiness and firmness of the tread, the careful dress on the guides, the uniform intervals between the companies, all eyes directly to the front, and the tattered and bullet-riven flags, festooned with flowers, all attracted universal notice. Many good people, up to that time, had looked upon our Western army as a sort of mob; but the world then saw, and recognized the fact, that it was an army in the proper sense, well organized, well commanded and disciplined; and there was no wonder that it had swept through the South like a tornado. For six hours and a half that strong tread of the Army of the West resounded along Pennsylvania Avenue; not a soul of that vast crowd of spectators left his place; and, when the rear of the column had passed by, thousands of the spectators still lingered to express their sense of confidence in the strength of a Government which could claim such an army.

The real difficulty was, and will be again, to obtain an adequate number of good soldiers. We tried almost every system known to modern nations, all with more or less success—voluntary enlistments, the draft, and bought substitutes—and I think that all officers of experience will confirm my assertion that the men who voluntarily enlisted at the outbreak of the war were the best, better than the conscript, and far better than the bought substitute. When a regiment is once organized in a State and mustered into the service of the United States, the officers and men become subject to the same laws of discipline and government as the regular troops. They are in no sense "militia," but compose a part of the Army of the United States, only retain their State title for convenience, and yet may be principally recruited from the neighborhood of their original organization. Once organized, the regiment should be kept full by recruits, and when it becomes difficult to obtain more recruits the pay should be raised by Congress, instead of tempting new men by exaggerated bounties. I believe it would have been more economical to have raised the pay of the soldier to thirty or even fifty dollars a month than to have held out the promise of three hundred and even six hundred dollars in the form of bounty. Toward the close of the war, I have often heard the soldiers complain that the "stay-at-home" men got better pay, bounties, and food, than they who were exposed to all the dangers and vicissitudes of the battles and marches at the front. The feeling of the soldiers should be that, in every event, the sympathy and preference of his government is for him who fights, rather than for him who is on provost or guard duty to the rear, and, like most men, he measures this by the amount of pay. Of course, the soldier must be trained to obedience and should be "content with his wages;" but whoever has commanded an army in the field knows the difference between a willing, contented mass of men and one that feels a cause of grievance. There is a soul to an army as well as to the individual man, and no general can accomplish the full work of his army unless he commands the soul of his men, as well as their bodies and legs.

The greatest mistake made in our civil war was in the mode of recruitment and promotion. When a regiment became reduced by the necessary wear and tear of service, instead of being filled up at the bottom, and the vacancies among the officers filled from the best non-commissioned officers and men, the habit was to raise new regiments, with new colonels, captains, and men, leaving the old and experienced battalions to dwindle away into mere skeleton organizations. I believe with the volunteers this matter was left to the States exclusively, and I remember that Wisconsin kept her regiments filled with recruits, whereas other States generally filled their quotas by new regiments, and the result was that we estimated a Wisconsin regiment equal to an ordinary brigade. I believe that five hundred new men added to an old and experienced regiment were more valuable than a thousand men in the form of a new regiment, for the former by association with good, experienced captains, lieutenants, and non-commissioned officers, soon became veterans, whereas the latter were generally unavailable for a year.

On a road, marching by the flank, it would be considered "good order" to have five thousand men to a mile, so that a full corps of thirty thousand men would extend six miles, but with the average trains and batteries of artillery the probabilities are that it would draw out to ten miles. On a long and regular march the divisions and brigades should alternate in the lead, the leading division should be on the road by the earliest dawn and march at the rate of about two miles, or, at most, two and a half miles an hour, so as to reach camp by noon. Even then the rear divisions and trains will hardly reach camp much before night. Theoretically, a marching column should preserve such order that by simply halting and facing to the right or left, it would be in line of battle; but this is rarely the case, and generally deployments are made "forward," by conducting each brigade by the flank obliquely to the right or left to its approximate position in line of battle, and there deployed. In such a line of battle, a brigade of three thousand infantry would occupy a mile of "front;" but for a strong line of battle five thousand men with two batteries should be allowed to each mile, or a division would habitually constitute a double line with skirmishers and a reserve on a mile of "front."

The "feeding" of an army is a matter of the most vital importance, and demands the earliest attention of the general intrusted with a campaign. To be strong, healthy, and capable of the largest measure of physical effort, the soldier needs about three pounds gross of food per day, and the horse or mule about twenty pounds. When a general first estimates the quantity of food and forage needed for an army of fifty or one hundred thousand men, he is apt to be dismayed, and here a good staff is indispensable, though the general cannot throw off on them the responsibility. He must give the subject his personal attention, for the army reposes in him alone, and should never doubt the fact that their existence overrides in importance all other considerations. Once satisfied of this, and that all has been done that can be, the soldiers are always willing to bear the largest measure of privation. Probably no army ever had a more varied experience in this regard than the one I commanded in 1864–'65.

Our base of supply was at Nashville, supplied by railways and the Cumberland River, thence by rail to Chattanooga, a "secondary base," and thence forward on a single-track railroad. The stores came forward daily, but I endeavored to have on hand a full supply for twenty days in advance. These stores were habitually in the wagon-trains, distributed to corps, divisions, and regiments, in charge of experienced quartermasters and commissaries, and became subject to the orders of the generals commanding these bodies. They were generally issued on provision returns, but these had to be closely scrutinized, for too often the colonels would make requisitions for pro-

4

visions for more men than they reported for battle. Of course, there are always a good many non-combatants with an army, but, after careful study, I limited their amount to twenty-five per cent of the "effective strength," and that was found to be liberal. An ordinary army wagon drawn by six mules may be counted on to carry three thousand pounds net, equal to the food of a full regiment for one day, but, by driving along beef cattle, a commissary may safely count the contents of one wagon as sufficient for two days' food for a regiment of a thousand men; and as a corps should have food on hand for twenty days ready for detachment, it should have three hundred such wagons, as a provision-train; and for forage, ammunition, clothing, and other necessary stores, it was found necessary to have three hundred more wagons, or six hundred wagons in all, for a *corps d'armée*.

On long marches the artillery and wagon-trains should always have the right of way, and the troops should improvise roads to one side, unless forced to use a bridge in common, and all trains should have escorts to protect them, and to assist them in bad places. To this end there is nothing like actual experience, only, unless the officers in command give the subject their personal attention, they will find their wagon-trains loaded down with tents, personal baggage, and even the arms and knapsacks of the escort. Each soldier should, if not actually "sick or wounded," carry his musket and equipments containing from forty to sixty rounds of ammunition, his shelter-tent, a blanket or overcoat, and an extra pair of pants, socks, and drawers, in the form of a scarf, worn from the left shoulder to the right side in lieu of knapsack, and in his haversack he should carry some bread, cooked meat, salt, and coffee. I do not believe a soldier should be loaded down too much, but, including his clothing, arms, and equipment, he can carry about fifty pounds without impairing his health or activity. A simple calculation will show that by such a distribution a corps will thus carry the equivalent of five hundred wagon-loads—an immense relief to the trains.

Where an army is near one of our many large navigable rivers, or has the safe use of a railway, it can usually be supplied with the full army ration, which is by far the best furnished to any army in America or Europe; but when it is compelled to operate away from such a base and is dependent on its own train of wagons, the commanding officer must exercise a wise discretion in the selection of his stores. In my opinion there is no better food for man than beef cattle driven on the hoof, issued liberally, with salt, bacon, and bread. Coffee has also become almost indispensable, though many substitutes were found for it, such as Indian-corn, roasted, ground, and boiled as coffee; the sweet-potato, and the seed of the okra-plant prepared in the same way. All these were used by the people of the South, who for years could procure no coffee, but I noticed that the women always begged of us some *real* coffee, which seems to satisfy a natural yearning or craving more powerful than can be accounted for on the theory of habit. Therefore I would always advise that the coffee and sugar ration be carried along, even at the expense of bread, for which there are many substitutes. Of these, Indian-corn is the best and most abundant. Parched in a frying-pan, it is excellent food, or if ground, or pounded and boiled with meat of any sort, it makes a most nutritious meal. The potato, both Irish and sweet, forms an excellent substitute for bread, and at Savannah we found the rice also suitable, both for men and animals. For the former it should be cleaned of its husk in a hominy block, easily prepared out of a log, and sifted with a coarse cornbag; but for horses it should be fed in the straw. During the Atlanta campaign we were supplied by our regular commissaries with all sorts of patent compounds, such as desiccated vegetables, and concentrated milk, meat-biscuit, and sausages, but somehow the men preferred the simpler and more familiar forms of food, and usually styled these "desecrated vegetables and consecrated milk." We were also supplied liberally with lime-juice, sauerkraut, and pickles, as an antidote to scurvy, and I now recall the extreme anxiety of my medical director, Dr. Kittoe, about the scurvy, which he reported at one time as spreading and imperiling the army. This occurred at a crisis about Kennesaw, when the railroad was taxed to its utmost capacity to provide the necessary ammunition, food, and forage, and could not possibly bring us an adequate supply of potatoes and cabbage, the usual antiscorbutics, when providentially the blackberries ripened and proved an admirable antidote, and I have known the skirmish-line, without orders, to fight a respectable battle for the possession of some old fields that were full of blackberries. Soon, thereafter, the green corn or roasting-ear came into season, and I heard no more of the scurvy. Our country abounds with plants which can be utilized for a prevention to the scurvy; besides the above are the persimmon, the sassafras root and bud, the wild-mustard, the "agave," turnip tops, the dandelion cooked as greens, and a decoction of the ordinary pineleaf.

For the more delicate and costly articles of food for the sick we relied mostly on the agents of the Sanitary Commission. I do not wish to doubt the value of these organizations, which gained so much applause during our civil war, for no one can question the motives of these charitable and generous people; but to be honest I must record an opinion that the Sanitary Commission should limit its operations to the hospitals at the rear, and should never appear at the front. They were generally local in feeling, aimed to furnish their personal friends and neighbors with a better class of food than the Government supplied, and the consequence was, that one regiment of a brigade would receive potatoes and fruit which would be denied another regiment close by. Jealousy would be the inevitable result, and in an army all parts should be equal; there should be no "partiality, favor, or affection." The Government should supply all essential wants, and in the hospitals to the rear will be found abundant opportunities for the exercise of all possible charity and generosity. During the war I several times gained the ill-will of the agents of the Sanitary Commission because I forbade their coming to the front unless they would consent to distribute their stores equally among all, regardless of the parties who had contributed them.

The sick, wounded, and dead of an army are the subjects of the greatest possible anxiety and add an immense amount of labor to the well men. Each regiment in an active campaign should have a surgeon and two assistants always close at hand, and each brigade and division should have an experienced surgeon as a medical director. The great majority of wounds and of sickness should be treated by the regimental surgeon, on the ground, under the eye of the colonel. As few should be sent to the brigade or division hospital as possible, for the men always receive better care with their own regiment than with strangers, and as a rule the cure is more certain; but when men receive disabling wounds, or have sickness likely to become permanent, the sooner they go far to the rear the better for all. The tent or the shelter of a tree is a better hospital than a house, whose walls absorb fetid and poisonous emanations and then give them back to the atmosphere. To men accustomed to the open air, who live on the plainest food, wounds seem to give less pain, and are attended with less danger to life than to ordinary soldiers in barracks.

Wounds which, in 1861, would have sent a man to the hospital for months, in 1865 were regarded as mere scratches, rather the subject of a joke than of sorrow. To new soldiers the sight of blood and death always has a sickening effect, but soon men become accustomed to it, and I have heard them exclaim on seeing a dead comrade borne to the rear, "Well, Bill has turned up *his* toes to the daisies." Of course, during a skirmish or battle, armed men should *never* leave their ranks to attend a dead or wounded comrade—this should be seen to in advance by the colonel, who should designate his musicians or company cooks as hospital attendants, with a white rag on their arm to indicate their office. A wounded man should go himself, if able, to the surgeon near at hand, or, if he need help, he should receive it from one of the attendants and not a comrade. It is wonderful how soon the men accustom themselves to these simple rules. In great battles these matters call for a more enlarged attention, and then it becomes the duty of the division general to see that proper stretchers and field-hospitals are ready for the wounded, and trenches are dug for the dead. There should be no real neglect of the dead, because it has a bad effect on the living; for each soldier values himself and comrade as highly as though he were living in a good house at home.

The regimental chaplain, if any, usually attends the burials from the hospital, should make notes and communicate details to the captain of the company, and to the family at home. Of course it is usually impossible to mark the grave with names, dates, etc., and consequently the names of the "unknown" in our national cemeteries equal about one-half of all the dead.

Very few of the battles in which I participated were fought as described in European text-books, in great masses, in perfect order, manoeuvring by corps, divisions, and brigades. We were generally in a wooded country, and, though our lines were deployed according to tactics, the men generally fought in strong skirmish-lines, taking advantage of the shape of ground, and of every cover. We were generally the assailants, and in wooded and broken countries the "defensive" had a positive advantage over us, for they were always ready, had cover, and always knew the ground to their immediate front; whereas we, their assailants, had to grope our way over unknown ground, and generally found a cleared field or prepared entanglements that held us for a time under a close and withering fire. Rarely did the opposing lines in compact order come into actual contact, but when, as at Peach-Tree Creek and Atlanta, the lines did become commingled, the men fought individually in every possible style, more frequently with the musket clubbed than with the bayonet, and in some instances the men clinched like wrestlers, and went to the ground together. Europeans frequently criticised our war, because we did not always take full advantage of a victory; the true reason was, that habitually the woods served as a screen, and we often did not realize the fact that our enemy had retreated till he was already miles away and was again intrenched, having left a mere skirmish-line to cover the movement, in turn to fall back to the new position.

Our war was fought with the muzzle-loading rifle. Toward the close I had one brigade armed with breech-loading "Spencer's;" the cavalry generally had breech-loading carbines, "Spencer's" and "Sharp's," both of which were good arms.

When a regiment is deployed as skirmishers, and crosses an open field or woods, under heavy fire, if each man runs forward from tree to tree, or stump to stump, and yet preserves a good general alignment, it gives great confidence to the men themselves, for they always keep their eyes well to the right and left, and watch their comrades; but when some few hold back, stick too close or too long to a comfortable log, it often stops the line and defeats the whole object. There is such a thing as individual courage, which has a value in war, but familiarity with danger, experience in war and its common attendants, and personal habit, are equally valuable traits, and these are the qualities with which we usually have to deal in war. All men naturally shrink from pain and danger and only incur their risk from some higher motive, or from habit; so that I would define true courage to be a perfect sensibility of the measure of danger and a mental willingness to incur it, rather than that insensibility to danger of which I have heard far more than I have seen. The most courageous men are generally unconscious of possessing the quality; therefore, when one professes it too openly, by words or bearing, there is reason to mistrust it. I would further illustrate my meaning by describing a man of true courage to be one who possesses all his faculties and senses perfectly when serious danger is actually present.

Modern wars have not materially changed the relative values or proportions of the several arms of service: infantry, artillery, cavalry, and engineers. If any thing, the infantry has been increased in value. Cavalry against cavalry, and as auxiliary to infantry, will always be valuable, while all great wars will, as heretofore, depend chiefly on the infantry. Artillery is more valuable with new and inexperienced troops than with veterans. In the early stages of the war the field-guns often bore the proportion of six to a thousand men; but toward the close of the war one gun, or at most two, to a thousand men, was deemed enough. Sieges, such as characterized the wars of the last century, are too slow for this period of the world. Earth-forts, and especially field-works, will hereafter play an important part in wars, because they enable a minor force to hold a superior one in check for a *time*, and time is a most valuable element in all wars. The habit of intrenching certainly does have the effect of making new troops timid. When a line of battle is once covered by a good parapet, made by the engineers or by the labor of the men themselves, it does require an effort to make them leave it in the face of danger; but when the enemy is intrenched, it becomes absolutely necessary to permit each brigade and division of the troops immediately opposed to throw up a corresponding trench for their own protection in case of a sudden sally. We invariably did this in all our recent campaigns, and it had no ill effect, though sometimes our troops were a little too slow in leaving their well-covered lines to assail the enemy in position or on retreat. Even our skirmishers were in the habit of rolling logs together, or of making a lunette of rails, with dirt in front, to cover their bodies; and, though it revealed their position, I cannot say that it worked a bad effect; so that, as a rule, it may safely be left to the men themselves. On the "defensive," there is no doubt of the propriety of fortifying; but in the assailing army the general must watch closely to see that his men do not neglect an opportunity to drop his precautionary defenses, and act promptly on the "offensive" at every chance.

I have many a time crept forward to the skirmish-line to avail myself of the cover of the pickets' "little fort," to observe more closely some expected result; and always talked familiarly with the men and was astonished to see how well they comprehended the general object and how accurately they were informed of the state of facts existing miles away from their particular corps. Soldiers are very quick to catch the general drift and purpose of a campaign and are always sensible when they are well commanded or well cared for. Once impressed with this fact, and that they are making progress, they bear cheerfully any amount of labor and privation.

For the rapid transmission of orders in an army covering a large space of ground, the magnetic telegraph is by far the best, though habitually the paper and pencil, with good mounted orderlies, answer every purpose. I have little faith in the signal-service by flags and torches, though we always used them; because, almost invariably when they were most needed, the view was cut off by intervening trees, or by mists and fogs. But the value of the magnetic telegraph in war cannot be exaggerated, as was illustrated by the perfect concert of action between the armies of Virginia and Georgia during 1864. Hardly a day intervened when General Grant did not know the exact state of facts with me, more than fifteen hundred miles away as the wires ran. So on the field a thin insulated wire may be run on improvised stakes or from tree to tree for six or more miles in a couple of hours, and I have seen operators so skillful, that by cutting the wire they would receive a message with their tongues from a distant station. As a matter of course, the ordinary commercial wires along the railways form the usual telegraph-lines for an army, and these are easily repaired and extended as the army advances, but each army and wing should have a small party of skilled men to put up the fieldwire, and take it down when done. This is far better than the signal-flags and torches. Our commercial telegraph-lines will always supply for war enough skillful operators.

The value of railways is also fully recognized in war quite as much as, if not more so than, in peace. The Atlanta campaign would simply have been impossible without the use of the railroads from Louisville to Nashville—one hundred and eighty-five miles—from Nashville to Chattanooga—one hundred and fifty-one miles—and from Chattanooga to Atlanta—one hundred and thirty-seven miles. Every mile of this "single track" was so delicate, that one man could in a minute have broken or moved a rail, but our trains usually carried along the tools and means to repair such a break. We had, however, to maintain strong guards and garrisons at each important bridge or trestle—the destruction of which would have necessitated time for rebuilding. For the protection of a bridge, one or two log block-houses, two stories high, with a piece of ordnance and a small infantry guard, usually sufficed. The block-house had a small parapet and ditch about it, and the roof was made shot-proof by earth piled on. These points could usually be reached only by a dash of the enemy's cavalry, and many of these block-houses successfully resisted serious attacks by both cavalry and artillery. The only block-house that was actually captured on the main was the one described near Allatoona.

Our trains from Nashville forward were operated under military rules, and ran about ten miles an hour in gangs of four trains of ten cars each. Four such groups of trains daily made one hundred and sixty cars, of ten tons each, carrying sixteen hundred tons, which exceeded the absolute necessity of the army, and allowed for the accidents that were common and inevitable. But, as I have recorded, that single stem of railroad, four hundred and seventy-three miles long, supplied an army of one hundred thousand men and thirty-five thousand animals for the period of one hundred and ninety-six days, viz., from May 1 to November 12, 1864. To have delivered regularly that amount of food and forage by ordinary wagons would have required thirty-six thousand eight hundred wagons of six mules each, allowing each wagon to have hauled two tons twenty miles each day, a simple impossibility in roads such as then existed in that region of country. Therefore, I reiterate that the Atlanta campaign was an impossibility without these railroads; and only then, because we had the men and means to maintain and defend them, in addition to what were necessary to overcome the enemy. Habitually, a passenger-car will carry fifty men with their necessary baggage. Box-cars, and even platform-cars, answer the purpose well enough, but they should always have rough board-seats. For sick and wounded men, box-cars filled with straw or bushes were usually employed. Personally, I saw but little of the practical working of the railroads, for I only turned back once as far as Resaca; but I had daily reports from the engineer in charge, and officers who came from the rear often explained to me the whole thing, with a description of the wrecked trains all the way from Nashville to Atlanta. I am convinced that the risk to life to the engineers and men on that railroad fully equaled that on the skirmish-line, called for as high an order of courage, and fully equaled it in importance. Still, I doubt if there be any necessity in time of peace to organize a corps specially to work the military railroads in time of war, because in peace these same men gain all the necessary experience, possess all the daring and courage of soldiers, and only need the occasional protection and assistance of the necessary train-guard, which may be composed of the furloughed men coming and going, or of details made from the local garrisons to the rear.

Engineer troops attached to an army are habitually employed in supervising the construction of forts or field works of a nature more permanent than the lines used by the troops in motion, and in repairing roads and making bridges. I had several regiments of this kind that were most useful, but as a rule we used the infantry, or employed parties of freedmen, who worked on the trenches at night while the soldiers slept, and these in turn rested by day. Habitually the repair of the railroad and its bridges was committed to hired laborers, like the English navvies, under the supervision of Colonel W. W. Wright, a railroad-engineer, who was in the military service at the time, and his successful labors were frequently referred to in the official reports of the campaign.

For the passage of rivers, each army corps had a pontoon-train with a detachment of engineers, and, on reaching a river, the leading infantry division was charged with the labor of putting it down. Generally the single pontoon-train could provide for nine hundred feet of bridge, which sufficed; but when the rivers were very wide two such trains would be brought together, or the single train was supplemented by a trestle-bridge, or bridges made on crib-work, out of timber found near the place. The pontoons in general use were skeleton frames, made with a hinge, so as to fold back and constitute a wagon-body. In this same wagon were carried the cotton canvas cover, the anchor and chains, and a due proportion of the balks, chesses, and lashings. All the troops became very familiar with their mechanism and use, and we were rarely delayed by reason of a river, however broad.

In relation to guards, pickets, and vedettes, I doubt if any discoveries or improvements were made during our war, or in any of the modern wars in Europe. These precautions vary with the nature of the country and the situation of each army. When advancing or retreating in line of battle, the usual skirmish-line constitutes the picket-line, and may have "reserves," but usually the main line of battle constitutes the reserve.

For flank-guards and rear-guards, one or more companies should be detached under their own officers, instead of making up the guard by detailing men from the several companies.

For regimental or camp guards, the details should be made according to existing army regulations; and all the guards should be posted early in the evening, so as to afford each sentinel or vedette a chance to study his ground before it becomes too dark.

In like manner as to the staff. The more intimately it comes into contact with the troops, the more useful and valuable it becomes. The almost entire separation of the staff from the line, as now practised by us, has proved mischievous, and the great retinues of staff-officers with which some of our earlier generals began the war were simply ridiculous. I don't believe in a chief of staff at all, and any general commanding an army, corps, or division, that has a staff-officer who professes to know more than his chief, is to be pitied. Each regiment should have a competent adjutant, quartermaster, and commissary, with two or three medical officers. Each brigade commander should have the same staff, with the addition of a couple of young aides-de-camp, habitually selected from the subalterns of the brigade, who should be good riders and intelligent enough to give and explain the orders of their general.

The same staff will answer for a division. The general in command of a separate army, and of a *corps d'armée*, should have the same professional assistance, with two or more good engineers, and his adjutant-general should exercise all the functions usually ascribed to a chief of staff, viz., he should possess the ability to comprehend the scope of operations, and to make verbally and in writing all the orders and details necessary to carry into effect the views of his general, as well as to keep the returns and records of events for the information of the next higher authority, and for history. A bulky staff implies a division of responsibility, slowness of action, and indecision, whereas a small staff implies activity and concentration of purpose. The smallness of General

13

Grant's staff throughout the civil war forms the best model for future imitation. So of tents, officers' furniture, etc., etc. In real war these should all be discarded, and an army is efficient for action and motion exactly in the inverse ratio of its *impedimenta*. Tents should be omitted altogether, save one to a regiment for an office, and a few for the division hospital. Officers should be content with a tent fly, improvising poles and shelter out of bushes. The *tente d'abri*, or shelter-tent, carried by the soldier himself, is all-sufficient. Officers should never seek for houses, but share the condition of their men.

To be at the head of a strong column of troops, in the execution of some task that requires brain, is the highest pleasure of war—a grim one and terrible, but which leaves on the mind and memory the strongest mark; to detect the weak point of an enemy's line; to break through with vehemence and thus lead to victory; or to discover some key-point and hold it with tenacity; or to do some other distinct act which is afterward recognized as the real cause of success. These all become matters that are never forgotten. Other great difficulties, experienced by every general, are to measure truly the thousand-and-one reports that come to him in the midst of conflict; to preserve a clear and well-defined purpose at every instant of time, and to cause all efforts to converge to that end.

To do these things he must know perfectly the strength and quality of each part of his own army, as well as that of his opponent, and must be where he can personally see and observe with his own eyes, and judge with his own mind. No man can properly command an army from the rear, he must be "at its front;" and when a detachment is made, the commander thereof should be informed of the object to be accomplished, and left as free as possible to execute it in his own way; and when an army is divided up into several parts, the superior should always attend that one which he regards as most important. Some men think that modern armies may be so regulated that a general can sit in an office and play on his several columns as on the keys of a piano; this is a fearful mistake. The directing mind must be at the very head of the army—must be seen there, and the effect of his mind and personal energy must be felt by every officer and man present with it, to secure the best results. Every attempt to make war easy and safe will result in humiliation and disaster.

Lastly, mail facilities should be kept up with an army if possible, that officers and men may receive and send letters to their friends, thus maintaining the home influence of infinite assistance to discipline. Newspaper correspondents with an army, as a rule, are mischievous. They are the world's gossips, pick up and retail the camp scandal, and gradually drift to the headquarters of some general, who finds it easier to make reputation at home than with his own corps or division. They are also tempted to prophesy events and state facts which, to an enemy, reveal a purpose in time to guard against it. Moreover, they are always bound to see facts colored by the partisan or political character of their own patrons, and thus bring army officers into the political controversies of the day, which are always mischievous and wrong. Yet, so greedy are the people at large for war news, that it is doubtful whether any army commander can exclude all reporters, without bringing down on himself a clamor that may imperil his own safety. Time and moderation must bring a just solution to this modern difficulty.

I will now conclude by a copy of my general orders taking leave of the army, which ended my connection with the war, though I afterward visited and took a more formal leave of the officers and men on July 4, 1865, at Louisville, Kentucky:

HEADQUARTERS MILITARY DIVISION OF THE MISSISSIPPI,
IN THE FIELD, WASHINGTON, D. C., *May* 30, 1865.

The general commanding announces to the Armies of the Tennessee and Georgia that the time has come for us to part. Our work is done, and armed enemies no longer defy us. Some of you will go to your homes, and others will be retained in military service till further orders.

And now that we are all about to separate, to mingle with the civil world, it becomes a pleasing duty to recall to mind the situation of national affairs when, but little more than a year ago, we were gathered about the cliffs of Lookout Mountain, and all the future was wrapped in doubt and uncertainty.

Three armies had come together from distant fields, with separate histories, yet bound by one common cause—the union of our country, and the perpetuation of the Government of our inheritance. There is no need to recall to your memories Tunnel Hill, with Rocky-Face Mountain and Buzzard-Roost Gap, and the ugly forts of Dalton behind.

We were in earnest, and paused not for danger and difficulty, but dashed through Snake-Creek Gap and fell on Resaca; then on to the Etowah, to Dallas, Kennesaw; and the heats of summer found us on the banks of the Chattahoochee, far from home, and dependent on a single road for supplies. Again we were not to be held back by any obstacle, and crossed over and fought four hard battles for the possession of the citadel of Atlanta. That was the crisis of our history. A doubt still clouded our future, but we solved the problem, destroyed Atlanta, struck boldly across the State of Georgia, severed all the main arteries of life to our enemy, and Christmas found us at Savannah.

Waiting there only long enough to fill our wagons, we again began a march which, for peril, labor, and results, will compare with any ever made by an organized army. The floods of the Savannah, the swamps of the Combahee and Edisto, the "high hills" and rocks of the Santee, the flat quagmires of the Pedee and Cape Fear Rivers, were all passed in mid-winter, with its floods and rains, in the face of an accumulating enemy; and, after the battles of Averysboro' and Bentonsville, we once more came out of the wilderness, to meet our friends at Goldsboro'. Even then we paused only long enough to get new clothing, to reload our wagons, again pushed on to Raleigh and beyond, until we met our enemy suing for peace, instead of war, and offering to submit to the injured laws of his and our country. As long as that enemy was defiant, nor mountains nor rivers, nor swamps, nor hunger, nor cold, had checked us; but when he, who had fought us hard and persistently, offered submission, your general thought it wrong to pursue him farther, and negotiations followed, which resulted, as you all know, in his surrender.

How far the operations of this army contributed to the final overthrow of the Confederacy and the peace which now dawns upon us, must be judged by others, not by us; but that you have done all that men could do has been admitted by those in authority, and we have a right to join in the universal joy that fills our land because the war is *over*, and our Government stands vindicated before the world by the joint action of the volunteer armies and navy of the United States.

To such as remain in the service, your general need only remind you that success in the past was due to hard work and discipline, and that the same work and discipline are equally important in the future. To such as go home, he will only say that our favored country is so grand, so extensive, so diversified in climate, soil, and productions, that every man may find a home and occupation suited to his taste; none should yield to the natural impatience sure to result from our past life of excitement and adventure. You will be invited to seek new adventures abroad; do not yield to the temptation, for it will lead only to death and disappointment.

Your general now bids you farewell, with the full belief that, as in war you have been good soldiers, so in peace you will make good citizens; and if, unfortunately, new war should arise in our country, "Sherman's army" will be the first to buckle on its old armor, and come forth to defend and maintain the Government of our inheritance.

By order of Major-General W. T. Sherman,
L. M. DAYTON, *Assistant Adjutant General.*

CHATTANOOGA TO KENNESAW

ON the 18th day of March, 1864, at Nashville, Tennessee, I relieved Lieutenant-General Grant in command of the Military Division of the Mississippi. General Grant was in the act of starting East to assume command of all the armies of the United States, but more particularly to give direction in person to the Armies of the Potomac and James, operating against Richmond; and I accompanied him as far as Cincinnati on his way, to avail myself of the opportunity to discuss privately many little details incident to the contemplated changes, and of preparation for the great events then impending. After my return I addressed myself to the task of organization and preparation, which involved the general security of the vast region of the South which had been already conquered, more especially the several routes of supply and communication with the active armies at the front, and to organize a large army to move into Georgia, coincident with the advance of the Eastern armies against Richmond.

I returned to Nashville from Cincinnati about the 25th of March, and started at once, in a special car attached to the regular train, to inspect my command at the front, going to Pulaski, Tennessee, where I found General G. M. Dodge; thence to Huntsville, Alabama, where I had left a part of my personal staff and the records of the department; and there I found General McPherson, who had arrived from Vicksburg, and had assumed command of the Army of the Tennessee. General McPherson accompanied me, and we proceeded by the cars to Stevenson and Bridgeport to Chattanooga, where we spent a day or two with General George H. Thomas, and then continued on to Knoxville, where was General Schofield. He returned with us to Chattanooga, stopping by the way a few hours at Loudon, where were the headquarters of the Fourth Corps. About the end of March, therefore, the three army commanders and myself were together at Chattanooga. We had nothing like a council of war, but conversed freely and frankly on all matters of interest then in progress or impending. We all knew that, as soon as the spring was fairly open, we should have to move directly against our antagonist, General Joseph E. Johnston, then securely intrenched at Dalton, thirty miles distant; and the purpose of our conference at the time was to ascertain our own resources and to distribute to each part of the army its appropriate share of work. We discussed every possible contingency likely to arise, and I simply instructed each army commander to make immediate preparations for a hard campaign, regulating the distribution of supplies that were coming up by rail from Nashville as equitably as possible. We also agreed on some subordinate changes in the organization of the three separate armies which were destined to take the field. These changes required the consent of the President and were all in due time approved.

The great question of the campaign was one of supplies. Nashville, our chief depot, was itself partially in a hostile country, and even the routes of supply from Louisville to Nashville by rail, and by way of the Cumberland River, had to be guarded. Chattanooga, our starting-point, was one hundred and thirty-six miles in front of Nashville, and every foot of the way, especially the many bridges, trestles, and culverts, had to be strongly guarded against the acts of a local hostile population and of the enemy's cavalry. Then, of course, as we advanced into Georgia, it was manifest that we should have to repair the railroad, use it, and guard it likewise. General Thomas's army was much the largest of the three, was best provided, and contained the best corps of engineers, railroad managers, and repair parties, as well as the best body of spies and provost-marshals. On him we were therefore compelled in a great measure to rely for these most useful branches of service. He had so long exercised absolute command and control over the railroads in his department, that the other armies were jealous, and these thought the Army of the Cumberland got the lion's share of the supplies and other advantages of the railroads. I found a good deal of feeling in the Army of the Tennessee on this score, and therefore took supreme control of the roads myself, placed all the army commanders on an equal footing, and gave to each the same control, so far as orders of transportation for men and stores were concerned. Thomas's spies brought him frequent and accurate reports of Joseph Johnston's army at Dalton, giving its strength anywhere between forty and fifty thousand men, and these were being reenforced by troops from Mississippi, and by the Georgia militia. General Johnston seemed to be acting purely on the defensive, so that we had

18

time and leisure to take all our measures deliberately and fully. I fixed the date of May 1st, when all things should be in readiness for the grand forward movement, and then returned to Nashville; General Schofield going back to Knoxville, and McPherson to Huntsville, Thomas remaining at Chattanooga.

On the 2d of April, at Nashville, I wrote to General Grant, then at Washington, reporting to him the results of my visit to the several armies, and asked his consent to the several changes proposed, which was promptly given by telegraph. I then addressed myself specially to the troublesome question of transportation and supplies. I found the capacity of the railroads from Nashville forward to Decatur and Chattanooga so small, especially in the number of locomotives and cars, that it was clear that they were barely able to supply the daily wants of the armies then dependent on them, with no power of accumulating a surplus in advance. The cars were daily loaded down with men returning from furlough, with cattle, horses, etc.; and, by reason of the previous desolation of the country between Chattanooga and Knoxville, General Thomas had authorized the issue of provisions to the suffering inhabitants.

We could not attempt an advance into Georgia without food, ammunition, etc.; and ordinary prudence dictated that we should have an accumulation at the front, in case of interruption to the railway by the act of the enemy, or by common accident. Accordingly, on the 6th of April, I issued a general order, limiting the use of the railroad-cars to transporting only the essential articles of food, ammunition, and supplies for the army proper, forbidding any further issues to citizens, and cutting off all civil traffic; requiring the commanders of posts within thirty miles of Nashville to haul out their own stores in wagons; requiring all troops destined for the front to march and all beef cattle to be driven on their own legs. This was a great help, but of course it naturally raised a howl. Some of the poor Union people of East Tennessee appealed to President Lincoln, whose kind heart responded promptly to their request. He telegraphed me to know if I could not modify or repeal my orders; but I answered him that a great campaign was impending, on which the fate of the nation hung; that our railroads had but a limited capacity, and could not provide for the necessities of the army and of the people too; that one or the other must quit, and we could not until the army of Joseph Johnston was conquered. Mr. Lincoln seemed to acquiesce, and I advised the people to obtain and drive out cattle from Kentucky, and to haul out their supplies by the wagon-road from the same quarter, by way of Cumberland Gap. By these changes I nearly or quite doubled our daily accumulation of stores at the front, and yet even this was not found enough.

I accordingly called together in Nashville the master of transportation, Colonel Anderson, the chief quartermaster, General J. L. Donaldson, and the chief commissary, General Amos Beckwith, for conference. I assumed the strength of the army to move from Chattanooga into Georgia at one hundred thousand men, and the number of animals to be fed, both for cavalry and draught, at thirty-five thousand; then, allowing for occasional wrecks of trains, which were very common, and for the interruption of the road itself by guerrillas and regular raids, we estimated it would require one hundred and thirty cars, of ten tons each, to reach Chattanooga daily, to be reasonably certain of an adequate supply. Even with this calculation, we could not afford to bring forward hay for the horses and mules, nor more than five pounds of oats or corn per day for each animal. I was willing to risk the question of forage in part, because I expected to find wheat and corn fields, and a good deal of grass, as we advanced into Georgia at that season of the year. The problem then was to deliver at Chattanooga and beyond one hundred and thirty car-loads daily, leaving the beef cattle to be driven on the hoof, and all the troops in excess of the usual train-guards to march by the ordinary roads. Colonel Anderson promptly explained that he did not possess cars or locomotives enough to do this work. I then instructed and authorized him to hold on to all trains that arrived at Nashville from Louisville, and to allow none to go back until he had secured enough to fill the requirements of our problem. At the time he only had about sixty serviceable locomotives, and about six hundred cars of all kinds, and he represented that to provide for all contingencies he must have at least one hundred locomotives and one thousand cars.

The department and army commanders had to maintain strong garrisons in their respective departments, and also to guard their respective lines of supply. I therefore, in my mind, aimed to prepare out of these three armies, by the 1st of May, 1864, a compact army for active operations in Georgia, of about the following numbers of men:

Army of the Cumberland	50,000
Army of the Tennessee	35,000
Army of the Ohio	15,000
Total	100,000

Kennesaw's Bombardment —

and, to make these troops as mobile as possible, I made the strictest possible orders in relation to wagons and all species of incumbrances and impedimenta whatever. Each officer and soldier was required to carry on his horse or person food and clothing enough for five days. To each regiment was allowed but one wagon and one ambulance, and to the officers of each company one pack-horse or mule.

Each division and brigade was provided a fair proportion of wagons for a supply-train, and these were limited in their loads to carry food, ammunition, and clothing. Tents were forbidden to all save the sick and wounded, and one tent only was allowed to each headquarters for use as an office. These orders were not absolutely enforced, though in person I set the example and did not have a tent, nor did any officer about me have one; but we had wall tent-flies, without poles, and no tent-furniture of any kind. We usually spread our flies over saplings, or on fence-rails or posts improvised on the spot. Most of the general officers, except Thomas, followed my example strictly; but he had a regular headquarters-camp. I frequently called his attention to the orders on this subject, rather jestingly than seriously. He would break out against his officers for having such luxuries, but, needing a tent himself, and being good-natured and slow to act, he never enforced my orders perfectly. In addition to his regular wagon-train, he had a big wagon which could be converted into an office, and this we used to call "Thomas's circus." Several times during the campaign I found quartermasters hid away in some comfortable nook to the rear, with tents and mess-fixtures which were the envy of the passing soldiers; and I frequently broke them up and distributed the tents to the surgeons of brigades. Yet my orders actually reduced the transportation, so that I doubt if any army ever went forth to battle with fewer impedimenta, and where the regular and necessary supplies of food, ammunition, and clothing, were issued, as called for, so regularly and so well.

My personal staff was then composed of Captain J. C. McCoy, aide-de-camp; Captain L. M. Dayton, aide-de-camp; Captain J. C. Audenried, aide-de-camp; Brigadier-General J. D. Webster, chief of staff; Major R. M. Sawyer, assistant adjutant-general; Captain Montgomery Rochester, assistant adjutant-general. These last three were left at Nashville in charge of the office, and were empowered to give orders in my name, communication being generally kept up by telegraph.

Subsequently were added to my staff, and accompanied me in the field, Brigadier-General W. F. Barry, chief of artillery; Colonel O. M. Poe, chief of engineers; Colonel L. C. Easton, chief quartermaster; Colonel Amos Beckwith, chief commissary; Captain Thomas G. Baylor, chief of ordnance; Surgeon E. D. Kittoe, medical director; Brigadier-General J. M. Corse, inspector-general; Lieutenant-Colonel C. Ewing, inspector-general; and Lieutenant-Colonel Willard Warner, inspector-general.

These officers constituted my staff proper at the beginning of the campaign, which remained substantially the same till the close of the war, with very few exceptions: Surgeon John Moore, United States Army, relieved Surgeon Kittoe of the volunteers (about Atlanta) as medical director; Major Henry Hitchcock joined as judge-advocate, and Captain G. Ward Nichols reported as an extra aide-de-camp (after the fall of Atlanta) at Gaylesville, just before we started for Savannah.

During the whole month of April the preparations for active war were going on with extreme vigor, and my letter-book shows an active correspondence with Generals Grant, Halleck, Thomas, McPherson, and Schofield on thousands of matters of detail and arrangement. When the time for action approached, viz., May 1, 1864, the actual armies prepared to move into Georgia resulted as follows, present for battle:

Army of the Cumberland, Major-General THOMAS.

	Men.
Infantry	54,568
Artillery	2,377
Cavalry	3,828
Aggregate	60,773

Number of field-guns, 130.

Army of the Tennessee, Major-General MCPHERSON.

	Men.
Infantry	22,437
Artillery	1,404
Cavalry	624
Aggregate	24,465

Guns, 96.

Army of the Ohio, Major-General SCHOFIELD.

	Men.
Infantry	11,183
Artillery	679
Cavalry	1,697
Aggregate	13,559

Guns, 28.

Grand aggregate, 98,797 men and 254 guns.

These figures do not embrace the cavalry divisions which were still incomplete, viz., of General Stoneman, at Lexington, Kentucky, and of General Garrard, at Columbia, Tennessee, who were then rapidly collecting horses, and joined us in the early stage of the campaign.

At first I intended to open the campaign about May 1st, by moving Schofield on Dalton from Cleveland, Thomas on the same objective from Chattanooga, and McPherson on Rome and Kingston from Gunter's Landing. My intention was merely to threaten Dalton in front, and to direct McPherson to act vigorously against the railroad below Resaca, far to the rear of the enemy. But by reason of his being short of his estimated strength by the four divisions before referred to, and thus being reduced to about twenty-four thousand men, I did not feel justified in placing him so far away from the support of the main body of the army, and therefore subsequently changed the plan of campaign, so far as to bring that army up to Chattanooga, and to direct it thence through Ship's Gap against the railroad to Johnston's rear, at or near Resaca, distant from Dalton only eighteen miles, and in full communication with the other armies by roads behind Rocky-face Ridge, of about the same length.

On the 10th of April I received General Grant's letter of April 4th from Washington, which formed the basis of all the campaigns of the year 1864, and subsequently received another of April 19th, written from Culpepper, Virginia, in his own handwriting, both of which are here given entire. These letters embrace substantially all the orders he ever made on this particular subject, and these, it will be seen, devolved on me the details both as to the plan and execution of the campaign by the armies under my immediate command. These armies were to be directed against the rebel army commanded by General Joseph E. Johnston, then lying on the defensive, strongly

23

intrenched at Dalton, Georgia; and I was required to follow it up closely and persistently, so that in no event could any part be detached to assist General Lee in Virginia; General Grant undertaking in like manner to keep Lee so busy that he could not respond to any calls of help by Johnston. Neither Atlanta, nor Augusta, nor Savannah, was the objective, but the "army of Jos. Johnston," go where it might.

HEADQUARTERS ARMIES OF THE UNITED STATES, ⎱
WASHINGTON, D. C., *April 4,* 1864. ⎰

Major-General W. T. SHERMAN, *commanding Military Division of the Mississippi.*

GENERAL: It is my design, if the enemy keep quiet and allow me to take the initiative in the spring campaign, to work all parts of the army together, and somewhat toward a common centre. For your information I now write you my programme, as at present determined upon.

I have sent orders to Banks, by private messenger, to finish up his present expedition against Shreveport with all dispatch; to turn over the defense of Red River to General Steele and the navy, and to return your troops to you, and his own to New Orleans; to abandon all of Texas, except the Rio Grande, and to hold that with not to exceed four thousand men; to reduce the number of troops on the Mississippi to the lowest number necessary to hold it, and to collect from his command not less than twenty-five thousand men. To this I will add five thousand from Missouri. With this force he is to commence operations against Mobile as soon as he can. It will be impossible for him to commence too early.

Gillmore joins Butler with ten thousand men, and the two operate against Richmond from the south side of James River. This will give Butler thirty-three thousand men to operate with, W. F. Smith commanding the right wing of his forces, and Gillmore the left wing. I will stay with the Army of the Potomac, increased by Burnside's corps of not less than twenty-five thousand effective men, and operate directly against Lee's army, wherever it may be found.

Sigel collects all his available force in two columns, one, under Ord and Averill, to start from Beverly, Virginia, and the other, under Crook, to start from Charleston, on the Kanawha, to move against the Virginia & Tennessee Railroad.

Crook will have all cavalry, and will endeavor to get in about Saltville, and move east from there to join Ord. His force will be all cavalry, while Ord will have from ten to twelve thousand men of all arms.

You I propose to move against Johnston's army, to break it up, and to get into the interior of the enemy's country as far as you can, inflicting all the damage you can against their war resources.

I do not propose to lay down for you a plan of campaign, but simply to lay down the work it is desirable to have done, and leave you free to execute it in your own way. Submit to me, however, as early as you can, your plan of operations.

As stated, Banks is ordered to commence operations as soon as he can. Gillmore is ordered to report at Fortress Monroe by the 18th inst., or as soon thereafter as practicable. Sigel is concentrating now. None will move from their places of rendezvous until I direct, except Banks. I want to be ready to move by the 25th inst., if possible; but all I can now direct is that you get ready as soon as possible. I know you will have difficulties to encounter in getting through the mountains to where supplies are abundant, but I believe you will accomplish it.

From the expedition from the Department of West Virginia I do not calculate on very great results; but it is the only way I can take troops from there. With the long line of railroad Sigel has to protect, he can spare no troops, except to move directly to his front. In this way he must get through to inflict great damage on the enemy, or the enemy must detach from one of his armies a large force to prevent it. In other words, if Sigel can't skin himself, he can hold a leg while some one else skins.

I am, general, very respectfully, your obedient servant,

U. S. GRANT, *Lieutenant-General.*

HEADQUARTERS MILITARY DIVISION OF THE MISSISSIPPI,
NASHVILLE, TENNESSEE, *April* 10, 1864.

Lieutenant-General U. S. GRANT, *Commander-in-Chief, Washington, D. C.*

DEAR GENERAL: Your two letters of April 4th are now before me, and afford me infinite satisfaction. That we are now all to act on a common plan, converging on a common centre, looks like enlightened war.

Like yourself, you take the biggest load, and from me you shall have thorough and hearty coöperation. I will not let side issues draw me off from your main plans in which I am to knock Jos. Johnston, and to do as much damage to the resources of the enemy as possible. I have heretofore written to General Rawlins and to Colonel Comstock (of your staff) somewhat of the method in which I propose to act. I have seen all my army, corps, and division commanders, and have signified only to the former, viz., Schofield, Thomas, and McPherson, our general plans, which I inferred from the purport of our conversation here and at Cincinnati.

First, I am pushing stores to the front with all possible dispatch, and am completing the army organization according to the orders from Washington, which are ample and perfectly satisfactory.

It will take us all of April to get in our furloughed veterans, to bring up A. J.

Smith's command, and to collect provisions and cattle on the line of the Tennessee. Each of the armies will guard, by detachments of its own, its rear communications.

At the signal to be given by you, Schofield, leaving a select garrison at Knoxville and Loudon, with twelve thousand men will drop down to the Hiawassee, and march against Johnston's right by the old Federal road. Stoneman, now in Kentucky, organizing the cavalry forces of the Army of the Ohio, will operate with Schofield on his left front—it may be, pushing a select body of about two thousand cavalry by Ducktown or Elijah toward Athens, Georgia.

Thomas will aim to have forty-five thousand men of all arms, and move straight against Johnston, wherever he may be, fighting him cautiously, persistently, and to the best advantage. He will have two divisions of cavalry, to take advantage of any offering.

McPherson will have nine divisions of the Army of the Tennessee, if A. J. Smith gets here, in which case he will have full thirty thousand of the best men in America. He will cross the Tennessee at Decatur and Whitesburg, march toward Rome, and feel for Thomas. If Johnston falls behind the Coosa, then McPherson will push for Rome; and if Johnston falls behind the Chattahoochee, as I believe he will, then McPherson will cross over and join Thomas.

McPherson has no cavalry, but I have taken one of Thomas's divisions, viz., Garrard's six thousand strong, which is now at Columbia, mounting, equipping, and preparing. I design this division to operate on McPherson's right, rear, or front, according as the enemy appears. But the moment I detect Johnston falling behind the Chattahoochee, I propose to cast off the effective part of this cavalry division, after crossing the Coosa, straight for Opelika, West Point, Columbus, or Wetumpka, to break up the road between Montgomery and Georgia. If Garrard can do this work well, he can return to the Union army; but should a superior force interpose, then he will seek safety at Pensacola and join Banks, or, after rest, will act against any force that he can find east of Mobile, till such time as he can reach me.

Should Johnston fall behind the Chattahoochee, I will feign to the right, but pass to the left and act against Atlanta or its eastern communications, according to developed facts.

This is about as far ahead as I feel disposed to look, but I will ever bear in mind that Johnston is at all times to be kept so busy that he cannot in any event send any part of his command against you or Banks.

If Banks can at the same time carry Mobile and open up the Alabama River, he will in a measure solve the most difficult part of my problem, viz., "provisions." But in that I must venture. Georgia has a million of inhabitants. If they can live, we should not starve. If the enemy interrupt our communications, I will be absolved from all obligations to subsist on our own resources, and will feel perfectly justified in taking whatever and wherever we can find.

I will inspire my command, if successful, with the feeling that beef and salt are all that is absolutely necessary to life, and that parched corn once fed General Jackson's army on that very ground.

As ever, your friend and servant,

W. T. SHERMAN, *Major-General.*

HEADQUARTERS ARMIES IN THE FIELD, \
CULPEPPER COURT-HOUSE, VIRGINIA, *April* 19, 1864.)

Major-General W. T. SHERMAN, *commanding Military Division of the Mississippi.*

GENERAL: Since my letter to you of April 4th I have seen no reason to change any portion of the general plan of campaign, if the enemy remain still and allow us to take the initiative. Rain has continued so uninterruptedly until the last day or two that it will be impossible to move, however, before the 27th, even if no more should fall in the mean time. I think Saturday, the 30th, will probably be the day for our general move.

Colonel Comstock, who will take this, can spend a day with you, and fill up many little gaps of information not given in any of my letters.

What I now want more particularly to say is, that if the two main attacks, yours and the one from here, should promise great success, the enemy may, in a fit of desperation, abandon one part of their line of defense, and throw their whole strength upon the other, believing a single defeat without any victory to sustain them better than a defeat all along their line, and hoping too, at the same time, that the army, meeting with no resistance, will rest perfectly satisfied with their laurels, having penetrated to a given point south, thereby enabling them to throw their force first upon one and then on the other.

With the majority of military commanders they might do this.

But you have had too much experience in traveling light, and subsisting upon the country, to be caught by any such *ruse.* I hope my experience has not been thrown away. My directions, then, would be, if the enemy in your front show signs of joining Lee, follow him up to the full extent of your ability. I will prevent the concentration of Lee upon your front, if it is in the power of this army to do it.

The Army of the Potomac looks well, and, so far as I can judge, officers and men feel well.   Yours truly,

U. S. GRANT, *Lieutenant-General.*

Lieutenant-General GRANT, *commanding Armies of the United States, Culpepper, Virginia.*

GENERAL: I now have, at the hands of Colonel Comstock, of your staff, the letter of April 19th, and am as far prepared to assume the offensive as possible. I only ask as much time as you think proper, to enable me to get up McPherson's two divisions from Cairo. Their furloughs will expire about this time, and some of them should now be in motion for Clifton, whence they will march to Decatur, to join General Dodge.

McPherson is ordered to assemble the Fifteenth Corps near Larkin's, and to get the Sixteenth and Seventeenth Corps (Dodge and Blair) at Decatur at the earliest possible moment. From these two points he will direct his forces on Lebanon, Summerville, and Lafayette, where he will act against Johnston, if he accept battle at Dalton; or move in the direction of Rome, if the enemy give up Dalton, and fall behind the Oostenaula or Etowah. I see that there is some risk in dividing our forces, but Thomas and Schofield will have strength enough to cover all the valleys as far as Dalton; and, should Johnston turn his whole force against Mc-Pherson, the latter will have his bridge at Larkin's, and the route to Chattanooga *via* Wills's Valley and the Chattanooga Creek, open for retreat; and if Johnston attempt to leave Dalton, Thomas will have force enough to push on through Dalton to Kingston, which will checkmate him. My own opinion is that Johnston will be compelled to hang to his railroad, the only possible avenue of supply to his army, estimated at from forty-five to sixty thousand men.

At Lafayette all our armies will be together, and if Johnston stands at Dalton we must attack him in position. Thomas feels certain that he has no material increase of force, and that he has not sent away Hardee, or any part of his army. Supplies are the great question. I have materially increased the number of cars daily. When I got here, the average was from sixty-five to eighty per day. Yesterday the report was one hundred and ninety-three; to-day, one hundred and thirty-four; and my estimate is that one hundred and forty-five cars per day will give us a day's supply and a day's accumulation.

McPherson is ordered to carry in wagons twenty days' rations, and to rely on the depot at Ringgold for the renewal of his bread. Beeves are now being driven on the hoof to the front; and the commissary, Colonel Beckwith, seems fully alive to the importance of the whole matter.

Our weakest point will be from the direction of Decatur, and I will be forced to risk something from that quarter, depending on the fact that the enemy has no force available with which to threaten our communications from that direction.

Colonel Comstock will explain to you personally much that I cannot commit to paper. I am, with great respect, W. T. SHERMAN, *Major-General.*

On the 28th of April I removed my headquarters to Chattanooga, and prepared for taking the field in person. General Grant had first indicated the 30th of April as the day for the simultaneous advance, but subsequently changed the day to May 5th. McPherson's troops were brought forward rapidly to Chattanooga, partly by rail and partly by marching. Thomas's troops were already in position (his advance being out as far as Ringgold—eighteen miles), and Schofield was marching down by Cleveland to Red Clay and Catoosa Springs. On the 4th of May, Thomas was in person at Ringgold, his left at Catoosa, and his right at Leet's Tan-yard. Schofield was at Red Clay, closing upon Thomas's left; and McPherson was moving rapidly into Chattanooga, and out toward Gordon's Mill. On the 5th I rode out to Ringgold, and on the very day appointed by General Grant from his headquarters in Virginia the great campaign was begun.

My general headquarters and official records remained back at Nashville, and I had near me only my personal staff and inspectors-general, with about half a dozen wagons, and a single company of Ohio sharp-shooters as headquarters or camp guard. I also had a small company of irregular Alabama cavalry, used mostly as orderlies and couriers. No wall-tents were allowed, only the flies. Our mess establishment was less in bulk than that of any of the brigade commanders; nor was this from an indifference to the ordinary comforts of life, but because I wanted to set the example, and gradually to convert all parts of that army into a mobile machine, willing and able to start at a minute's notice and to subsist on the scantiest food. To reap absolute success might involve the necessity even of dropping all wagons and to subsist on the chance food which the country was known to contain. I had obtained not only the United States census-tables of 1860, but a compilation made by the Controller of the State of Georgia for the purpose of taxation, containing in considerable detail the "population and statistics" of every county in Georgia. One of my aides acted as assistant adjutant-general, with an order-book, letter-book, and writing-paper, that filled a small chest not much larger than an ordinary candle-box. The only reports and returns called for were the ordinary tri-monthly returns of "effective strength."

The 6th of May was given to Schofield and McPherson to get into position, and on the 7th

General Thomas moved in force against Tunnel Hill, driving off a mere picket-guard of the enemy, and I was agreeably surprised to find that no damage had been done to the tunnel or the railroad. From Tunnel Hill I could look into the gorge by which the railroad passed through a straight and well-defined range of mountains, presenting sharp palisade faces, and known as "Rocky Face." The gorge itself was called the "Buzzard Roost." We could plainly see the enemy in this gorge and behind it, and Mill Creek which formed the gorge, flowing toward Dalton, had been dammed up, making a sort of irregular lake, filling the road, thereby obstructing it, and the enemy's batteries crowned the cliffs on either side. The position was very strong, and I knew that such a general as was my antagonist, Joseph Johnston, who had been there six months, had fortified it to the maximum. Therefore I had no intention to attack the position seriously in front, but depended on McPherson to capture and hold the railroad to its rear, which would force Johnston to detach largely against him, or rather, as I expected, to evacuate his position at Dalton altogether. My orders to Generals Thomas and Schofield were merely to press strongly at all points in front, ready to rush in on the first appearance of "let go," and, if possible, to catch our enemy in the confusion of retreat.

All the movements of the 7th and 8th were made exactly as ordered, and the enemy seemed quiescent, acting purely on the defensive.

I had constant communication with all parts of the army, and on the 9th McPherson's head of column entered and passed through Snake Creek, perfectly undefended, and accomplished a complete surprise to the enemy. At its farther *débouché* he met a cavalry brigade, easily driven, which retreated hastily north toward Dalton, and doubtless carried to Johnston the first serious intimation that a heavy force of infantry and artillery was to his rear and within a few miles of his railroad. I got a short note from McPherson that day (written at 2 p.m., when he was within a mile and a half of the railroad, above and near Resaca), and we all felt jubilant. I renewed orders to Thomas and Schofield to be ready for the instant pursuit of what I expected to be a broken and disordered army, forced to retreat by roads to the east of Resaca, which were known to be very rough and impracticable.

That night I received further notice from McPherson that he had found Resaca too strong for a surprise; that in consequence he had fallen back three miles to the mouth of Snake-Creek Gap and was there fortified. I wrote him the next day the following letters:

30

HEADQUARTERS MILITARY DIVISION OF THE MISSISSIPPI, }
IN THE FIELD, TUNNEL HILL, GEORGIA, *May 11, 1864 — Morning.* }

Major-General McPHERSON, *commanding Army of the Tennessee, Sugar Valley, Georgia.*

GENERAL: I received by courier (in the night) yours of 5 and 6:30 p.m. of yesterday.

You now have your twenty-three thousand men, and General Hooker is in close support, so that you can hold all of Jos. Johnston's army in check should he abandon Dalton. He cannot afford to abandon Dalton, for he has fixed it up on purpose to receive us, and he observes that we are close at hand, waiting for him to quit. He cannot afford a detachment strong enough to fight you, as his army will not admit of it.

Strengthen your position; fight any thing that comes; and threaten the safety of the railroad all the time. But, to tell the truth, I would rather the enemy would stay in Dalton two more days, when he may find in his rear a larger party than he expects in an open field. At all events, we can then choose our own ground, and he will be forced to move out of his works. I do not intend to put a column into Buzzard-Roost Gap at present.

See that you are in easy communication with me and with all headquarters. After to-day the supplies will be at Ringgold. Yours,

W. T. SHERMAN, *Major-General commanding.*

HEADQUARTERS MILITARY DIVISION OF THE MISSISSIPPI, }
IN THE FIELD, TUNNEL HILL, GEORGIA, *May 11, 1864 — Evening.* }

General McPHERSON, *Sugar Valley.*

GENERAL: The indications are that Johnston is evacuating Dalton. In that event, Howard's corps and the cavalry will pursue; all the rest will follow your route. I will be down early in the morning.

Try to strike him if possible about the forks of the road.

Hooker must be with you now, and you may send General Garrard by Summerville to threaten Rome and that flank. I will cause all the lines to be felt at once.

W. T. SHERMAN, *Major-General commanding.*

McPherson had startled Johnston in his fancied security, but had not done the full measure of his work. He had in hand twenty-three thousand of the best men of the army, and could have walked into Resaca (then held only by a small brigade), or he could have placed his whole force astride the railroad above Resaca and there have easily withstood the attack of all of Johnston's army, with the knowledge that Thomas and Schofield were on his heels. Had he done so, I am certain that Johnston would not have ventured to attack him in position, but would have retreated eastward by Spring Place, and we should have captured half his army and all his artillery and wagons at the very beginning of the campaign.

Such an opportunity does not occur twice in a single life, but at the critical moment McPherson seems to have been a little timid. Still, he was perfectly justified by his orders, and fell back and assumed an unassailable defensive position in Sugar Valley, on the Resaca side of Snake-Creek Gap. As soon as informed of this, I determined to pass the whole army through Snake-Creek Gap, and to move on Resaca with the main army.

But during the 10th, the enemy showed no signs of evacuating Dalton, and I was waiting for the arrival of Garrard's and Stoneman's cavalry, known to be near at hand, so as to secure the full advantages of victory, of which I felt certain. Hooker's Twentieth Corps was at once moved down to within easy supporting distance of McPherson; and on the 11th, perceiving signs of evacuation of Dalton, I gave all the orders for the general movement, leaving the Fourth Corps and Stoneman's cavalry in observation in front of Buzzard-Roost Gap, and directing all the rest of the army to march through Snake-Creek Gap, straight on Resaca. The roads were only such as the country afforded, mere rough wagon-ways, and these converged to the single narrow track through Snake-Creek Gap; but during the 12th and 13th the bulk of Thomas's and Schofield's armies were got through, and deployed against Resaca, McPherson on the right, Thomas in the centre, and Schofield on the left. Johnston, as I anticipated, had abandoned all his well-prepared defenses at Dalton, and was found inside of Resaca with the bulk of his army, holding his divisions well in hand, acting purely on the defensive, and fighting well at all points of conflict. A complete line of intrenchments was found covering the place, and this was strongly manned at all points. On the 14th we closed in, enveloping the town on its north and west, and during the 15th we had a day of continual battle and skirmish. At the same time I caused two pontoon-bridges to be laid across the Oostenaula River at Lay's Ferry, about three miles below the town, by which we could threaten Calhoun, a station on the railroad seven miles below Resaca. At the same time, May 14th, I dispatched General Garrard, with his cavalry division, down the Oostenaula by the Rome road, with orders to cross over, if possible, and to attack or threaten the railroad at any point below Calhoun and above Kingston.

Death of Gen Polk
Pine Mountain
Kennesaw

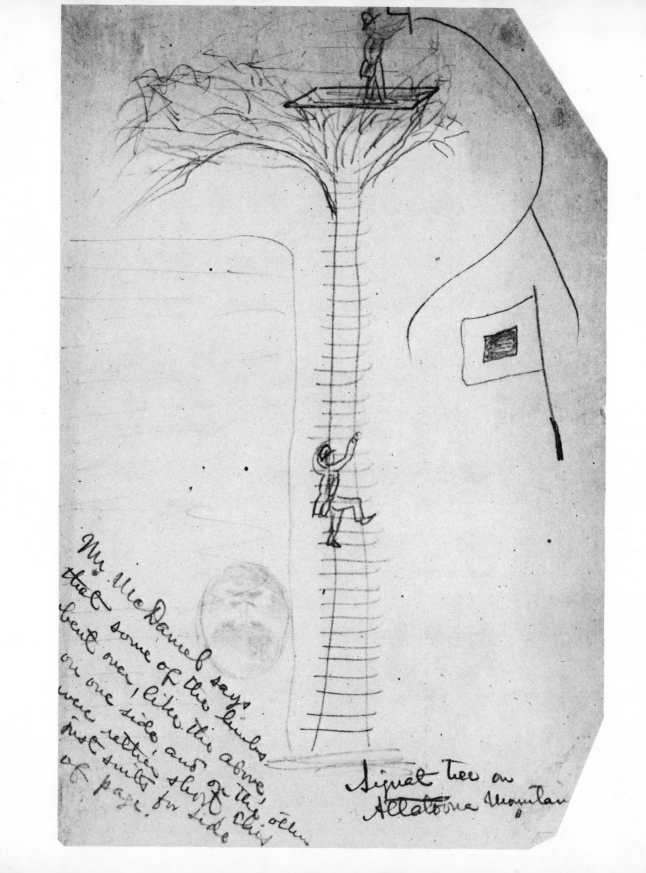

Mr. McDaniel says
that some of the limbs
bent over, like this above,
on one side, and on the other
were rather sharp. This
has suited shape on this
of page on side

Signal tree on
Allatoona Mountain

During the 15th, without attempting to assault the fortified works, we pressed at all points, and the sound of cannon and musketry rose all day to the dignity of a battle. Toward evening McPherson moved his whole line of battle forward, till he had gained a ridge overlooking the town, from which his field-artillery could reach the railroad-bridge across the Oostenaula. The enemy made several attempts to drive him away, repeating the sallies several times, and extending them into the night; but in every instance he was repulsed with bloody loss. Hooker's corps had also some heavy and handsome fighting that afternoon and night on the left, where the Dalton road entered the intrenchments, capturing a four-gun intrenched battery, with its men and guns; and generally all our men showed the finest fighting qualities. Howard's corps had followed Johnston down from Dalton, and was in line; Stoneman's division of cavalry had also got up, and was on the extreme left, beyond the Oostenaula.

On the night of May 15th Johnston got his army across the bridges, set them on fire, and we entered Resaca at daylight. Our loss up to that time was about six hundred dead and thirty-three hundred and seventy-five wounded—mostly light wounds that did not necessitate sending the men to the rear for treatment. That Johnston had deliberately designed in advance to give up such strong positions as Dalton and Resaca, for the purpose of drawing us farther south, is simply absurd. Had he remained in Dalton another hour, it would have been his total defeat, and he only evacuated Resaca because his safety demanded it. The movement by us through Snake-Creek Gap was a total surprise to him. My army about doubled his in size, but he had all the advantages of natural positions, of artificial forts and roads, and of concentrated action. We were compelled to grope our way through forests, across mountains, with a large army, necessarily more or less dispersed. Of course, I was disappointed not to have crippled his army more at that particular stage of the game; but, as it resulted, these rapid successes gave us the initiative, and the usual impulse of a conquering army.

Johnston having retreated in the night of May 15th, immediate pursuit was begun. A division of infantry was at once dispatched down the valley toward Rome, to support Garrard's cavalry, and the whole army was ordered to pursue, McPherson by Lay's Ferry, on the right, Thomas directly by the railroad, and Schofield by the left, by the old road that crossed the Oostenaula above Echota or Newtown. We hastily repaired the railroad-bridge at Resaca, which had been partially burned, and built a temporary floating-bridge out of timber and materials found on the spot; so that Thomas got his advance corps over during the 16th, and marched as far as Calhoun, where he came into communication with McPherson's troops, which had crossed the Oostenaula at Lay's Ferry by our pontoon-bridges, previously laid. Inasmuch as the bridge at Resaca was overtaxed, Hooker's Twentieth Corps was also diverted to cross by the fords and ferries above Resaca, in the neighborhood of Echota.

On the 17th, toward evening, the head of Thomas's column, Newton's division, encountered the rear-guard of Johnston's army near Adairsville. I was near the head of column at the time, trying to get a view of the position of the enemy from an elevation in an open field. My party attracted the fire of a battery; a shell passed through the group of staff-officers and burst just beyond, which scattered us promptly. The next morning the enemy had disappeared, and our pursuit was continued to Kingston, which we reached during Sunday forenoon, the 19th.

From Resaca the railroad runs nearly due south, but at Kingston it makes junction with another railroad from Rome, and changes direction due east. At that time McPherson's head of column was about four miles to the west of Kingston, at a country place called "Woodlawn;" Schofield and Hooker were on the direct roads leading from Newtown to Cassville, diagonal to the route followed by Thomas. Thomas's head of column, which had followed the country roads alongside of the railroad, was about four miles east of Kingston, toward Cassville, when about noon I got a message from him that he had found the enemy, drawn up in line of battle, on some extensive, open ground, about half-way between Kingston and Cassville, and that appearances indicated a willingness and preparation for battle.

Hurriedly sending orders to McPherson to resume the march, to hasten forward by roads leading to the south of Kingston, so as to leave for Thomas's troops and trains the use of the main road and to come up on his right, I rode forward rapidly, over some rough gravel hills, and about six miles from Kingston found General Thomas, with his troops deployed; but he reported that the enemy had fallen back in echelon of divisions, steadily and in superb order, into Cassville. I knew that the roads by which Generals Hooker and Schofield were approaching would lead them to a seminary near Cassville, and that it was all-important to secure the point of junction of these roads with the main road along which we were marching. Therefore I ordered General Thomas to push forward his deployed lines as rapidly as possible; and, as night was approaching, I ordered two field-batteries to close up at a gallop on some woods which lay between us and the town of

34

Cassville. We could not see the town by reason of these woods, but a high range of hills just back of the town was visible over the tree-tops. On these hills could be seen fresh-made parapets and the movements of men, against whom I directed the artillery to fire at long range. The stout resistance made by the enemy along our whole front of a couple of miles indicated a purpose to fight at Cassville; and, as the night was closing in, General Thomas and I were together, along with our skirmish-line near the seminary, on the edge of the town, where musket-bullets from the enemy were cutting the leaves of the trees pretty thickly about us. Either Thomas or I remarked that that was not the place for the two senior officers of a great army, and we personally went back to the battery, where we passed the night on the ground. During the night I had reports from McPherson, Hooker, and Schofield. The former was about five miles to my right rear, near the "nitre-caves;" Schofield was about six miles north, and Hooker between us, within two miles. All were ordered to close down on Cassville at daylight, and to attack the enemy wherever found. Skirmishing was kept up all night, but when day broke the next morning, May 20th, the enemy was gone, and our cavalry was sent in pursuit. These reported him beyond the Etowah River. We were then well in advance of our railroad-trains, on which we depended for supplies; so I determined to pause a few days to repair the railroad, which had been damaged but little, except at the bridge at Resaca, and then to go on.

Nearly all the people of the country seemed to have fled with Johnston's army; yet some few families remained, and from one of them I procured the copy of an order which Johnston had made at Adairsville, in which he recited that he had retreated as far as strategy required, and that his army must be prepared for battle at Cassville. The newspapers of the South, many of which we found, were also loud in denunciation of Johnston's falling back before us without a serious battle, simply resisting by his skirmish-lines and by his rear-guard. But his friends proclaimed that it was all *strategic*; that he was deliberately drawing us farther and farther into the meshes, farther and farther away from our base of supplies, and that in due season he would not only halt for battle, but assume the bold offensive. Of course it was to my interest to bring him to battle as soon as possible, when our numerical superiority was at the greatest; for he was picking up his detachments as he fell back, whereas I was compelled to make similar and stronger detachments to repair the railroads as we advanced, and to guard them. I found at Cassville many evidences of preparation for a grand battle, among them a long line of fresh intrenchments on the hill beyond the town, extending nearly three miles to the south, embracing the railroad-crossing. I was also convinced that the whole of Polk's corps had joined Johnston from Mississippi and that he had in hand three full corps, Hood's, Polk's, and Hardee's, numbering about sixty thousand men, and could not then imagine why he had declined battle, and did not learn the real reason till after the war was over, and then from General Johnston himself.

In the autumn of 1865, taking a steamer, I found as fellow-passengers Generals Johnston and Frank Blair. We were, of course, on the most friendly terms, and on our way up we talked over our battles again, played cards, and questioned each other as to particular parts of our mutual conduct in the game of war. I told Johnston that I had seen his order of preparation, in the nature of an address to his army, announcing his purpose to retreat no more, but to accept battle at Cassville. He answered that such was his purpose; that he had left Hardee's corps in the open fields to check Thomas, and gain time for his formation on the ridge, just behind Cassville; and it was this corps which General Thomas had seen deployed, and whose handsome movement in retreat he had reported in such complimentary terms. Johnston described how he had placed Hood's corps on the right, Polk's in the centre, and Hardee's on the left. He said he had ridden over the ground, given to each corps commander his position and orders to throw up parapets during the night; that he was with Hardee on his extreme left as the night closed in, and as Hardee's troops fell back to the position assigned them for the intended battle of the next day; and that, after giving Hardee some general instructions, he and his staff rode back to Cassville. As he entered the town he met Generals Hood and Polk. Hood inquired of him if he had had any thing to eat, and he said no, that he was both hungry and tired, when Hood invited him to go and share a supper which had been prepared for him at a house close by. At the supper they discussed the chances of the impending battle, when Hood spoke of the ground assigned him as being enfiladed by our Union artillery, which Johnston disputed, when General Polk chimed in with the remark the General Hood was right; that the cannon-shots fired by us at nightfall had enfiladed their general line of battle, and that for this reason he feared they could not hold their men. General Johnston was surprised at this, for he understood General Hood to be one of those who professed to criticise his strategy, contending that, instead of retreating, he should have risked a battle. General Johnston said he was provoked, accused them of having been in conference, with being beaten before battle, and added that he was unwilling to engage in a critical battle with an

36

army so superior to his own in numbers, with two of his three corps commanders dissatisfied with the ground and positions assigned them. He then and there made up his mind to retreat still farther south, to put the Etowah River and the Allatoona range between us; and he at once gave orders to resume the retrograde movement. The rebel army did retreat that night, leaving us masters of all the country above the Etowah River.

For the purposes of rest, to give time for the repair of the railroads, and to replenish supplies, we lay by some few days in that quarter—Schofield with Stoneman's cavalry holding the ground at Cassville Depot, Cartersville, and the Etowah Bridge; Thomas holding his ground near Cassville, and McPherson that near Kingston. The officer intrusted with the repair of the railroads was Colonel W. W. Wright, a railroad-engineer, who, with about two thousand men, was so industrious and skillful that the bridge at Resaca was rebuilt in three days, and cars loaded with stores came forward to Kingston on the 24th. The telegraph also brought us the news of the bloody and desperate battles of the Wilderness, in Virginia, and that General Grant was pushing his operations against Lee with terrific energy. I was therefore resolved to give my enemy no rest.

In early days (1844), when a lieutenant of the Third Artillery, I had been sent from Charleston, South Carolina, to Marietta, Georgia, to assist Inspector-General Churchill to take testimony concerning certain losses of horses and accoutrements by the Georgia Volunteers during the Florida War; and after completing the work at Marietta we transferred our party over to Bellefonte, Alabama. I had ridden the distance on horseback, and had noted well the topography of the country, especially that about Kennesaw, Allatoona, and the Etowah River. I therefore knew that the Allatoona Pass was very strong, would be hard to force, and resolved not even to attempt it, but to turn the position, by moving from Kingston to Marietta *via* Dallas; accordingly I made orders on the 20th to get ready for the march to begin on the 23d. The Army of the Cumberland was ordered to march for Dallas, by Euharlee and Stilesboro; Davis's division, then in Rome, by Van Wert; the Army of the Ohio to keep on the left of Thomas, by a place called Burnt Hickory; and the Army of the Tennessee to march for a position a little to the south, so as to be on the right of the general army, when grouped about Dallas.

The movement contemplated leaving our railroad, and to depend for twenty days on the contents of our wagons; and as the country was very obscure, mostly in a state of nature, densely wooded, and with few roads, our movements were necessarily slow. We crossed the Etowah by several bridges and fords, and took as many roads as possible, keeping up communication by cross-roads, or by couriers through the woods. I personally joined General Thomas, who had the centre, and was consequently the main column, or "column of direction." The several columns followed generally the valley of the Euharlee, a tributary coming into the Etowah from the south, and gradually crossed over a ridge of mountains, parts of which had once been worked over for gold, and were consequently full of paths and unused wagon-roads or tracks. A cavalry picket of the enemy at Burnt Hickory was captured, and had on his person an order from General Johnston, dated at Allatoona, which showed that he had detected my purpose of turning his position, and it accordingly became necessary to use great caution, lest some of the minor columns should fall into ambush, but, luckily the enemy was not much more familiar with that part of the country than we were. On the other side of the Allatoona range, the Pumpkin-Vine Creek, also a tributary of the Etowah, flowed north and west; Dallas, the point aimed at, was a small town on the other or east side of this creek, and was the point of concentration of a great many roads that led in every direction. Its possession would be a threat to Marietta and Atlanta, but I could not then venture to attempt either, till I had regained the use of the railroad, at least as far down as its *débouché* from the Allatoona range of mountains. Therefore, the movement was chiefly designed to compel Johnston to give up Allatoona.

Kingston, Georgia
May 20th, 1864

Dearest Ellen,

I have no doubt you will complain of neglect on my part, but you have sense enough to see that my every minute has been taken. According to appointment with General Grant, I got everything as far ready as possible on the 5th and started from Chattanooga on the 6th. Troops had to be marched and collected from all parts of the country without attracting attention, and I got McPherson up to Chattanooga and on Johnston's flank before he suspected anything more than a detachment of Thomas's command.

Dalton lies in a valley, but the road passes through a gap which was a most formidable place. I drew Johnston's attention to it, whilst I moved the army round through a gap thirty miles further south and appeared on his rear and flank.

He hastily evacuated Dalton and succeeded in getting into Resaca, eighteen miles, where he had prepared a strong position. This we attacked at all points, getting closer and closer, whilst I got a bridge across the Oostenaula and again threatened his rear.

Again he started and we chased him fighting all the way to Cassville, and today the army is pushing him across the Etowah. Having a railroad, and familiar with all the byways, he has got off, but at a cost of about 6000 men—we have a thousand prisoners, have killed and wounded 5000 and have ourselves lost less than 4000. We have had no time to count noses. The enemy burned the railroad bridge at Oostenaula but we have repaired it now and have the telegraph and cars to the very rear of our army.

The whole movement has been rapid, skillful and successful, but will be measured by subsequent events. Difficulties arise as we go, for I have to drop men to guard our roads, whereas our enemy gathers up his guards and collects other reinforcements. I will cross the Etowah and Chattahoochee and swing round Atlanta. If I can break up that nest it will be a splendid achievement. Grant's battles in Virginia are fearful but necessary. Immense slaughter is necessary to prove that our Northern armies can and will fight. That, once impressed, will be an immense moral power.

Banks's utter failure is awful, as that force should now be at Mobile. It may be that Canby can straighten out matters. Banks was so intent on civil government that he underrated the military features of his territory. All attempts at civil government in the midst of war are folly. I am in good health and see no reason to apprehend any reverse though I shall be duly cautious, as we have a large army skillfully commanded at my front. Love to all,

W. T. Sherman

Kingston, Georgia
May 22nd, 1864

Dearest Ellen:

Tomorrow we start again for Atlanta. I would like to go back and give you a connected narrative of events, but I know it would take more time than I can devote to it, and I suppose you will have curiosity enough to read everything with Sherman at the top of the page. I believe the world now admits my right to maintain public silence and recognizes it as a military power. The officers and soldiers, too, have realized that by bringing up McPherson's army with secrecy and dispatch and putting it through Snake Creek Gap unobserved that I saved them the terrible door of death that Johnston had prepared for them in the Buzzard Roost. We were forced to attack at Resaca and there, too, by catching the strong and weak points I enabled the army to fight at as little disadvantage as possible; and following up quick and strong we gave Johnston no time to fortify, though every pass was barricaded all the way down. I think we inflicted more loss on the enemy than we sustained ourselves, and up to this time we have taken fifteen guns, 2500 prisoners and a large lot of property. Of course, being compelled to guard our commu-

nications, our strength is diminished as we advance and that of the enemy increases. I have no doubt we must have a terrific battle at some point near the Chattahoochee. The main roads cross the Etowah thirteen miles from here and for six miles lay among hills that afford strong positions. These I must avoid and shall move due south to Dallas and thence to Marietta and the Chattahoochee Bridge. You will no doubt recognize this very country as the one I was in twenty years ago and to which I took such a fancy. Yesterday I rode my lines and passed quite close to Colonel Tumlin's place, the same where the big mounds are, where I stopped in going from Marietta to Bellefonte and back. I will probably pass by those same big mounds tomorrow. The weather is oppressively hot and roads dusty. I do hope we will have rain as it is choking to soldiers and mules. Our large trains make a fearful dust.

I will put up a map to go to you by this mail by which you can trace our progress. Thomas is my center and has about 45,000 men. McPherson my right, 25,000; and Schofield my left, 15,000; in all 85,000 men, a vast army to feed and to move. I can't move about as I did with 15,000 or 20,000 men. I think I have the best army in the country, and if I can't take Atlanta and stir up Georgia considerably I am mistaken. Our greatest danger is from cavalry in which arm of service the enemy is superior to us in quantity and quality, cutting our wagons or railroads. I have on hand, however, enough for twenty days and in that time I ought to determine a good deal. You will no doubt have full accounts of the fighting—at Rocky Face I made our display to attract attention away from McPherson. At Resaca we had several pretty sharp fights—one, Hooker pressing down from the north, another the Fifteenth Corps dashing for position close to the enemy's flank and holding it against repeated night assaults, and Sweeny's Division holding the pontoon bridge at Lay's Ferry—all well and handsomely done. In pursuit, I tried hard to strike in behind Johnston with my cavalry, but they did not accomplish it. But we did force the enemy to abandon the line of the Coosa and Etowah which was the first step in the game. Our next is to force him behind the Chattahoochee and last to take Atlanta and disturb the peace of the inhabitants of central Georgia and prevent reinforcements going to Lee. If that Banks's force could only go to Mobile now, there would not be a shadow of doubt of full success.

Yours ever,
W. T. Sherman

On the 25th all the columns were moving steadily on Dallas—McPherson and Davis away off to the right, near Van Wert; Thomas on the main road in the centre, with Hooker's Twentieth Corps ahead, toward Dallas; and Schofield to the left rear. For the convenience of march, Hooker had his three divisions on separate roads, all leading toward Dallas, when, in the afternoon, as he approached a bridge across Pumpkin-Vine Creek, he found it held by a cavalry force, which was driven off, but the bridge was on fire. This fire was extinguished, and Hooker's leading division followed the retreating cavalry on a road leading due east toward Marietta, instead of Dallas. This leading division, about four miles out from the bridge, struck a heavy infantry force, which was moving down from Allatoona toward Dallas, and a sharp battle ensued. I came up in person soon after, and as my map showed that we were near an important cross-road called "New Hope," from a Methodist meeting-house there of that name, I ordered General Hooker to secure it if possible that night. He asked for a short delay, till he could bring up his other two divisions, viz., of Butterfield and Ward, but before these divisions had got up and were deployed, the enemy had also gained corresponding strength. The woods were so dense, and the resistance so spirited, that Hooker could not carry the position, though the battle was noisy, and prolonged far into the night. This point, "New Hope," was the accidental intersection of the road leading from Allatoona to Dallas with that from Van Wert to Marietta, was four miles northeast of Dallas, and from the bloody fighting there for the next week was called by the soldiers "Hell-Hole."

The night was pitch-dark, it rained hard, and the convergence of our columns toward Dallas produced much confusion. I am sure similar confusion existed in the army opposed to us, for we were all mixed up. I slept on the ground, without cover, alongside of a log, got little sleep, resolved at daylight to renew the battle, and to make a lodgment on the Dallas and Allatoona road if possible, but the morning revealed a strong line of intrenchments facing us, with a heavy force of infantry and guns. The battle was renewed, and without success. McPherson reached Dallas that morning, viz., the 26th, and deployed his troops to the southeast and east of the town, placing Davis's division of the Fourteenth Corps, which had joined him on the road from Rome, on his left; but this still left a gap of at least three miles between Davis and Hooker. Meantime, also, General Schofield was closing up on Thomas's left.

Satisfied that Johnston in person was at New Hope with all his army, and that it was so much nearer my objective, the railroad, than Dallas, I concluded to draw McPherson from Dallas to Hooker's right, and gave orders accordingly; but McPherson also was confronted with a heavy force, and, as he began to withdraw according to his orders, on the morning of the 28th he was fiercely assailed on his right; a bloody battle ensued, in which he repulsed the attack, inflicting heavy loss on his assailants, and it was not until the 1st of June that he was enabled to withdraw from Dallas, and to effect a close junction with Hooker in front of New Hope. Meantime Thomas and Schofield were completing their deployments, gradually overlapping Johnston on his right, and thus extending our left nearer and nearer to the railroad, the nearest point of which was Acworth, about eight miles distant. All this time a continual battle was in progress by strong skirmish-lines, taking advantage of every species of cover and both parties fortifying each night by rifle-trenches with head-logs, many of which grew to be as formidable as first-class works of defense. Occasionally one party or the other would make a dash in the nature of a sally, but usually it sustained a repulse with great loss of life. I visited personally all parts of our lines nearly every day, was constantly within musket-range, and though the fire of musketry and cannon resounded day and night along the whole line, varying from six to ten miles, I rarely saw a dozen of the enemy at any one time; and these were always skirmishers dodging from tree to tree, or behind logs on the ground, or who occasionally showed their heads above the hastily-constructed but remarkably strong rifle-trenches. On the occasion of my visit to McPherson on the 30th of May, while standing with a group of officers, among whom were Generals McPherson, Logan, Barry, and Colonel Taylor, my former chief of artillery, a Minié-ball passed through Logan's coat-sleeve, scratching the skin, and struck Colonel Taylor square in the breast; luckily he had in his pocket a famous memorandum-book, in which he kept a sort of diary, about which we used to joke him a good deal; its thickness and size saved his life, breaking the force of the ball, so that after traversing the book it only penetrated the breast to the ribs, but it knocked him down and disabled him for the rest of the campaign.

On the 1st of June General McPherson closed in upon the right, and, without attempting further to carry the enemy's strong position at New Hope Church, I held our general right in close contact with it, gradually, carefully, and steadily working by the left, until our strong infantry-lines had reached and secured possession of all the wagon-roads between New Hope, Allatoona, and Acworth, when I dispatched Generals Garrard's and Stoneman's divisions of cavalry into Allatoona, the first around by the west end of the pass and the latter by the direct road. Both reached their destination without opposition, and orders were at once given to repair the railroad forward from Kingston to Allatoona, embracing the bridge across the Etowah River. Thus the real object of my move on Dallas was accomplished, and on the 4th of June I was preparing to draw off from New Hope Church, and to take position on the railroad in front of Allatoona, when, General Johnston himself having evacuated his position, we effected the change without further battle, and moved to the railroad, occupying it from Allatoona and Acworth forward to Big Shanty, in sight of the famous Kennesaw Mountain.

Thus, substantially in the month of May, we had steadily driven our antagonist from the strong positions of Dalton, Resaca, Cassville, Allatoona, and Dallas; had advanced our lines in strong, compact order from Chattanooga to Big Shanty, nearly a hundred miles of as difficult country as was ever fought over by civilized armies; and thus stood prepared to go on, anxious to fight, and confident of success as soon as the railroad communications were complete to bring forward the necessary supplies. It is now impossible to state accurately our loss of life and men in any one separate battle; for the fighting was continuous, almost daily, among trees and bushes, on ground where one could rarely see a hundred yards ahead.

The aggregate loss in the several corps for the month of May, sent to the Adjutant-General's office in the usual monthly returns, were:

Killed and missing	1,863
Wounded	7,436
Total	9,299

General Joseph E. Johnston, whose effective strength at the end of May was 64,456, states his losses:

Killed	721
Wounded	4,672
Total	5,393

These figures include only the killed and wounded, whereas my statement of losses embraces the "missing," which are usually "prisoners," and of these we captured, during the whole campaign of four and a half months, exactly 12,983. Assuming a due proportion for the month of May—one-fourth—makes 3,245 to be added to the killed and wounded given above, making an aggregate loss in Johnston's army, from Dalton to New Hope, of 8,638, against ours of 9,299.

I always estimated my force at about double the enemy and could afford to lose two to one without disturbing our relative proportion; but I also reckoned that, in the natural strength of the

43

country, in the abundance of mountains, streams, and forests, he had a fair offset to our numerical superiority, and therefore endeavored to act with reasonable caution while moving on the vigorous "offensive."

With the drawn battle of New Hope Church, and our occupation of the natural fortress of Allatoona, terminated the month of May and the first stage of the campaign.

BATTLES ABOUT KENNESAW

On the 1st of June our three armies were well in hand, in the broken and densely-wooded country fronting the enemy intrenched at New Hope Church, about five miles north of Dallas. General Stoneman's division of cavalry had occupied Allatoona, on the railroad, and General Garrard's division was at the western end of the pass, about Stilesboro. Colonel W. W. Wright of the Engineers was busily employed in repairing the railroad and rebuilding the bridge across the Etowah River, which had been destroyed by the enemy on his retreat; and the armies were engaged in a general and constant skirmish along a front of about six miles—McPherson the right, Thomas the centre, and Schofield on the left. By gradually covering our front with parapet, and extending to the left, we approached the railroad toward Acworth and overlapped the enemy's right. By the 4th of June we had made such progress that Johnston evacuated his lines in the night, leaving us masters of the situation, when I deliberately shifted McPherson's army to the extreme left, at and in front of Acworth, with Thomas's about two miles on his right, and Schofield's on his right—all facing east. Heavy rains set in about the 1st of June, making the roads infamous; but our marches were short, as we needed time for the repair of the railroad, so as to bring supplies forward to Allatoona Station. On the 6th I rode back to Allatoona, seven miles, found it all that was expected, and gave orders for its fortification and preparation as a secondary base. General Blair arrived at Acworth on the 8th with his two divisions of the Seventeenth Corps —the same which had been on veteran furlough—had come up from Cairo by way of Clifton, on the Tennessee River, and had followed our general route to Allatoona, where he had left a garrison of about fifteen hundred men. His effective strength, as reported, was nine thousand. These, with new regiments and furloughed men who had joined early in the month of May, equaled our losses from battle, sickness, and by detachments; so that the three armies still aggregated about one hundred thousand effective men.

15 NW of Marietta
June 1st, 1864

Dearest Ellen,

We are still hammering away but not making as much progress as I could wish. High chestnut and huckleberry ridges with narrow & difficult roads make a poor country to handle a large army in and it enables the enemy to ambush us, and stop our Roads, and embarrass us generally. I have got east of the Allatoona mountains but not yet out into the cleared country. Maj. Taylor was shot yesterday square in the breast and his life saved by that famous note book. He will be able to travel in a few days, but will suffer some months. The ball entered his right breast & coursed round to his back. Maj. [unclear] died some hours after his wound. Young [Wise?] was shot in the face but not killed. Without any grand battles we have had innumerable short sharp encounters, in which generally we have the advantage. My health is good. Love to all. No letters from you for a month.

W. T. S.

Acworth, Georgia
June 9th, 1864

Dearest Ellen,

I don't know that you can find this place on your map, but it is on the main road from Chattanooga into Georgia, seven miles in front of Allatoona, twelve from Marietta and thirty from Atlanta. The army lies about this place, extending east, north and south. We are replenishing our wagons with ammunition, forage and provisions. The railroad to our rear is all in good order except the bridge across the Etowah burned by the enemy, which will soon be done. I am forced to move with due deliberation to gain time for other combinations from Memphis and New Orleans, on Mobile, etc. But we will soon move forward to the Chattahoochee, eleven miles beyond Marietta. Johnston may fight us at the ridge of hills just this side of Marietta, but I think I can dislodge him and this will leave the great battle on or near the Chattahoochee, the passage of which he must dispute. He has a strong, well-disciplined army, but I think we can whip him on any thing like fair terms. So I will not run hot-headed against any works prepared for us. He thinks he checked us at Dallas. I went there to avoid the Allatoona Pass and as soon as I had drawn his army there, I slipped my cavalry into Allatoona Pass and round the main army on its front, a perfect success. I never designed to attack his hastily prepared works at Dallas and New Hope Church, and, as soon as he saw I was making for the railroad around his right flank, he abandoned his works and we occupied them for a moment and moved by the best road to our present position. We have captured several of their mails and it is wonderful to see how the soldiers talk of driving me back to the Ohio, and their returning to their loving families in Tennessee and Kentucky. I fear they count without their host, as they will have an awful reckoning if they attempt to pass over or around this army.

The paucity of news from this army at this time in Northern papers is most satisfactory to me. My circular was exactly right. Every officer and soldier should keep his friends and family advised of his own adventures and situation, whilst the busy and mischievous scribblers for newspapers are discountenanced. I know my course is right and meets the unqualified approval of all good soldiers. The press is angry at my term, "the cheap flattery of the press." We all know that generals and aspirants bribe these fellows by the loan of government horses and other conveniences not at their individual cost, but at the cost of the United States, and in return receive the cheap flattery of the press. The press caused the war, the press gives it point and bitterness, and as long as the press, both North and South, is allowed to fan the flames of discord and hostility, so long must the war last. The Southern press is just the same, and as long as people look to the press for truth and counsel, so long will war and anarchy prevail. The liberty of the press, like that of individuals, must be restrained to just limits consistent with the good of the whole, and every fool must not be allowed to print and publish falsehood and scandal as he pleases.

Blair is up and many detachments have come forward, so my army today is stronger than when I first sallied from Chattanooga.

I have received no letters from you of late and suppose you think it unsafe—only one mail has been captured by the enemy and that an unimportant one. I got the short telegraph of yesterday saying all was well. I feel anxious to hear from you more often, but know you are all in a safe and bountiful country. All my staff are well and have not been harmed—Colonel Taylor was wounded as he accompanied me in a tour of the lines. He is here, but will go home as soon as the railroad is done. Major [Geary?] was killed at Dallas and [unclear] wounded. No others of your acquaintance hurt, but of course the real battle is not yet fought. When it does come I will take good care to have it a big and decisive one.

Yours ever,
W. T. Sherman

On the 10th of June the whole combined army moved forward six miles to "Big Shanty," a station on the railroad, whence we had a good view of the enemy's position, which embraced three prominent hills, know as Kennesaw, Pine Mountain, and Lost Mountain. On each of these hills the enemy had signal-stations and fresh lines of parapets. Heavy masses of infantry could be distinctly seen with the naked eye, and it was manifest that Johnston had chosen his ground well, and with deliberation had prepared for battle; but his line was at least ten miles in extent—too long, in my judgment, to be held successfully by his force, then estimated at sixty thousand. As his position, however, gave him a perfect view over our field, we had to proceed with due caution. McPherson had the left, following the railroad, which curved around the north base of Kennesaw; Thomas the centre, obliqued to the right, deploying below Kennesaw and facing Pine Hill; and Schofield, somewhat refused, was on the general right, looking south, toward Lost Mountain.

On the 11th the Etowah bridge was done; the railroad was repaired up to our very skirmish-line, close to the base of Kennesaw, and a loaded train of cars came to Big Shanty. The locomotive, detached, was run forward to a water-tank within the range of the enemy's guns on Kennesaw, whence the enemy opened fire on the locomotive; but the engineer was not afraid, went on to the tank, got water, and returned safely to his train, answering the guns with the screams of his engine, heightened by the cheers and shouts of our men.

The rains continued to pour and made our developments slow and dilatory, for there were no roads, and these had to be improvised by each division for its own supply-train from the depot in Big Shanty to the camps. Meantime each army was deploying carefully before the enemy, intrenching every camp, ready as against a sally. The enemy's cavalry was also busy in our rear, compelling us to detach cavalry all the way back as far as Resaca, and to strengthen all the infantry posts as far as Nashville.

Big Shanty, Georgia
June 12th, 1864

Dearest Ellen,

I have received Phil's dispatch announcing the birth to us of another son. It took me somewhat by surprise but was not altogether unexpected. Well, I am glad you are over the terrible labor and hope that it is the last you will have to endure. Of course I am pleased to know the sex of the child as he must succeed to the place left vacant by Willy, though I fear we will never again be able to lavish on any one the love we had for him.

Still we hardly know ourselves what is in store for us. I agree with you that we should retain Willy's name vacant for his memory and that, though dead to this world, he yet lives fresh in our memories. Whatever name you give this child will be acceptable to me. Charles as a common family name would do, but I will suggest now that you may name him as you choose only that it be simple and common. I received within the past few days a great number of letters, among them a few from you, all in a heap, but all were short, and those for Charley* were delivered. I have not [told?] to Charley the birth of the child and don't know as I will till he finds it out, and I am now so used to conceal my thoughts that no one can suspect my knowledge till I reveal it. You say that pending the important events now transpiring you cannot write. I feel so, too. That it should have devolved on me to guide one of the two great armies on which may depend the fate of our people for the next hundred years I somewhat regret. Yet you know I have been drawn into it by a slow and gradual process which I could not avoid. Grant was forced into his position and I likewise. I think thus far I have played my game well. Had my plans been executed with the vim I contemplated, I should have forced Johnston to fight the decisive battle in the Oostenaula Valley between Dalton and Resaca, but McPherson was a little overcautious, and we cannot move vast armies of this size with the rapidity of thought or of small bodies.

For the past ten days, our movements have been vastly retarded by rains. It has rained hard all the time and today harder than ever, a steady cold rain. I am in an old house with a fire burning, which is not uncomfortable. Johnston has 60,000 infantry, 15,000 cavalry and a good deal of militia. We must have a terrific battle, and he wants to choose and fortify his ground. He also aims to break my roads to the rear. I wish we could make an accumulation of stores somewhere near, but the railroad is taxed to its utmost to supply our daily wants.

The country is stripped of cattle, horses, hogs and grain, but there are large fine fields of growing oats, wheat and corn which our horses and mules devour as we advance. Thus far we have been well supplied, and I hope it will continue, though I expect to hear any day of Forrest breaking into Tennessee from some quarter. John Morgan is in Kentucky, but I attach little importance to him or his raid as we don't draw anything from Kentucky, and there are plenty of troops there to capture and destroy him. Forrest is a more dangerous man. I am in hopes that an expedition sent out from Memphis on Tupelo about the first of June will give him full employment. I have also ordered A. J. Smith with the force he brought out of Red River to move against Mobile by way of diversion. Johnston is now between me and Marietta. As soon as these clouds and storms clear away I will study his position and determine to assault his line or turn it and force him back of the Chattahoochee. As long as I press him close and prevent his sending anything

---

* Sherman's brother-in-law.

to Lee I fulfill my part of the Grand Plan. In the mean time Grant will give Lee all the fighting he wants until he is sick of the war. Every man in America should now be armed, and all who will not help should be put in petticoats and deprived of the right to vote in the affairs of the after Nation. I will telegraph you on all important occasions. Hoping you will soon be well and contented, I am as ever your,

W. T. Sherman

By the 14th the rain slackened, and we occupied a continuous line of ten miles, intrenched, conforming to the irregular position of the enemy, when I reconnoitred, with a view to make a break in their line between Kennesaw and Pine Mountain. When abreast of Pine Mountain I noticed a rebel battery on its crest, with a continuous line of fresh rifle-trench about half-way down the hill. Our skirmishers were at the time engaged in the woods about the base of this hill between the lines, and I estimated the distance to the battery on the crest at about eight hundred yards. Near it, in plain view, stood a group of the enemy, evidently observing us with glasses. General Howard, commanding the Fourth Corps, was near by, and I called his attention to this group and ordered him to compel it to keep behind its cover. He replied that his orders from General Thomas were to spare artillery-ammunition. This was right, according to the general policy, but I explained to him that we must keep up the *morale* of a bold offensive, that he must use his artillery, force the enemy to remain on the timid defensive, and ordered him to cause a battery close by to fire three volleys.

In a conversation with General Johnston, after the war, he explained that on that day he had ridden in person from Marietta to Pine Mountain, held by Bates's division, and was accompanied by Generals Hardee and Polk. When on Pine Mountain, reconnoitring, quite a group of soldiers, belonging to the battery close by, clustered about him. He noticed the preparations of our battery to fire and cautioned these men to scatter. They did so, and he likewise hurried behind the parapet, from which he had an equally good view of our position; but General Polk, who was dignified and corpulent, walked back slowly, not wishing to appear too hurried or cautious in the presence of the men, and was struck across the breast by an unexploded shell, which killed him instantly.

I was on horseback, a couple of hundred yards off, before my orders to fire were executed, had no idea that our shot had taken effect, and continued my ride down along the line to Schofield's extreme flank, returning late in the evening to my headquarters at Big Shanty, where I occupied an abandoned house. In a cotton-field back of that house was our signal-station, on the roof of an old gin-house. The signal-officer reported that by studying the enemy's signals he had learned the "key," and that he could read their signals. He explained to me that he had translated a signal about noon, from Pine Mountain to Marietta, "Send an ambulance for General Polk's body;" and later in the day another, "Why don't you send an ambulance for General Polk?" From this we inferred that General Polk had been killed, but how or where we knew not; and this inference was confirmed later in the same day by the report of some prisoners who had been captured.

On the 15th we advanced our general lines, intending to attack at any weak point discovered between Kennesaw and Pine Mountain; but Pine Mountain was found to be abandoned, and Johnston had contracted his front somewhat, on a direct line, connecting Kennesaw with Lost Mountain. Thomas and Schofield thereby gained about two miles of most difficult country, and McPherson's left lapped well around the north end of Kennesaw. We captured a good many prisoners, among them a whole infantry regiment, the Fourteenth Alabama, three hundred and twenty strong.

On the 16th the general movement was continued, when Lost Mountain was abandoned by the enemy. Our right naturally swung around, so as to threaten the railroad below Marietta, but Johnston had still further contracted and strengthened his lines, covering Marietta and all the roads below.

On the 17th and 18th the rain again fell in torrents, making army movements impossible, but we devoted the time to strengthening our positions, more especially the left and centre, with a view gradually to draw from the left to add to the right; and we had to hold our lines on the left extremely strong, to guard against a sally from Kennesaw against our depot at Big Shanty. Garrard's division of cavalry was kept busy on our left, McPherson had gradually extended to his right, enabling Thomas to do the same still farther; but the enemy's position was so very strong and everywhere it was covered by intrenchments, that we found it as dangerous to assault as a permanent fort. We in like manner covered our lines of battle by similar works, and even our skirmishers learned to cover their bodies by the simplest and best forms of defensive works, such as rails or logs, piled in the form of a simple lunette, covered on the outside with earth thrown up at night.

The enemy and ourselves used the same form of rifle-trench, varied according to the nature of the ground: the trees and bushes were cut away for a hundred yards or more in front, serving as an abatis or entanglement; the parapets varied from four to six feet high, the dirt taken from a ditch outside and from a covered way inside, and this parapet was surmounted by a "head-log," composed of the trunk of a tree from twelve to twenty inches at the butt, lying along the interior crest of the parapet and resting in notches cut in other trunks which extended back, forming an inclined plane, in case the head-log should be knocked inward by a cannon-shot. The men of both armies became extremely skillful in the construction of these works, because each man realized their value and importance to himself, so that it required no orders for their construction. As soon as a regiment or brigade gained a position within easy distance for a sally, it would set to work with a will and would construct such a parapet in a single night; but I endeavored to spare the soldiers this hard labor by authorizing each division commander to organize out of the freedmen who escaped to us a pioneer corps of two hundred men, who were fed out of the regular army supplies, and I promised them ten dollars a month, under an existing act of Congress. These pioneer detachments became very useful to us during the rest of the war, for they could work at night while our men slept; they in turn were not expected to fight and could therefore sleep by day. Our enemies used their slaves for a similar purpose, but usually kept them out of the range of fire by employing them to fortify and strengthen the position to their rear *next* to be occupied in their general retrograde. During this campaign hundreds if not thousands of miles of similar intrenchments were built by both armies, and as a rule whichever party attacked one of them got the worst of it.

On the 19th of June the rebel army again fell back on its flanks, to such an extent that for a time I supposed it had retreated to the Chattahoochee River, fifteen miles distant; but as we pressed forward we were soon undeceived, for we found it still more concentrated, covering Marietta and the railroad. These successive contractions of the enemy's line encouraged us and discouraged him. On the 20th Johnston's position was unusually strong. Kennesaw Mountain was his salient; his two flanks were refused and covered by parapets and by Noonday and Nose's Creeks. His left flank was his weak point, so long as he acted on the "defensive," whereas, had he designed to contract the extent of his line for the purpose of getting in reserve a force with which to strike offensively from his right, he would have done a wise act, and I was compelled to presume that such was his object. We were also so far from Nashville and Chattanooga that we were naturally sensitive for the safety of our railroad and depots, so that the left (McPherson) was held *very strong*.

About this time came reports that a large cavalry force of the enemy had passed around our left flank, evidently to strike this very railroad somewhere below Chattanooga. I therefore reenforced the cavalry stationed from Resaca to Cassville, and ordered forward from Huntsville, Alabama, the infantry division of General John E. Smith, to hold Kingston securely.

While we were thus engaged about Kennesaw, General Grant had his hands full with Lee in Virginia. General Halleck was the chief of staff at Washington, and to him I communicated almost daily. On the 21st of June I reported to him tersely and truly the condition of facts on that day: "This is the nineteenth day of rain, and the prospect of fair weather is as far off as ever. The roads are impassable; the fields and woods become quagmires after a few wagons have crossed over. Yet we are at work all the time. The left flank is across Noonday Creek, and the right is across Nose's Creek. The enemy still holds Kennesaw, a conical mountain, with Marietta behind it, and has his flanks retired, to cover that town and the railroad behind. I am all ready to attack the moment the weather and roads will permit troops and artillery to move with any thing like life."

The weather has a wonderful effect on troops: in action and on the march, rain is favorable; but in the woods, where all is blind and uncertain, it seems almost impossible for an army covering ten miles of front to act in concert during wet and stormy weather. Still I pressed operations with the utmost earnestness, aiming always to keep our fortified lines in absolute contact with the enemy, while with the surplus force we felt forward, from one flank or the other, for his line of communication and retreat. On the 22d of June I rode the whole line, and ordered General Thomas in person to advance his extreme right corps (Hooker's); and instructed General Schofield, by letter, to keep his entire army, the Twenty-third Corps, as a strong right flank in close support of Hooker's deployed line. During this day the sun came out, with some promise of clear weather, and I had got back to my bivouac about dark, when a signal-message was received, dated—

General SHERMAN:

We have repulsed two heavy attacks, and feel confident, our only apprehension being from our extreme right flank. Three entire corps are in front of us.

Major-General HOOKER.

Hooker's corps belonged to Thomas's army; Thomas's headquarters were two miles nearer to Hooker than mine; and Hooker, being an old army officer, knew that he should have reported this fact to Thomas and not to me; I was, moreover, specially disturbed by the assertion in his report that he was uneasy about his *right flank*, when Schofield had been specially ordered to protect that. I first inquired of my adjutant, Dayton, if he were certain that General Schofield had received his orders, and he answered that the envelope in which he had sent them was receipted by General Schofield himself. I knew, therefore, that General Schofield must be near by, in close support of Hooker's right flank. General Thomas had before this occasion complained to me of General Hooker's disposition to "switch off," leaving wide gaps in his line, so as to be independent, and to make *glory* on his own account. I therefore resolved not to overlook this breach of discipline and propriety. The rebel army was only composed of three corps; I had that very day ridden six miles of their lines, found them everywhere strongly occupied, and therefore Hooker could not have encountered "three entire corps." Both McPherson and Schofield had also complained to me of this same tendency of Hooker to widen the gap between his own corps and his proper army (Thomas's), so as to come into closer contact with one or other of the wings, asserting that he was the senior by commission to both McPherson and Schofield, and that in the event of battle he should assume command over them, by virtue of his older commission.

They appealed to me to protect them. I had heard during that day some cannonading and heavy firing down toward the "Kulp House," which was about five miles southeast of where I was, but this was nothing unusual, for at the same moment there was firing along our lines full ten miles in extent. Early the next day (23d) I rode down to the "Kulp House," which was on a road leading from Powder Springs to Marietta, about three miles distant from the latter. On the way I passed through General Butterfield's division of Hooker's corps, which I learned had not been engaged at all in the battle of the day before; then I rode along Geary's and Ward's divisions, which occupied the field of battle, and the men were engaged in burying the dead. I found General Schofield's corps on the Powder Springs road, its head of column abreast of Hooker's right, therefore constituting "a strong right flank," and I met Generals Schofield and Hooker together. As rain was falling at the moment, we passed into a little church standing by the road-side, and I there showed General Schofield Hooker's signal-message of the day before. He was very angry, and pretty sharp words passed between them, Schofield saying that his head of column had been, at the time of the battle, actually in advance of Hooker's line; that the attack or sally of the enemy struck his troops before it did Hooker's; that General Hooker knew of it at the time; and he offered to go out and show me that the dead men of his advance division were lying farther out than any of Hooker's. General Hooker pretended not to have known this fact. I then asked him why he had called on me for help, until he had used all of his own troops; asserting that I had just seen Butterfield's division, and had learned from him that he had not been engaged the day before at all; and I asserted that the enemy's sally must have been made by one corps (Hood's), in place of three, and that it had fallen on Geary's and Ward's divisions, which had repulsed the attack handsomely. As we rode away from that church General Hooker was by my side, and I told him that such a thing must not occur again; in other words, I reproved him more gently than the occasion demanded, and from that time he began to sulk. General Hooker had come from the East with great fame as a "fighter," and at Chattanooga he was glorified by his "battle above the clouds," which I fear turned his head. He seemed jealous of all the army commanders, because in years, former rank, and experience, he thought he was our superior.

On the 23d of June I telegraphed to General Halleck this summary, which I cannot again better state:

> We continue to press forward on the principle of an advance against fortified positions. The whole country is one vast fort, and Johnston must have at least fifty miles of connected tenches, with abatis and finished batteries. We gain ground daily, fighting all the time. On the 21st General Stanley gained a position near the south end of Kennesaw, from which the enemy attempted in vain to drive him; and the same day General T. J. Wood's division took a hill, which the enemy assaulted three times at night without success, leaving more than a hundred dead on the ground. Yesterday the extreme right (Hooker and Schofield) advanced on the Powder Springs road to within three miles of Marietta. The enemy made a strong

effort to drive them away, but failed signally, leaving more than two hundred dead on the field. Our lines are now in close contact, and the fighting is incessant, with a good deal of artillery-fire. As fast as we gain one position the enemy has another all ready, but I think he will soon have to let go Kennesaw, which is the key to the whole country. The weather is now better, and the roads are drying up fast. Our losses are light, and, notwithstanding the repeated breaks of the road to our rear, supplies are ample.

Near Marietta, Georgia
June 26th, 1864

Dearest Ellen,

Phil's dispatch of the 11th is my last from Lancaster. I have a letter which you must have written just before the birth of our child. I am anxious to hear more in detail. I have written but little because my thoughts and mind have been so intent on other matters. Johnston has fallen back several times abandoning long lines of entrenchments. But he still occupies a good position with Kennesaw Mountain as the apex of his triangle embracing Marietta. His wing fell back for miles one day and I thought he had gone, but not so.

We have worked our way forward until we are in close contact, constant skirmishing and picket firing. He is afraid to come at us, and we have been cautious about dashing against his breastworks, that are so difficult to undertake in this hilly and wooded country. My lines are ten miles long and every change necessitates a large amount of work. Still we are now all ready, and I must attack direct or turn the position. Both will be attended with loss and difficulty, but one or the other must be attempted.

This is Sunday and I will write up all my letters, and tomorrow will pitch in at some one or more points.

I am now 105 miles from Chattanooga, and all our provisions have to come over that single road, which is almost daily broken somewhere, but thus far our supplies have been ample. We have devoured the land and our animals eat up the wheat and corn fields close. All the people retire before us and desolation is behind. To realize what war is one should follow our tracks. I am very anxious to hear from you and the youngsters. I suppose Tom feels the pride of having a younger brother to rule over and control. May the child grow up and possess the courage, confidence and kindness of heart of our poor Willy. I would gladly surrender all the honors and fame of this life if I could see him once more in his loving confidence and faith in us. But we must now think of the living and prepare them for our exodus, which may be near at hand.

Though not conscious of danger at this moment, I know the country swarms with thousands who would shoot me and thank their God they had slain a monster; and yet I have been more kindly disposed to the people of the South than any general officer of the whole army.

Yours ever,
W. T. Sherman

During the 24th and 25th of June General Schofield extended his right as far as prudent, so as to compel the enemy to thin out his lines correspondingly, with the intention to make two strong assaults at points where success would give us the greatest advantage. I had consulted Generals Thomas, McPherson, and Schofield, and we all agreed that we could not with prudence stretch out any more, and therefore there was no alternative but to attack "fortified lines," a thing carefully avoided up to that time. I reasoned, if we could make a breach anywhere near the rebel centre, and thrust in a strong head of column, that with the one moiety of our army we could hold in check the corresponding wing of the enemy, and with the other sweep in flank and overwhelm the other half. The 27th of June was fixed as the day for the attempt, and in order to oversee the whole, and to be in close communication with all parts of the army, I had a place cleared on the top of a hill to the rear of Thomas's centre, and had the telegraph-wires laid to it. The points of attack were chosen, and the troops were all prepared with as little demonstration as possible.

About 9 a.m. of the day appointed, the troops moved to the assault, and all along our lines for ten miles a furious fire of artillery and musketry was kept up. At all points the enemy met us with determined courage and in great force. McPherson's attacking column caught up the face of the lesser Kennesaw, but could not reach the summit. About a mile to the right Thomas's assaulting column reached the parapet, where Brigadier-General Harker was shot down mortally wounded, and Brigadier-General Daniel McCook, my old law-partner, was desperately wounded, from the effects of which he afterward died. By 11:30 the assault was in fact over and had failed. We had not broken the rebel line at either point, but our assaulting columns held their ground within a few yards of the rebel trenches and there covered themselves with parapet. McPherson lost about five hundred men and several valuable officers, and Thomas lost nearly two thousand men. This was the hardest fight of the campaign up to that date. Johnston admitted his loss in killed and wounded at 808.

While the battle was in progress at the centre, Schofield crossed Olley's Creek on the right and gained a position threatening Johnston's line of retreat; and, to increase the effect, I ordered Stoneman's cavalry to proceed rapidly still farther to the right, to Sweetwater. Satisfied of the bloody cost of attacking intrenched lines, I at once thought of moving the whole army to the railroad at a point about ten miles below Marietta, or to the Chattahoochee River itself. All the orders were issued to bring forward supplies enough to fill our wagons, intending to strip the railroad back to Allatoona, and leave that place as our depot, to be covered as well as possible by Garrard's cavalry. General Thomas, as usual, shook his head, deeming it risky to leave the railroad; but something had to be done, and I had resolved on this move, as reported in my dispatch to General Halleck on July 1st:

> General Schofield is now south of Olley's Creek, and on the head of Nickajack. I have been hurrying down provisions and forage, and to-morrow night propose to move McPherson from the left to the extreme right, back of General Thomas. This will bring my right within three miles of the Chattahoochee River, and about five miles from the railroad. By this movement I think I can force Johnston to move his whole army down from Kennesaw to defend his railroad and the Chattahoochee, when I will (by the left flank) reach the railroad below Marietta; but in this I must cut loose from the railroad with ten days' supplies in wagons. Johnston may come out of his intrenchments to attack Thomas, which is exactly what I want, for General Thomas is well intrenched on a line parallel with the enemy south of Kennesaw. I think that Allatoona and the line of the Etowah are strong enough for me to venture on this move. The movement is substantially down the Sandtown road straight for Atlanta.

McPherson drew out of his lines during the night of July 2d, leaving Garrard's cavalry, dismounted, occupying his trenches, and moved to the rear of the Army of the Cumberland, stretching down the Nickajack; but Johnston detected the movement, and promptly abandoned Marietta and Kennesaw. I expected as much, for, by the earliest dawn of the 3d of July, I was up at a large spy-glass mounted on a tripod, which Colonel Poe, United States Engineers, had at his bivouac close by our camp. I directed the glass on Kennesaw, and saw some of our pickets crawling

58

up the hill cautiously; soon they stood upon the very top, and I could plainly see their movements as they ran along the crest just abandoned by the enemy. In a minute I roused my staff and started them off with orders in every direction for a pursuit by every possible road, hoping to catch Johnston in the confusion of retreat, especially at the crossing of the Chattahoochee River.

Near Marietta, Georgia
June 30th, 1864

Dearest Ellen,

I got Mary Ewing's letter, also that of Susan [unclear], telling me of your serious illness after the birth of the new baby, but I had got Phil's dispatch saying you had been very sick but were much better and on the mend. I have no doubt your anxiety on many accounts has caused your illness but now having a new object of interest I hope your interest will revive and return you rapidly to health.

It is enough to make the whole world start at the awful amount of death and destruction that now stalks abroad. Daily for the past two months has the work progressed, and I see no signs of a remission till one or both and all the armies are destroyed, when I suppose the balance of the people will tear each other up, as Grant says, reenacting the story of the Kilkenny cats. I begin to regard the death and mangling of a couple thousand men as a small affair, a kind of morning dash. And it may be well that we become so hardened. Each day is killed or wounded some valuable officers and men, the bullets coming from a concealed foe. I suppose the papers are impatient why I don't push on more rapidly to Atlanta, but those who are here are satisfied with the progress. It is as much as our railroad can do to supply us bread, meat and corn, and I cannot leave the railroad to swing on Johnston's flank or rear without giving him the railroad, which I cannot do without having a good supply on hand. I am moving heaven and earth to accomplish this, in which event I shall leave the railroad and move to the Chattahoochee, threatening to cross which will I think force him to do that very thing, when I will swing round on the road again. In that event he may be all ready and attempt to hold both road and river, but my opinion is he has not force enough to do both. In that event you will be without news of us for ten days. I think we can whip his army in fair battle, but behind the hills and trunks our loss of life and limb on the first assault could reduce us too much. In other words, at this distance from home we cannot afford the losses of such terrible assaults as Grant has made. I have only one source of supply. Grant had several in succession. One of my chief objects was to prevent Joe Johnston from detaching against Grant till he got below Richmond and that I have done. I have no idea of besieging Atlanta but may cross the Chattahoochee and circle round Atlanta, breaking up its roads.

As you begin to get well, I fear you will begin to fret again about changing your abode. If you are not comfortable at home try and rent some house, not the small one of Martin's you bespoke, but get Martin or Phil to find some other and live as quietly and comfortably as possible. The worst of the war is not yet begun. The civil strife at the North has to come yet and the tendency to anarchy to be cured. Look at matters in Kentucky and Missouri and down the Mississippi and Arkansas, where shallow people have been taught to believe the war is over, and you will see trouble enough to convince you I was right in my view of the case from the first. Stay as quietly as you can at Lancaster till Grant and I have our downfall, or are disposed of and then if we can do better will be time enough to change. In such a quiet place as Lancaster you can hardly realize the truth that is so plain and palpable to me. I hardly think Johnston will give me a chance to fight a decisive battle unless at such a disadvantage that I ought not to accept, and he is so situated that when threatened or pressed too hard he draws off leaving us a barren victory. He will thus act all summer, unless he gains a great advantage in position or succeeds in breaking our roads. My love to all the children and folks and believe me always.

Yours,
W. T. Sherman

Our losses, from June 1st to July 3d, were all substantially sustained about Kennesaw and Marietta, and it was really a continuous battle, lasting from the 10th day of June till the 3d of July, when the rebel army fell back from Marietta toward the Chattahoochee River. Our losses were:

Killed and missing	1,790
Wounded	5,740
Total	7,530

Johnston makes his statement of losses for pretty much the same period, from June 4th to July 4th:

Killed	468
Wounded	3,480
Total	3,948

BATTLES ABOUT ATLANTA

On the 3d of July, by moving McPherson's entire army from the extreme left, at the base of Kennesaw to the right, below Olley's Creek, and stretching it down the Nickajack toward Turner's Ferry of the Chattahoochee, we forced Johnston to choose between a direct assault on Thomas's intrenched position, or to permit us to make a lodgment on his railroad below Marietta, or even to cross the Chattahoochee. Of course, he chose to let go Kennesaw and Marietta and fall back on an intrenched camp prepared by his orders in advance on the north and west bank of the Chattahoochee, covering the railroad-crossing and his several pontoon-bridges. I confess I had not learned beforehand of the existence of this strong place and had counted on striking him an effectual blow in the expected confusion of his crossing the Chattahoochee, a broad and deep river then to his rear. Ordering every part of the army to pursue vigorously on the morning of the 3d of July, I rode into Marietta, just quitted by the rebel rear-guard, and was terribly angry at the cautious pursuit by Garrard's cavalry, and even by the head of our infantry columns. But Johnston had in advance cleared and multiplied his roads, whereas ours had to cross at right angles from the direction of Powder Springs toward Marietta, producing delay and confusion. By night Thomas's head of column ran up against a strong rear-guard intrenched at Smyrna camp-ground, six miles below Marietta, and there on the next day we celebrated our Fourth of July, by a noisy but not a desperate battle, designed chiefly to hold the enemy there till Generals McPherson and Schofield could get well into position below him, near the Chattahoochee crossings.

It was here that General Noyes lost his leg. I came very near being shot myself while reconnoitring in the second story of a house on our picket-line, which was struck several times by cannon-shot, and perfectly riddled with musket-balls.

During the night Johnston drew back all his army and trains inside his intrenched camp at the Chattahoochee, which proved one of the strongest pieces of field-fortification I ever saw. We closed up against it and were promptly met by a heavy and severe fire. On personally reconnoitring, I saw the abatis and the strong redoubts, which satisfied me of the preparations that had been made by Johnston. While I was with General Jeff C. Davis, a poor Negro came out of the abatis, blanched with fright, said he had been hidden under a log all day, with a perfect storm of shot, shells, and musket-balls passing over him, till a short lull had enabled him to creep out and make himself known to our skirmishers, who in turn had sent him back to where we were. This Negro explained that he with about a thousand slaves had been at work a month or more on these very lines, which, as he explained, extended from the river about a mile above the railroad-bridge to Turner's Ferry below, being in extent from five to six miles.

Therefore, on the 5th of July we had driven our enemy to cover in the valley of the Chattahoochee, and we held possession of the river above for eighteen miles as far as Roswell and below ten miles to the mouth of the Sweetwater. Moreover, we held the high ground and could overlook his movements, instead of his looking down on us, as was the case at Kennesaw.

From a hill just back of Vining's Station I could see the houses in Atlanta, nine miles distant, and the whole intervening valley of the Chattahoochee; could observe the preparations for our reception on the other side, the camps of men and large trains of covered wagons; and supposed, as a matter of course, that Johnston had passed the river with the bulk of his army, and that he had only left on our side a corps to cover his bridges; but in fact he had only sent across his cavalry and trains. Between Howard's corps at Paice's Ferry and the rest of Thomas's army was a space concealed by dense woods, in crossing which I came near riding into a detachment of the enemy's cavalry; and later in the same day Colonel Frank Sherman, of Chicago, then on General Howard's staff, did actually ride straight into the enemy's camp, supposing that our lines were continuous. He was carried to Atlanta, and for some time the enemy supposed they were in possession of the commander-in-chief of the opposing army.

I knew that Johnston would not remain long on the west bank of the Chattahoochee, for I could easily practise on that ground to better advantage our former tactics of intrenching a moiety in his front, and with the rest of our army cross the river and threaten either his rear or the city of Atlanta itself, which city was of vital importance to the existence not only of his own army, but of the Confederacy itself. In my dispatch of July 6th to General Halleck, at Washington, I state that—

Johnston (in his retreat from Kennesaw) has left two breaks in the railroad— one above Marietta and one near Vining's Station. The former is already repaired, and Johnston's army has heard the sound of our locomotives. The telegraph is finished to Vining's Station, and the field-wire has just reached my bivouac, and will be ready to convey this message as soon as it is written and translated into cipher.

I propose to study the crossings of the Chattahoochee, and, when all is ready, to move quickly. As a beginning, I will keep the troops and wagons well back from the river, and only display to the enemy our picket-line, with a few field-batteries along at random. I have already shifted Schofield to a point in our left rear, whence he can in a single move reach the Chattahoochee at a point above the railroad-bridge, where there is a ford. At present the waters are turbid and swollen from recent rains; but if the present hot weather lasts, the water will run down very fast. We have pontoons enough for four bridges, but, as our crossing will be resisted, we must manœuvre some. All the regular crossing-places are covered by forts, apparently of long construction; but we shall cross in due time, and, instead of attacking Atlanta direct, or any of its forts, I propose to make a circuit, destroying all its railroads. This is a delicate movement, and must be done with caution. Our army is in good condition and full of confidence; but the weather is intensely hot, and a good many men have fallen with sunstroke. The country is high and healthy, and the sanitary condition of the army is good.

Of course, I expected every possible resistance in crossing the Chattahoochee River, and had made up my mind to feign on the right but actually to cross over by the left. We had already secured a crossing-place at Roswell, but one nearer was advisable; General Schofield had examined the river well, found a place just below the mouth of Soap's Creek which he deemed advantageous, and was instructed to effect an early crossing there and to intrench a good position on the other side, viz., the east bank. But, preliminary thereto, I had ordered General Rousseau, at Nashville, to collect, out of the scattered cavalry in Tennessee, a force of a couple of thousand men, to make a rapid march for Opelika, to break up the railroad-links between Georgia and Alabama, and then to make junction with me about Atlanta.

Rousseau, when he reported to me in person before Atlanta, on the 23d of July, stated his entire loss to have been only twelve killed and thirty wounded. He brought in four hundred captured mules and three hundred horses, and also told me a good story. He said he was far down in Alabama, below Talladega, one hot, dusty day, when the blue clothing of his men was gray with dust; he had halted his column along a road, and he in person, with his staff, had gone to the house of a planter, who met him kindly on the front-porch. He asked for water, which was brought, and as the party sat on the porch in conversation he saw, in a stable-yard across the road, quite a number of good mules. He remarked to the planter, "My good sir, I fear I must take some of your mules." The planter remonstrated, saying he had already contributed liberally to the *good cause*; that it was only last week he had given General Roddy ten mules. Rousseau replied, "Well, in this war you should be at least neutral—that is, you should be as liberal to us as to Roddy" (a rebel cavalry general). "Well, ain't you on our side?" "No," said Rousseau; "I am General Rousseau, and all these men you see are Yanks." "Great God! is it possible? Are these Yanks? Who ever supposed they would come away down here in Alabama?" Of course, Rousseau took his ten mules.

Schofield effected his crossing at Soap's Creek very handsomely on the 9th, capturing the small guard that was watching the crossing. By night he was on the high ground beyond, strongly intrenched, with two good pontoon-bridges finished, and was prepared, if necessary, for an assault by the whole Confederate army. The same day Garrard's cavalry also crossed over at Roswell, drove away the cavalry-pickets and held its ground till relieved by Newton's division of Howard's corps, which was sent up temporarily, till it in turn was relieved by Dodge's Sixteenth Corps of the Army of the Tennessee, which was the advance of the whole of that army.

That night Johnston evacuated his trenches, crossed over the Chattahoochee, burned the railroad-bridge and his pontoon and trestle bridges, and left us in full possession of the north or west bank—besides which, we had already secured possession of the two good crossings at Roswell and Soap's Creek. I have always thought Johnston neglected his opportunity there, for he had lain comparatively idle while we got control of both banks of the river above him.

Dearest Ellen,

It is now more than two months since I left Chattanooga and I think during all this time I have but one letter from you. I fear you have been more ill than I had supposed but I hope that it in no manner resulted from uneasiness about me. I have been very well all the time but necessarily so employed that I could not write much. All my letters partake more of the dispatch kind than anything else and I have settled down so that I dislike to write a regular letter. Charley and Dayton have often written and I have no doubt you have followed us in our tedious and dangerous journey. We are now on the Chattahoochee in plain view of the city of Atlanta, nine miles off. The enemy and the Chattahoochee lie below us, and intense heat prevails; but I think I shall succeed. At all events you know I never turn back. I see by the papers that too much stress was laid on the repulse of June 27th. I was forced to make the effort, and it should have succeeded; but the officers and men have become so used to my avoiding excessive danger and forcing back the enemy by strategy that they hate to assault. But to assault is sometimes necessary, for its effect on the enemy. Had that assault succeeded, I could have then fought Johnston with the advantage on my side, instead of his having all the benefit of forts, ground, creeks, etc. As it was I did not give him rest but forced him across the Chattahoochee, which was the first great object. I have already got Schofield and Garrard across the River, and therefore can cross the army when I choose. I sent to General Webster my pay accounts for May, and after paying some small accounts he was to send a check for the balance to you. He writes me he has done so. I want you to write to Professor Albert E. Church, U. S. Military Academy, West Point, and ask him what is my assessment towards the National Monument that is being erected there in memory of the West Point graduates that have fallen in this war. It is about $27—when the exact figure is thus ascertained send him a check. Also subscribe for the United States Service Magazine of which Professor H. [Coffie?] of Philadelphia is Editor. It is a monthly magazine and will be good authority. I see he proposes to publish in the August number a sketch of my life, compiled by authority of a friend of mine. I wrote to Coffie to know what friend and he answered, Bowman. I don't know what data Bowman has but, of course, I know he will deal in more eulogy and generalisms than I would prefer, but cannot avoid it. I wish the letter of resignation I made in Louisiana embraced in any sketch of me, and I remember you said you had a copy. If you have it still, make a copy and send it to Bowman, if you know where he is or to Professor Coffie who will see to it. If you cannot attend to these matters get Phil or some one else to do it for you. The distant booming of cannons and sharp rattle of musketry is now so familiar that it feels unnatural unless they are constant. The army is very large and extends from Roswell factory at the north around to Sandtown, but my center is directly in front of Atlanta. I will have to manœuver some hereabouts to drive the enemy and to gain time to accumulate stores by rail to enable me to operate beyond reach of the railroad. Thus far our supplies have been ample and the country is high, mountainous, with splendid water and considerable forage in the nature of fields of growing wheat, oats and corn, but we sweep across it leaving it as bare as a desert. The people all flee before us. The task of feeding this vast host is a more difficult one than to fight. I hope by this time you are well, and that the youngster is beginning to develop so you can make a guess what he is to be. I should like to have your opinion of him though it will be a prejudiced one. I should like Minnie and Lizzie and Tom to write more frequently. They must not expect me to write letters for them; they must understand my present family is numbered by hundreds of thousands, all of whom look to me to provide for their wants. I shall not attempt an official account of this campaign until it approaches completion. Give my love to your father and all the young folks.

Yours ever
W. T. Sherman

Chattahoochee, Georgia
July 13th, 1864

Dearest Ellen,

I have not written as often as I should, still as often as you should expect in the midst of the incessant war in which I have been engaged for the past two months. I have not heard a word from you since the birth of our son and only two short telegrams from Phil. I have telegraphed twice and elicited no reply. Charley does not hear from Lancaster either, but today heard from Sis at Chauncy, and she said you were doing well at last accounts. Still I supposed you must be dangerously ill or that your letters miscarried. But today Ellen Lynch's letter came addressed in your hand and postmarked July 6th. You should write occasionally or make Lizzie write or Minnie who must now be at home, or get some one for I should not be kept uneasy about you, when my mind is kept in such a stretch by the circumstances that surround me. I believe I have conducted this campaign as skilfully as possible, and when understood in all its details it will attract the notice of military judges. Still, much remains and I may be all the year. I do not pretend to see the end of this war, though I am far down in the very heart of the enemy's country. You will hear less of us hereafter. I have asked Mr. Stanton not to publish my daily dispatches because they give a clue to the enemy and I prefer silence. It is an element of reason. I wrote a long letter to Phil which will explain our position. In a few days I will cross the Chattahoochee and then will come the real struggle. I know we will whip Johnston in anything like a fair fight, but being on the defensive he can take great ad-

66

vantage of forts, field works and the nature of the ground which naturally favors him. But we have overcome all such obstacles thus far, and trust we can continue to do so, though it involves time. My army is as strong as the day we left Chattanooga and full of confidence. Weather is very hot, but we have plenty of water and the country is mountainous and healthy. I am in very good condition, and my horses are all well, which is important. Give my love to all the folks and have Minnie, Lizzie and Tom write to me. Describe the young one.

Yours ever,
W. T. Sherman

On the 13th I ordered McPherson, with the Fifteenth Corps, to move up to Roswell, to cross over, prepare good bridges, and to make a strong intrenched position on the farther side. Stoneman had been sent down to Campbellton, with orders to cross over and to threaten the railroad below Atlanta, if he could do so without too much risk; and General Blair, with the Seventeenth Corps, was to remain at Turner's Ferry, demonstrating as much as possible, thus keeping up the feint below while we were actually crossing above. Thomas was also ordered to prepare his bridges at Powers's and Paice's Ferries. By crossing the Chattahoochee above the railroad-bridge, we were better placed to cover our railroad and depots than below, though a movement across the river below the railroad, to the south of Atlanta, might have been more decisive. But we were already so far from home and would be compelled to accept battle whenever offered, with the Chattahoochee to *our* rear, that it became imperative for me to take all prudential measures the case admitted of, and I therefore determined to pass the river above the railroad-bridge—McPherson on the left, Schofield in the centre, and Thomas on the right.

On the 13th I reported to General Halleck as follows:

> All is well. I have now accumulated stores at Allatoona and Marietta, both fortified and garrisoned points. Have also three places at which to cross the Chattahoochee in our possession, and only await General Stoneman's return from a trip down the river, to cross the army in force and move on Atlanta.
>
> Stoneman is now out two days, and had orders to be back on the fourth or fifth day at furthest.

From the 10th to the 15th we were all busy in strengthening the several points for the proposed passage of the Chattahoochee, in increasing the number and capacity of the bridges, rearranging the garrisons to our rear, and in bringing forward supplies. On the 15th General Stoneman got back to Powder Springs and was ordered to replace General Blair at Turner's Ferry, and Blair, with the Seventeenth Corps, was ordered up to Roswell to join McPherson.

On the 17th we began the general movement against Atlanta, Thomas crossing the Chattahoochee at Powers's and Paice's, by pontoon-bridges; Schofield moving out toward Cross Keys, and McPherson toward Stone Mountain. We encountered but little opposition except by cavalry. On the 18th all the armies moved on a general right wheel, Thomas to Buckhead, forming line of battle facing Peach-Tree Creek; Schofield was on his left, and McPherson well over toward the railroad between Stone Mountain and Decatur, which he reached at 2 p.m. of that day, about four miles from Stone Mountain and seven miles east of Decatur, and there he turned toward Atlanta, breaking up the railroad as he progressed, his advance-guard reaching Decatur about night, where he came into communication with Schofield's troops, which had also reached Decatur. About 10 a.m. of that day (July 18th), when the armies were all in motion, one of General Thomas's staff-officers brought me a citizen, one of our spies, who had just come out of Atlanta, and had brought a newspaper of the same day or of the day before, containing Johnston's order relinquishing the command of the Confederate forces in Atlanta, and Hood's order assuming the command. I immediately inquired of General Schofield, who was his classmate at West Point, about Hood, as to his general character, etc., and learned that he was bold even to rashness and courageous in the extreme; I inferred that the change of commanders meant "fight." Notice of this important change was at once sent to all parts of the army, and every division commander was cautioned to be always prepared for battle in any shape. This was just what we wanted, to fight in open ground on any thing like equal terms, instead of being forced to run up against prepared intrenchments; but, at the same time, the enemy having Atlanta behind him, could choose the time and place of attack, and could at pleasure mass a superior force on our weakest points. Therefore, we had to be constantly ready for sallies.

On the 19th the three armies were converging toward Atlanta, meeting such feeble resistance that I really thought the enemy intended to evacuate the place. The troops had crossed Peach-Tree Creek, were deployed, but at the time were resting for noon, when, without notice, the enemy came pouring out of their trenches down upon them, they became commingled and fought in many places hand to hand. General Thomas happened to be near the rear of Newton's

division, and got some field-batteries in a good position, on the north side of Peach-Tree Creek, from which he directed a furious fire on a mass of the enemy, which was passing around Newton's left and exposed flank. After a couple of hours of hard and close conflict, the enemy retired slowly within his trenches, leaving his dead and many wounded on the field. Johnson's and Newton's losses were light, for they had partially covered their fronts with light parapet; but Hooker's whole corps fought in open ground and lost about fifteen hundred men. He reported four hundred rebel dead left on the ground and that the rebel wounded would number four thousand; but this was conjectural, for most of them got back within their own lines. We had, however, met successfully a bold sally, had repelled it handsomely, and were also put on our guard; and the event illustrated the future tactics of our enemy.

Colonel Tom Reynolds was shot through the leg. When the surgeons were debating the propriety of amputating it in his hearing, he begged them to spare the leg, as it was very valuable, being an "imported leg." He was of Irish birth, and this well-timed piece of wit saved his leg, for the surgeons thought, if he could perpetrate a joke at such a time, they would trust to his vitality to save his limb.

During the night, I had full reports from all parts of our line, most of which was partially intrenched as against a sally, and finding that McPherson was stretching out too much on his left flank, I wrote him a note early in the morning not to extend so much by his left; for we had not troops enough to completely invest the place, and I intended to destroy utterly all parts of the Augusta Railroad to the east of Atlanta, then to withdraw from the left flank and add to the right. In that letter I ordered McPherson not to extend any farther to the left, but to employ General Dodge's corps, then forced out of position, to destroy every rail and tie of the railroad, from Decatur up to his skirmish-line, and I wanted McPherson to be ready, as soon as General Garrard returned from Covington (whither I had sent him), to move to the extreme right of Thomas, so as to reach if possible the Macon railroad below Atlanta. In the morning we found the strong line of parapet, "Peach-Tree line," to the front of Schofield and Thomas, abandoned, and our lines were advanced rapidly close up to Atlanta. For some moments I supposed the enemy intended to evacuate, and in person was on horseback at the head of Schofield's troops, who had advanced in front of the Howard House to some open ground, from which we could plainly see the whole rebel line of parapets, and I saw their men dragging up from the intervening valley, by the distillery, trees and saplings for abatis. Our skirmishers found the enemy down in this valley, and we could see the rebel main line strongly manned, with guns in position at intervals. Schofield was dressing forward his lines, and I could hear Thomas farther to the right engaged, when General McPherson and his staff rode up. We went back to the Howard House, a double frame-building with a porch and sat on the steps, discussing the chances of battle and of Hood's general character. McPherson had also been of the same class at West Point with Hood, Schofield, and Sheridan. We agreed that we ought to be unusually cautious and prepared at all times for sallies and for hard fighting, because Hood, though not deemed much of a scholar or of great mental capacity, was undoubtedly a brave, determined, and rash man; and the change of commanders at that particular crisis argued the displeasure of the Confederate Government with the cautious but prudent conduct of General Joseph Johnston.

McPherson was in excellent spirits, well pleased at the progress of events so far, and had come over purposely to see me about the order I had given him to use Dodge's corps to break up the railroad, saying that the night before he had gained a position on Leggett's Hill from which he could look over the rebel parapet and see the high smoke-stack of a large foundry in Atlanta; that before receiving my orders he had diverted Dodge's two divisions from the main road, along a diagonal one that led to his extreme left flank, then held by Giles A. Smith's division, for the purpose of strengthening that flank; and that he had sent some intrenching-tools there, to erect some batteries from which he intended to knock down that foundry, and otherwise to damage the buildings inside of Atlanta. He said he could put all his pioneers to work, and do with them in the time indicated all I had proposed to do with General Dodge's two divisions. Of course I assented at once, and we walked down the road a short distance, sat down by the foot of a tree where I had my map, and on it pointed out to him Thomas's position and his own. I then explained minutely that, after we had sufficiently broken up the Augusta road, I wanted to shift his whole army around by the rear to Thomas's extreme right, and hoped thus to reach the other railroad at East Point. While we sat there we could hear lively skirmishing going on near us down about the distillery, and occasionally round-shot from twelve- or twenty-four pound guns came through the trees in reply to those of Schofield, and we could hear similar sounds all along down the lines of Thomas to our right, and his own to the left; but presently the firing appeared a little more brisk, and then we heard an occasional gun back toward Decatur. I asked him what it meant. We took

70

my pocket-compass (which I always carried), and by noting the direction of the sound, we became satisfied that the firing was too far to our left rear to be explained by known facts, and he hastily called for his horse, his staff, and his orderlies.

McPherson was then in his prime, about thirty-four years old, over six feet high, and a very handsome man in every way, was universally liked, and had many noble qualities. He had on his boots outside his pantaloons, gauntlets on his hands, had on his major-general's uniform, and wore a sword-belt, but no sword. He hastily gathered his papers into a pocket-book, put it in his breast-pocket, and jumped on his horse, saying he would hurry down his line and send me back word what these sounds meant. Although the sound of musketry on our left grew in volume, I was not so much disturbed by it as by the sound of artillery back toward Decatur. I ordered Schofield at once to send a brigade back to Decatur and was walking up and down the porch of the Howard House, listening, when one of McPherson's staff, with his horse covered with sweat, dashed up to the porch, and reported that General McPherson was either "killed or a prisoner." He explained that when they had left me a few minutes before, they had ridden rapidly across to the railroad, the sounds of battle increasing as they neared the position occupied by General Giles A. Smith's division and that McPherson had sent first one, then another of his staff to bring some of the reserve brigades of the Fifteenth Corps over to the exposed left flank; that he had reached the head of Dodge's corps and had ordered it to hurry forward to the same point; that then, almost if not entirely alone, he had followed this road leading across the wooded valley behind the Seventeenth Corps, and had disappeared in these woods, doubtless with a sense of absolute security. The sound of musketry was there heard, and McPherson's horse came back, bleeding, wounded, and riderless. I ordered the staff-officer who brought this message to return at once, to find General Logan (the senior officer present with the Army of the Tennessee), to report the same facts to him, and to instruct him to drive back this supposed small force, which had evidently got around the Seventeenth Corps through the blind woods in rear of our left flank. I dispatched orders to General Thomas on our right, telling him of this strong sally, and my inference that the lines in his front had evidently been weakened by reason thereof and that he ought to take advantage of the opportunity to make a lodgment in Atlanta, if possible.

Meantime the sounds of the battle rose on our extreme left more and more furious, extending to the place where I stood, at the Howard House. Within an hour an ambulance came in bearing

McPherson's body. I had it carried inside of the Howard House and laid on a door wrenched from its hinges. Dr. Hewitt, of the army, was there, and I asked him to examine the wound. He opened the coat and shirt, saw where the ball had entered and where it came out, or rather lodged under the skin, and he reported that McPherson must have died in a few seconds after being hit; that the ball had ranged upward across his body and passed near the heart. He was dressed just as he left me, with gauntlets and boots on, but his pocket-book was gone. On further inquiry I learned that his body must have been in possession of the enemy some minutes, during which time it was rifled of the pocket-book, and I was much concerned lest the letter I had written him that morning should have fallen into the hands of some one who could read and understand its meaning. Fortunately the spot in the woods where McPherson was shot was regained by our troops in a few minutes, and the pocket-book found in the haversack of a prisoner of war captured at the time, and it and its contents were secured by one of McPherson's staff.

The reports that came to me from all parts of the field revealed clearly what was the game of my antagonist, and the ground somewhat favored him. The railroad and wagon-road from Decatur to Atlanta lie along the summit, from which the waters flow, by short, steep valleys, into the "Peach-Tree" and Chattahoochee, to the west, and by other valleys, of gentler declivity, toward the east (Ocmulgee). The ridges and level ground were mostly cleared, and had been cultivated as corn or cotton fields; but where the valleys were broken, they were left in a state of nature—wooded, and full of undergrowth. McPherson's line of battle was across this railroad, along a general ridge, with a gentle but cleared valley to his front, between him and the defenses of Atlanta; and another valley, behind him, was clear of timber in part, but to his left rear the country was heavily wooded. Hood, during the night of July 21st, had withdrawn from his Peach-Tree line, had occupied the fortified line of Atlanta, facing north and east, with Stewart's—formerly Polk's —corps and part of Hardee's, and with G. W. Smith's division of militia. His own corps, and part of Hardee's, had marched out to the road leading from McDonough to Decatur and had turned so as to strike the left and rear of McPherson's line "in air." At the same time he had sent Wheeler's division of cavalry against the trains parked in Decatur. Unluckily for us, I had sent away the whole of Garrard's division of cavalry during the night of the 20th, with orders to proceed to Covington, thirty miles east, to burn two important bridges across the Ulcofauhatchee and Yellow Rivers, to tear up the railroad, to damage it as much as possible from Stone Mountain eastward, and to be gone four days; so that McPherson had no cavalry in hand to guard that flank.

The enemy was therefore enabled, under cover of the forest, to approach quite near before he was discovered; indeed, his skirmish-line had worked through the timber and got into the field to the rear of Giles A. Smith's division of the Seventeenth Corps unseen, had captured Murray's battery of regular artillery, moving through these woods entirely unguarded, and had got possession of several of the hospital camps. The right of this rebel line struck Dodge's troops in motion; but, fortunately, this Sixteenth Corps had only to halt, face to the left, and was in line of battle; and this corps not only held in check the enemy, but drove him back through the woods. About the same time this same force had struck General Giles A. Smith's left flank, doubled it back, captured four guns in position and the party engaged in building the very battery which was the special object of McPherson's visit to me, and almost enveloped the entire left flank. The men, however, were skillful and brave and fought for a time with their backs to Atlanta. They gradually fell back, compressing their own line, and gaining strength by making junction with Leggett's division of the Seventeenth Corps, well and strongly posted on the hill. One or two brigades of the Fifteenth Corps, ordered by McPherson, came rapidly across the open field to the rear, from the direction of the railroad, filled up the gap from Blair's new left to the head of Dodge's column— now facing to the general left—thus forming a strong left flank, at right angles to the original line of battle. The enemy attacked, boldly and repeatedly, the whole of this flank, but met an equally fierce resistance; and on that ground a bloody battle raged from little after noon till into the night. A part of Hood's plan of action was to sally from Atlanta at the same moment; but this sally was not, for some reason, simultaneous, for the first attack on our extreme left flank had been checked and repulsed before the sally came from the direction of Atlanta. Meantime, Colonel Sprague, in Decatur, had got his teams harnessed up and safely conducted his train to the rear of Schofield's position, holding in check Wheeler's cavalry till he had got off all his trains, with the exception of three or four wagons. I remained near the Howard House, receiving reports and sending orders, urging Generals Thomas and Schofield to take advantage of the absence from their front of so considerable a body as was evidently engaged on our left and, if possible, to make a lodgment in Atlanta itself; but they reported that the lines to their front, at all accessible points, were strong, by nature and by art, and were fully manned. About 4 p.m. the expected sally came from Atlanta, directed mainly against Leggett's Hill and along the Decatur road. At Leggett's Hill they were met and bloodily repulsed. Along the railroad they were more successful. Sweeping over a small force with two guns, they reached our main line, broke through it, and got possession of De Gress's battery of four twenty-pound Parrotts, killing every horse and turning the guns against us. General Charles R. Wood's division of the Fifteenth Corps was on the extreme right of the Army of the Tennessee, between the railroad and the Howard House, where he connected with Schofield's troops. He reported to me in person that the line on his left had been swept back and that his connection with General Logan on Leggett's Hill was broken. I ordered him to wheel his brigades to the left, to advance in echelon, and to catch the enemy in flank. General Schofield brought forward all his available batteries, to the number of twenty guns, to a position to the left front of the Howard House, whence we could overlook the field of action, and directed a heavy fire over the heads of General Wood's men against the enemy; and we saw Wood's troops advance and encounter the enemy, who had secured possession of the old line of parapet which had been held by our men. His right crossed this parapet, which he swept back, taking it in flank; and, at the same time, the division which had been driven back along the railroad was rallied by General Logan in person and fought for their former ground. These combined forces drove the enemy into Atlanta, recovering the twenty-pound Parrott guns—but one of them was found "bursted" while in the possession of the enemy. The two six-pounders farther in advance were, however, lost and had been hauled back by the enemy into Atlanta. Poor Captain de Gress came to me in tears, lamenting the loss of his favorite guns; when they were regained he had only a few men left and not a single horse. He asked an order for a reequipment, but I told him he must beg and borrow of others till he could restore his battery, now reduced to three guns. How he did so I do not know, but in a short time he did get horses, men, and finally another gun, of the same special pattern, and served them with splendid effect till the very close of the war.

The battle of July 22d is usually called the battle of Atlanta. It extended from the Howard House to General Giles A. Smith's position, about a mile beyond the Augusta Railroad, and then back toward Decatur, the whole extent of ground being fully seven miles. In part the ground was clear and in part densely wooded. I rode over the whole of it the next day, and it bore the marks of a bloody conflict. The enemy had retired during the night inside of Atlanta, and we remained masters of the situation outside. I purposely allowed the Army of the Tennessee to fight this battle almost unaided, save by demonstrations on the part of General Schofield and Thomas against the

fortified lines to their immediate fronts, and by detaching, as described, one of Schofield's brigades to Decatur, because I knew that the attacking force could only be a part of Hood's army, and that, if any assistance were rendered by either of the other armies, the Army of the Tennessee would be jealous. Nobly did they do their work that day, and terrible was the slaughter done to our enemy, though at sad cost to ourselves, as shown by the following reports:

HEADQUARTERS MILITARY DIVISION OF THE MISSISSIPPI, |
IN THE FIELD, NEAR ATLANTA, *July* 23, 1864. |

General HALLECK, *Washington, D. C.*

Yesterday morning the enemy fell back to the intrenchments proper of the city of Atlanta, which are in a general circle, with a radius of one and a half miles, and we closed in. While we were forming our lines, and selecting positions for our batteries, the enemy appeared suddenly out of the dense woods in heavy masses on our extreme left, and struck the Seventeenth Corps (General Blair) in flank, and was forcing it back, when the Sixteenth Corps (General Dodge) came up and checked the movement, but the enemy's cavalry got well to our rear, and into Decatur, and for some hours our left flank was completely enveloped. The fight that resulted was continuous until night, with heavy loss on both sides. The enemy took one of our batteries (Murray's, of the Regular Army) that was marching in its place in column in the road, unconscious of danger. About 4 p.m. the enemy sallied against the division of General Morgan L. Smith, of the Fifteenth Corps, which occupied an abandoned line of rifle-trench near the railroad east of the city, and forced it back some four hundred yards, leaving in his hands for the time two batteries, but the ground and batteries were immediately after recovered by the same troops reenforced. I cannot well approximate our loss, which fell heavily on the Fifteenth and Seventeenth Corps, but count it as three thousand; I know that, being on the defensive, we have inflicted equally heavy loss on the enemy.

General McPherson, when arranging his troops about 11 a.m., and passing from one column to another, incautiously rode upon an ambuscade without apprehension, at some distance ahead of his staff and orderlies, and was shot dead.

W. T. SHERMAN, *Major-General commanding.*

HEADQUARTERS MILITARY DIVISION OF THE MISSISSIPPI,
IN THE FIELD, NEAR ATLANTA, GEORGIA, *July* 25, 1864—8 a.m.

Major-General HALLECK, *Washington, D. C.*

GENERAL: I find it difficult to make prompt report of results, coupled with some data or information, without occasionally making mistakes. McPherson's sudden death, and Logan succeeding to the command as it were in the midst of battle, made some confusion on our extreme left; but it soon recovered and made sad havoc with the enemy, who had practised one of his favorite games of attacking our left when in motion, and before it had time to cover its weak flank. After riding over the ground and hearing the varying statements of the actors, I directed General Logan to make an official report of the actual result, and I herewith inclose it.

Though the number of dead rebels seems excessive, I am disposed to give full credit to the report that our loss, though only thirty-five hundred and twenty-one killed, wounded, and missing, the enemy's dead alone on the field nearly equaled that number, viz., thirty-two hundred and twenty. Happening at that point of the line when a flag of truce was sent in to ask permission for each party to bury its dead, I gave General Logan authority to permit a temporary truce on that flank *alone*, while our labors and fighting proceeded at all others.

I also send you a copy of General Garrard's report of the breaking of the railroad toward Augusta. I am now grouping my command to attack the Macon road, and with that view will intrench a strong line of circumvallation with flanks, so as have as large an infantry column as possible, with all the cavalry to swing round to the south and east, to strike that road at or below East Point.

I have the honor to be, your obedient servant,

W. T. SHERMAN, *Major-General commanding.*

HEADQUARTERS DEPARTMENT AND ARMY OF THE TENNESSEE,
BEFORE ATLANTA, GEORGIA, *July* 24, 1864.

Major-General W. T. SHERMAN, *commanding Military Division of the Mississippi.*

GENERAL: I have the honor to report the following general summary of the result of the attack of the enemy on this army on the 22d inst.

Total loss, killed, wounded, and missing, thirty-five hundred and twenty-one, and ten pieces of artillery.

We have buried and delivered to the enemy, under a flag of truce sent in by them, in front of the Third Division, Seventeenth Corps, one thousand of their killed.

The number of their dead in front of the Fourth Division of the same corps, including those on the ground not now occupied by our troops, General Blair reports, will swell the number of their dead on his front to two thousand.

The number of their dead buried in front of the Fifteenth Corps, up to this hour, is three hundred and sixty, and the commanding officer reports that at least as many more are yet unburied, burying-parties being still at work.

The number of dead buried in front of the Sixteenth Corps is four hundred and twenty-two. We have over one thousand of their wounded in our hands, the larger number of the wounded being carried off during the night, after the engagement, by them.

We captured eighteen stands of colors, and have them now. We also captured five thousand stands of arms.

The attack was made on our lines seven times, and was seven times repulsed. Hood's and Hardee's corps and Wheeler's cavalry engaged us.

We have sent to the rear one thousand prisoners, including thirty-three commissioned officers of high rank.

We still occupy the field, and the troops are in fine spirits. A detailed and full report will be furnished as soon as completed.

Recapitulation.

Our total loss	3,521
Enemy's dead, thus far reported, buried, and delivered to them	3,220
Total prisoners sent North	1,017
Total prisoners, wounded, in our hands	1,000
Estimated loss of the enemy, at least	10,000

Very respectfully, your obedient servant,

John A. Logan, *Major-General.*

On the 22d of July General Rousseau reached Marietta, having returned from his raid on the Alabama road at Opelika, and on the next day General Garrard also returned from Covington, both having been measurably successful. The former was about twenty-five hundred strong, the latter about four thousand, and both reported that their horses were jaded and tired, needing shoes and rest. But, about this time, I was advised by General Grant, then investing Richmond, that the rebel government had become aroused to the critical condition of things about Atlanta, and that I must look out for Hood being greatly reenforced. I therefore was resolved to push matters, and at once set about the original purpose of transferring the whole of the Army of the Tennessee to our right flank, leaving Schofield to stretch out so as to rest his left on the Augusta road, then torn up for thirty miles eastward; and, as auxiliary thereto, I ordered all the cavalry to be ready to pass around Atlanta on both flanks, to break up the Macon road at some point below, so as to cut off all supplies to the rebel army inside, and thus to force it to evacuate, or come out and fight us on equal terms.

General Hooker was offended because he was not chosen to succeed McPherson; but his chances were not even considered; indeed, I had never been satisfied with him since his affair at the Kulp House and had been more than once disposed to relieve him of his corps, because of his repeated attempts to interfere with Generals McPherson and Schofield. I am told that he says that Thomas and I were jealous of him; but this is hardly probable, for we on the spot did not rate his fighting qualities as high as he did, and I am, moreover, convinced that both he and General Butterfield went to the rear for personal reasons. We were then two hundred and fifty miles in advance of our base, dependent on a single line of railroad for our daily food. We had a bold, determined foe in our immediate front, strongly intrenched, with communication open to his rear for supplies and reenforcements, and every soldier realized that we had plenty of hard fighting ahead, and that all honors had to be fairly earned. General Hooker, moreover, when he got back to Cincinnati, reported that we had run up against a rock at Atlanta, and that the country ought to be prepared to hear of disaster from that quarter.

Near Atlanta, Georgia
July 26th, 1864

Dearest Ellen,

I got your long letter and one from Minnie last night and telegraphed you in general terms that we are all well. We have Atlanta close aboard, as the sailors say, but it is a hard nut to handle. These fellows fight like Devils and Indians combined, and it calls for all my cunning and strength.

Instead of attacking the forts which are really unassailable, I must generally destroy the roads which make Atlanta a place worth having. This I have partially done. Two out of three are broken and we are now manœuvering for the third.

I lost my right bower in McPherson, but of course it is expected, for with all the natural advantages of bushes, cover of all kinds, we must all be killed. I mean the general officers. McPherson was riding within his lines behind his wing of the army, but the enemy had got round the flank and crept up one of those hollows with bushes that concealed them completely. It has been thus all the way from Chattanooga, and if Beaure-

gard can induce Davis to adopt the Indian policy of ambuscade, which he urged two years ago, but which Jeff thought rather derogatory to the high pretenses of his Cause to courage and manliness, every officer will be killed, for the whole country is a forest, so that an enemy can waylay every path and road, and could not be found. Poor Mac, he was killed dead instantly. I think I shall prefer Howard to succeed him. Charley is quite well—gone today to inspect some cavalry that must start tomorrow on a raid. Corse is relieved from my staff and given a division in Dodge's command. Charley ought to keep you advised of these things. The truth is I have other things to think of.

Yours ever,
W. T. S.

P.S. You have fallen into an error about McPherson. He was not out of his place or exposing himself more than I and every general does daily. He was to the rear of his lines, riding by a road he had passed twice that morning. The thing was an accident that resulted from the varied character of the country we are in, dense woods fill all the ravines and hollows, and what tilled, cleared ground there is is on the ridge levels, or the alluvium of creek bottoms. The hills are all chestnut ridges with quartz and granite boulders and gravel. You can't find one hundred acres of level, clear ground between here and Chattanooga, and not a day passes but what every general officer may be shot as McPherson was.

On the 25th of July the army stood thus: the Army of the Tennessee (General O. O. Howard commanding) was on the left, pretty much on the same ground it had occupied during the battle of the 22d, all ready to move rapidly by the rear to the extreme right beyond Proctor's Creek; the Army of the Ohio (General Schofield) was next in order, with its left flank reaching the Augusta Railroad; next in order, conforming closely with the rebel intrenchments of Atlanta, was General Thomas's Army of the Cumberland, in the order of—the Fourth Corps (Stanley's), the Twentieth Corps (Williams's), and the Fourteenth Corps (Palmer's). Palmer's right division (Jefferson C. Davis's) was strongly refused along Proctor's Creek. This line was about five miles long, and was intrenched as against a sally about as strong as was our enemy. The cavalry was assembled in two strong divisions; that of McCook (including the brigade of Harrison which had been brought in from Opelika by General Rousseau) numbered about thirty-five hundred effective cavalry, and was posted to our right rear, at Turner's Ferry, where we had a good pontoon-bridge; and to our left rear, at and about Decatur, were the two cavalry divisions of Stoneman, twenty-five hundred, and Garrard, four thousand, united for the time and occasion under the command of Major-General George Stoneman, a cavalry-officer of high repute. My plan of action was to move the Army of the Tennessee to the right rapidly and boldly against the railroad below Atlanta, and at the same time to send all the cavalry around by the right and left to make a lodgment on the Macon road about Jonesboro.

All the orders were given, and the morning of the 27th was fixed for commencing the movement. On the 26th I received from General Stoneman a note asking permission, after having accomplished his orders to break up the railroad at Jonesboro, to go on to Macon to rescue our prisoners of war known to be held there and then to push on to Andersonville, where was the great depot of Union prisoners, in which were penned at one time as many as twenty-three thousand of our men, badly fed and harshly treated. I wrote him an answer consenting substantially to his proposition, only modifying it by requiring him to send back General Garrard's division to its position on our left flank after he had broken up the railroad at Jonesboro. Promptly, all got off, and General Dodge's corps reached its position across Proctor's Creek the same evening, and early the next morning (the 28th) Blair's corps deployed on his right, both corps covering their front with the usual parapet; the Fifteenth Corps came up that morning on the right of Blair, strongly refused, and began to prepare the usual cover. As General Jeff C. Davis's division was left out of line, I ordered it on the evening before to march down toward Turner's Ferry, and then to take a road laid down on our maps which led from there toward East Point, ready to engage any enemy that might attack our general right flank, after the same manner as had been done to the left flank on the 22d.

Personally on the morning of the 28th I followed the movement and rode to the extreme right, where we could hear some skirmishing and an occasional cannon-shot. As we approached the ground held by the Fifteenth Corps, a cannon-ball passed over my shoulder and killed the horse of an orderly behind; and seeing that this gun enfiladed the road by which we were riding, we turned out of it and rode down into a valley, where we left our horses and walked up to the hill held by Morgan L. Smith's division of the Fifteenth Corps. Near a house I met Generals Howard and Logan, who explained that there was an intrenched battery to their front, with the appearance of a strong infantry support. I then walked up to the ridge, where I found General Morgan L. Smith. His men were deployed and engaged in rolling logs and fence-rails, preparing a

80

hasty cover. From this ridge we could overlook the open fields near a meeting-house known as "Ezra Church," close by the Poor-House. We could see the fresh earth of a parapet covering some guns that fired an occasional shot, and there was also an appearance of activity beyond. General Smith was in the act of sending forward a regiment from his right flank to feel the position of the enemy, when I explained to him and to Generals Logan and Howard that they must look out for General Jeff C. Davis's division, which was coming up from the direction of Turner's Ferry.

As the skirmish-fire warmed up along the front of Blair's corps, as well as along the Fifteenth Corps, I became convinced that Hood designed to attack this right flank, to prevent, if possible, the extension of our line in that direction. I regained my horse, and rode rapidly back to see that Davis's division had been dispatched as ordered. I found General Davis in person, who was unwell, and had sent his division that morning early, under the command of his senior brigadier, Morgan; but, as I attached great importance to the movement, he mounted his horse, and rode away to overtake and to hurry forward the movement, so as to come up on the left rear of the enemy, during the expected battle.

By this time the sound of cannon and musketry denoted a severe battle was in progress, which began seriously at 11½ a.m., and ended substantially by 4 p.m. It was a fierce attack by the enemy on our extreme right flank, well posted and partially covered. The most authentic account of the battle is given by General Logan, who commanded the Fifteenth Corps, in his official report to the Adjutant-General of the Army of the Tennessee, thus:

HEADQUARTERS FIFTEENTH ARMY CORPS, }
BEFORE ATLANTA, GEORGIA, *July* 29, 1864. }

Lieutenant-Colonel WILLIAM T. CLARK, *Assistant Adjutant-General, Army of the Tennessee, present.*

COLONEL: I have the honor to report that, in pursuance of orders, I moved my command into position on the right of the Seventeenth Corps, which was the extreme right of the army in the field, during the night of the 27th and morning of the 28th; and, while advancing in line of battle to a more favorable position, we were met by the rebel infantry of Hardee's and Lee's corps, who made a determined and desperate attack on us at 11½ a.m. of the 28th (yesterday).

My lines were only protected by logs and rails, hastily thrown up in front of them.

The first onset was received and checked, and the battle commenced and lasted until about three o'clock in the evening. During that time six successive charges were made, which were six times gallantly repulsed, each time with fearful loss to the enemy.

Later in the evening my lines were several times assaulted vigorously, but each time with like result.

The worst of the fighting occurred on General Harrow's and Morgan L. Smith's fronts, which formed the centre and right of the corps.

The troops could not have displayed greater courage, nor greater determination not to give ground; had they shown less, they would have been driven from their position.

Brigadier-Generals C. R. Woods, Harrow, and Morgan L. Smith, division commanders, are entitled to equal credit for gallant conduct and skill in repelling the assault.

My thanks are due to Major-Generals Blair and Dodge for sending me reenforcements at a time when they were much needed.

My losses were fifty killed, four hundred and forty-nine wounded, and seventy-three missing: aggregate, five hundred and seventy-two.

The division of General Harrow captured five battle-flags. There were about fifteen hundred or two thousand muskets left on the ground. One hundred and six prisoners were captured, exclusive of seventy-three wounded, who were sent to our hospital, and are being cared for by our surgeons.

Five hundred and sixty-five rebels have up to this time been buried, and about two hundred are supposed to be yet unburied.

A large number of their wounded were undoubtedly carried away in the night, as the enemy did not withdraw till near daylight. The enemy's loss could not have been less than six or seven thousand men.

A more detailed report will hereafter be made.

I am, very respectfully,

Your obedient servant,

JOHN A. LOGAN,
Major-General, commanding Fifteenth Army Corps.

This was, of course, the first fight in which General Howard had commanded the Army of the Tennessee, and he evidently aimed to gain the heart of his army, to which he was a stranger. He very properly left General Logan to fight his own corps, but exposed himself freely; and, after the firing had ceased, in the afternoon he walked the lines; the men, as reported to me, gathered about him in the most affectionate way, and he at once gained their respect and confidence. To this fact I at the time attached much importance, for it put me at ease as to the future conduct of that most important army.

At no instant of time did I feel the least uneasiness about the result on the 28th, but wanted to reap fuller results, hoping that Davis's division would come up at the instant of defeat, and catch the enemy in flank; but the woods were dense, the roads obscure, and as usual this division got on the wrong road, and did not come into position until about dark. In like manner, I thought that Hood had greatly weakened his main lines inside of Atlanta, and accordingly sent repeated orders to Schofield and Thomas to make an attempt to break in; but both reported that they found the parapets very strong and full manned.

Our men were unusually encouraged by this day's work, for they realized that we could compel Hood to come out from behind his fortified lines to attack us at a disadvantage. In conversation with me, the soldiers of the Fifteenth Corps, with whom I was on the most familiar terms, spoke of the affair of the 28th as the easiest thing in the world; that, in fact, it was a common slaughter of the enemy; they pointed out where the rebel lines had been and how they themselves had fired deliberately, had shot down their antagonists, whose bodies still lay unburied, and marked plainly their lines of battle, which must have halted within easy musket-range of our men, who were partially protected by their improvised line of logs and fence-rails. All bore willing testimony to the courage and spirit of the foe, who, though repeatedly repulsed, came back with increased determination some six or more times.

The next morning the Fifteenth Corps wheeled forward to the left over the battle-field of the day before, and Davis's division still farther prolonged the line, which reached nearly to the ever-to-be-remembered "Sandtown road."

Then, by further thinning out Thomas's line, which was well intrenched, I drew another division of Palmer's corps around to the right, to further strengthen that flank. I was impatient to hear from the cavalry raid, then four days out, and was watching for its effect, ready to make a bold push for the possession of East Point. General Garrard's division returned to Decatur on the 31st, and reported that General Stoneman had posted him at Flat Rock, while Stoneman went on. The month of July therefore closed with our infantry line strongly intrenched, but drawn out from the Augusta road on the left to the Sandtown road on the right, a distance of full ten measured miles.

The enemy, though evidently somewhat intimidated by the results of their defeats on the 22d and 28th, still presented a bold front at all points, with fortified lines that defied a direct assault. Our railroad was done to the rear of our camps, Colonel W. W. Wright having reconstructed the bridge across the Chattahoochee in six days; and our garrisons and detachments to the rear had so effectually guarded the railroad that the trains from Nashville arrived daily, and our substantial wants were well supplied.

Near Atlanta,
July 29th, 1864

Dearest Ellen,

Since crossing Chattahoochee I have been too busy to write. We have had three pretty hard battles. The enemy attacked my center as we were fairly across the Peachtree Creek, and got badly beaten. Next as we closed in on Atlanta he struck our extreme left and the fighting was desperate. He drove back a part of the left, but the men fought hard and when night closed our losses amounted to 3500 and we found nearly 3000 dead Rebels. Making the usual allowance, the enemy must have sustained a loss of 10,000. Yesterday I shifted the Army of the Tennessee to my extreme right, and in getting into position I was again attacked and repulsed the attack. The fight was mostly with the Fifteenth Corps. Logan commanded it. McPherson's death was a great loss to me. I depended much on him. In casting about for a successor I proposed Howard who is a man of mind and intellect. He is very honest, sincere and moral even to piety but brave, having lost an arm already. But he was a junior Major General to Hooker who took offense and has gone away. I don't regret it. He is envious, imperious and braggart. Self prevailed with him and knowing him intimately, I honestly preferred Howard. Yesterday's work justified my choice, for Howard's disposition and manner elicited the shouts of my old corps, and he at once stepped into the shoes of McPherson and myself. I have now Thomas, Schofield and Howard, all tried and approved soldiers. We are gradually drawing our lines close up to Atlanta, fortifying our front against their bold sallies, and I now have all the cavalry out against the roads between Atlanta and Macon. I am glad I beat Johnston, for he had the most exalted reputation with our old army as a strategist. Hood is a new man and a fighter and must be watched closer, as he is reckless of the lives of his men. It is wonderful with what faith they adhere to the belief that they whip us on all occasions, though we have them now almost penned up in Atlanta. If no reinforcements come, I think I will cut them off from all communication with the rest of the Confederacy. Bowman has sent me the proof sheets of the August number of the U. S. Service Magazine. The sketch is strong, but contains enough original matter to give it the coloring of truth.

I enclose you a letter for you which seems to be from the mother of your "Norah." I also repeat that I prefer that Minnie should return to that school at Cincinnati, and Lizzie go along if willing. I prefer you should stay at Lancaster at whatever sacrifice of feeling or personal aversion till we can see daylight ahead in this war. But if you will go, better to Cincinnati than Notre Dame. There you have no better medical attendance than you will find within reach of Lancaster. I don't pretend to see a wink ahead, and if I get killed, which is not improbable at any moment, you will of course be compelled to be at Lancaster. Yesterday a solid cannon shot passed me close and killed an orderly's horse (Charley's orderly) close behind me. In fact, I daily pass death in the most familiar shapes and you should base your calculations on that event. I got Minnie's letter. It is plainly and well written and I feel satisfied she has made good progress at her new school, and do not wish her to change. I have cut out of a magazine two rough wood cuts of Grant and myself which approximate likenesses. Keep them as samples. Charley and I are both well and my staff remains unchanged except I have given Corse to Dodge to command one of his divisions. Give my love to all the children and the folks generally.

Yours ever,
W. T. Sherman

The month, though hot in the extreme, had been one of constant conflict, without intermission, and on four separate occasions—July 4th, 20th, 22d, and 28th—these affairs had amounted to real battles, with casualty lists by the thousands. Our losses, as compiled from the official returns for July, 1864, are:

Killed and missing	3,804
Wounded	5,915
Total	9,719

Commencing with July 4th and terminating with July 31st, enemy losses were:

Killed	1,341
Wounded	7,500
Captured	2,000
Total	10,841

Dearest Ellen,

I got a letter from you last night and one for Charley, and was glad to hear you were getting along so well, and that the baby exhibits signs of healthy life. I have for some days been occupying a good house on the Buckhead Road about four miles north of Atlanta, but am going to move in the morning more to the right to be nearer where I expect the next battle. You have heard, doubtless, full accounts of the battles of the 20th, 22nd and 28th, in all which the enemy attacked a part of our lines in force but was always repulsed with heavy loss. But I fear we have sustained a reverse in some cavalry that I sent round by the rear to break the Macon road. It was commanded by McCook, a cousin of Davis. They reached the railroad and broke it; also burned a large number of the baggage wagons belonging to the enemy, and were on their way back when they were beset by heavy forces of cavalry about Newnan and I fear are overpowered and a great part killed or captured. Some 500 have got in and give confused accounts, but time enough has elapsed for the party to be back, and I hear nothing further of them. Somehow or other we cannot get cavalry. The enemy takes all the horses of the country, and we have to buy and our people won't sell. Stoneman is also only with a cavalry force attempting to reach our prisoners confined at Andersonville, but since McCook's misfortune I also have fears for his safety. I am now moving so as to get possession of the railroad out of Atlanta to the south—we already have possession of those to the north and east—where it will be difficult for Hood to maintain his army in Atlanta. This army is much reduced in strength by deaths, sickness and expiration of service. It looks hard to see regiments march away when their time is up. On the other side they have everybody, old and young and for indefinite periods. I have to have also along the railroad a large force to guard the supplies. So that I doubt if our army much exceeds that of Hood. No recruits are coming, for the draft is not till September, and then I suppose it will consist mostly of niggers and bought recruits that must be kept well to the rear. I sometimes think our people do not desire to succeed in war. They are so apathetic.

McPherson was shot dead. I had his body brought up to me, and sent it back to the railroad. He was shot high up in the breast with a bullet and must have fallen from his horse dead. Howard, who succeeds him, is a fine gentleman and a good officer. Hooker got mad because he was not appointed to the command and has gone North. This ought to damn him, showing that he is selfish and not patriotic. He was not suited to the command. I expect we will have a hard fight for the railroad about the day after tomorrow, and [it?] must be more heavy on us as we must attack. I am always glad when the enemy attacks, for the advantage then is with us. I see that Grant has sprung his mines at Petersburg and hope he will succeed in taking that town, as it will be a constant threat to Richmond, but Richmond itself can only be taken by regular siege. Atlanta is on high ground and the woods extend up to the forts which look strong and encircle the whole town. Most of the people are gone and it is now simply a big fort. I have been a little sick today but feel better. Weather very hot. Love to all.

Yours ever,
W. T. Sherman

CAPTURE OF ATLANTA

THE month of August opened hot and sultry, but our position before Atlanta was healthy, with ample supply of wood, water, and provisions. The troops had become habituated to the slow and steady progress of the siege; the skirmish-lines were held close up to the enemy, were covered by rifle-trenches or logs, and kept up a continuous clatter of musketry. The main lines were held farther back, adapted to the shape of the ground, with muskets loaded and stacked for instant use. The field-batteries were in select positions, covered by handsome parapets, and occasional shots from them gave life and animation to the scene. The men loitered about the trenches carelessly, or busied themselves in constructing ingenious huts out of the abundant timber, and seemed as snug, comfortable, and happy, as though they were at home. General Schofield was still on the extreme left, Thomas in the centre, and Howard on the right. Baird's and Jeff C. Davis's two divisions of the Fourteenth Corps were detached to the right rear and held in reserve.

I thus awaited the effect of the cavalry movement against the railroad about Jonesboro and had heard from General Garrard that Stoneman had gone on to Macon; during that day (August 1st) Colonel Brownlow, of a Tennessee cavalry regiment, came in to Marietta from General McCook, and reported that McCook's whole division had been overwhelmed, defeated, and captured at Newnan. Of course, I was disturbed by this wild report, though I discredited it, but made all possible preparations to strengthen our guards along the railroad to the rear, on the theory that the force of cavalry which had defeated McCook would at once be on the railroad about Marietta.

At the same time Garrard was ordered to occupy the trenches on our left, while Schofield's whole army moved to the extreme right and extended the line toward East Point. Thomas was also ordered still further to thin out his lines, so as to set free Johnson's other division of Palmer's Fourteenth Corps, which was moved to the extreme right rear and held in reserve ready to make a bold push from that flank to secure a footing on the Macon Railroad at or below East Point.

These changes were effected during the 2d and 3d days of August, when General McCook came in and reported the actual results of his cavalry expedition. He had crossed the Chattahoochee River below Campbellton by his pontoon-bridge; had then marched rapidly across to the Macon Railroad at Lovejoy's Station, where he had reason to expect General Stoneman; but, not hearing of him, he set to work, tore up two miles of track, burned two trains of cars, and cut away five miles of telegraph-wire. He also found the wagon-train belonging to the rebel army in Atlanta, burned five hundred wagons, killed eight hundred mules, and captured seventy-two officers and three hundred and fifty men. Finding his progress eastward, toward McDonough, barred by a superior force, he turned back to Newnan, where he found himself completely surrounded by infantry and cavalry. He had to drop his prisoners and fight his way out, losing about six hundred men in killed and captured, and then returned with the remainder to his position at Turner's Ferry. This was bad enough, but not so bad as had been reported by Colonel Brownlow. Meantime, rumors came that General Stoneman was down about Macon, on the east bank of the Ocmulgee. On the 4th of August Colonel Adams got to Marietta with his small brigade of nine hundred men belonging to Stoneman's cavalry, reporting, as usual, all the rest lost, and this was partially confirmed by a report which came to me all the way round by General Grant's headquarters before Richmond. A few days afterward Colonel Capron also got in, with another small brigade perfectly demoralized and confirmed the report that General Stoneman had covered the escape of these two small brigades, himself standing with a reserve of seven hundred men, with which he surrendered to a Colonel Iverson. Thus another of my cavalry divisions was badly damaged, and out of the fragments we hastily reorganized three small divisions under Brigadier-Generals Garrard, McCook, and Kilpatrick.

Stoneman had not obeyed his orders to attack the railroad *first* before going to Macon and Andersonville, but had crossed the Ocmulgee River high up near Covington and had gone down that river on the east bank. He reached Clinton and sent out detachments which struck the railroad leading from Macon to Savannah at Griswold Station, where they found and destroyed seventeen locomotives and over a hundred cars; then went on and burned the bridge across the Oconee and reunited the division before Macon. Stoneman shelled the town across the river, but could not cross over by the bridge, and returned to Clinton, where he found his retreat obstructed, as he supposed, by a superior force. There he became bewildered and sacrificed himself for the safety of his command. He occupied the attention of his enemy by a small force of seven hundred men, giving Colonels Adams and Capron leave, with their brigades, to cut their way back to me at Atlanta. The former reached us entire, but the latter was struck and scattered at some place farther north and came in by detachments. Stoneman surrendered and remained a prisoner until he was exchanged some time after, late in September.

I now became satisfied that cavalry could not, or would not, make a sufficient lodgment on the railroad below Atlanta, and that nothing would suffice but for us to reach it with the main army. I always expected to have a desperate fight to get possession of the Macon road, which was then the vital objective of the campaign. Its possession by us would, in my judgment, result in the capture of Atlanta and give us the fruits of victory, although the destruction of Hood's army was the real object to be desired. Yet Atlanta was known as the "Gate-City of the South," was full of foundries, arsenals, and machine-shops, and I knew that its capture would be the death-knell of the Southern Confederacy.

On the 4th of August I ordered General Schofield to make a bold attack on the railroad, anywhere about East Point, and ordered General Palmer to report to him for duty. He at once denied General Schofield's right to command him; but, after examining the dates of their respective commissions and hearing their arguments, I wrote to General Palmer.

August 4th—10:45 p.m.

From the statements made by yourself and General Schofield to-day, my decision is, that he ranks you as a major-general, being of the same date of present commission, by reason of his previous superior rank as *brigadier-general*. The movements of to-morrow are so important that the orders of the superior on that flank must be regarded as military orders, and not in the nature of cooperation. I did hope that there would be no necessity for my making this decision; but it is better for all parties interested that no question of rank should occur in actual battle. The

90

Sandtown road, and the railroad, if possible, must be gained to-morrow, if it costs half your command. I regard the loss of time this afternoon as equal to the loss of two thousand men.

And on the 5th I again wrote to General Palmer, arguing the point with him, advising him, as a friend, not to resign at that crisis lest his motives might be misconstrued and because it might damage his future career in civil life; but, at the same time, I felt it my duty to say to him that the operations on that flank, during the 4th and 5th, had not been satisfactory—not imputing to him, however, any want of energy or skill, but insisting that "the events did not keep pace with my desires." General Schofield had reported to me that night:

> I am compelled to acknowledge that I have totally failed to make any aggressive movement with the Fourteenth Corps. I have ordered General Johnson's division to replace General Hascall's this evening, and I propose to-morrow to take my own troops (Twenty-third Corps) to the right, and try to recover what has been lost by two days' delay. The force may likely be too small.

I sanctioned the movement and ordered two of Palmer's divisions—Davis's and Baird's—to follow *en échelon* in support of Schofield and summoned General Palmer to meet me in person. He came on the 6th to my headquarters and insisted on his resignation being accepted, for which formal act I referred him to General Thomas. He then rode to General Thomas's camp, where he made a written resignation of his office as commander of the Fourteenth Corps and was granted the usual leave of absence to go to his home in Illinois, there to await further orders. General Thomas recommended that the resignation be accepted; that Johnson, the senior division commander of the corps, should be ordered back to Nashville as chief of cavalry, and that Brigadier-General Jefferson C. Davis, the next in order, should be promoted major-general, and assigned to command the corps. These changes had to be referred to the President in Washington and were, in due time, approved and executed; and thenceforward I had no reason to complain of the slowness or inactivity of that splendid corps. It had been originally formed by General George H. Thomas, had been commanded by him in person, and had imbibed somewhat his personal character, steadiness, good order, and deliberation—nothing hasty or rash, but always safe, slow, and sure.

Dearest Ellen,

I have yours and Phil's long letters of August 1st and am willing you should move to Notre Dame and put the children at school. I was in hopes that you could [get?] along till this campaign was over without change but it may be well to act on the theory that this war cannot end in my day and therefore we might as well as bid adieu to any delusion of ever having a home. I did think that I might possibly be able to get as far north as Cincinnati, but that is just as unlikely as to get to north Indiana. I see the government has settled down on the policy of trusting to state agents gathering up niggers and vagabonds by high bounties to fill our armies, and as this kind of trash merely fill our hospitals and keep well to the rear, I suppose I have to fight till this army is used and then wait for a new revolution. It is now raining hard. We have been fighting all day along our line ten miles long. We tried to break through at one point to reach the railroad but failed, losing about 500 men. Since the enemy failed in his last attack on us, he has kept close inside his forts and extended them south as we devolved in that direction. I must persevere, but confess I would feel more sanguine if it were not for the fact I have stated. Agents are coming to me from Massachusetts, Rhode Island and Ohio to recruit Negroes, as fast as we catch them, to count as soldiers. I remonstrated to Mr. Lincoln in the strongest terms but he answered it was the law and I have to submit. Niggers won't work now, and half my army are driving wagons, loading and unloading cases, and doing work which the very Negroes we have captured might do, whilst these same niggers are soldiers on paper. But I cannot get any. The fact is, modern philanthropy will commit our oldest and best soldiers to labor whilst the nigger parades and [frolics?] in some remote and safe place. It is an insult to our race to count them as a part of the quota. If you go to South Bend, you had better make a regular move. Get a house and make arrangements to stay there till the children are educated.

You already have $4000 loaned on that Kansas Farm. Tell your father that I am unwilling you should have any more loaned so far away from where you will have to live in case of accident to me. Don't change the mortgage on the Lancaster Farm on any condition. For you cannot give these matters attention. Tell your father my peremptory orders are that you keep those debts as they now are, unless they can be converted into U. S. Bonds. Remember now that money is worth less than half than what it was, or in other words your $20,000 is now only about $8,000 in gold. You may now recall what I used to say, and what you deemed so extravagant, but the cost and duration of this war are beyond the calculation of any person. In all this country, women and children that used to be wealthy have been compelled to hoe the ground and plant potatoes and our soldiers eat them up. In Ohio it may not be so bad, but it will come that all will have to

work to raise food and clothing. If I take Atlanta, don't think the war ended. It has barely begun, for you must see the signs of division and strife at the North. How after the third year of war the enemy burns Chambersburg in Pennsylvania and Congress wants to put Negroes in our ranks and call them the equals of whites! You see my mind so [occupied?] on these matters that I can hardly keep to our private matters. But you must see that I cannot undertake to advise you in the matter of a home in the terrible uncertainty that involves us all. If we had any landmarks to tie to, any fixed hope or knowledge, I could reason about it, but we have nothing. Life, property, income, time and place are all so uncertain that the wisest can not see a wink ahead. How then can I even look to this winter or the next? Of course, I could not live in Lancaster or Notre Dame, and therefore you must seek a place of residence utterly without reference to me. I see the causes of annoyance you have at home. Still, I have always supposed that, go where you might, you would drift back to Lancaster and therefore preferred you should stay there till we could see daylight ahead. I thought it better for you to be near your father, if not in his house, for every month he will be more or less ill, and you will have to go, so that most of the time our family will be scattered. But you may try it and all I can advise is to save a little something, for I have no reasonable chance of surviving the war, unless the fickle changes of time dispenses [with?] Grant and me, and substitutes new favorites, when I might escape to California or some other distant land and await the next great change. I will draw my pay of our paymaster in a day or two and send you all the money I can spare. Hill's time is out on the 19th and I will owe him a good deal. Roger is already discharged. Indeed, the times of all our three-year men are out this month, and I will be left with a small army, with no hope of reinforcements till after the states have exhausted their efforts to recruit niggers down South. If I could keep my army up to its standard, I could go on, but our losses are from 300 to 1000 a day. I suppose we have lost a thousand today in battle, and the only way to keep up the balance is to kill an equal number, but the rascals keep behind good parapets, in the very hope to kill enough of my men thus to assume the offensive. Let me know when you propose to move, but try for once to let Minnie commence a term with a class. Better move at once, so she may be ready for the September term. I am glad to hear such good accounts of the youngster. We will need a large growth of population to replace the havoc of this age. I would like the children to write me occasionally.

Ever yours,
W. T. Sherman

Near Atlanta, Georgia
August 9th, 1864

Dearest Ellen,

I got your note of August 4th today, enclosing one for Charley, which I have handed him. Tell Mr. Hunter and Mrs. [unclear] it is idle to attempt the exchange of Dr. [unclear]. I have already lost Stoneman and near 2000 cavalry in attempting to rescue the prisoners at Macon. I get one hundred letters a day almost, asking me to effect the exchange or release of these prisoners. It is not in my power. The whole matter of exchanges is in the hands of Colonel [unclear] Commission at Washington. I am capturing and sending North hundreds of prisoners daily and have no intercourse with the enemy. I have not exchanged a single message, not even a flag of truce. I assented to the enemy sending a partial flag [of truce] to bury some dead, on a particular spot, but did not suspend the fire at any other. I have cannonaded Atlanta pretty heavily today, and our lines are extended full ten miles, but still the enemy is beyond. They have either a larger force than we estimate or their lines are well concealed by their forts. They occupy a high ridge and we are on densely wooded hill sides and slopes. To assault their position would cost more lives than we can spare, and to turn the position I would have to cut loose from our base, which is rather a risky business in a country devoid of all manner of supplies.

I drew two months' pay and send you it nearly all. I will not preach economy any more, and only will say that next month's pay is due to Hill and my [obligations?] here, which I have not paid for a long while. Though I eat nothing but rations, my mess costs me $50 or $60 a month. I have given my consent to your moving to South Bend, only take the whole family. There is no chance of my ever getting North again and therefore you can choose a house utterly regardless of my movements. I regard the war as hardly begun, and see no chance of escaping unless in the revolution of this fall and winter new favorites arise. The people of the North always have slackened their efforts to uniform our army when reinforcements are needed and then break out when it is too late. I suppose such will be the case this year. The whole South is now armed and the whole North should be, every man that can carry a musket. I have not yet seen young [unclear], indeed the cavalry is so far out on the flanks that I rarely see it.

Ever yours,
W. T. Sherman

On August 7th I telegraphed to General Halleck:

Have received to-day the dispatches of the Secretary of War and of General Grant, which are very satisfactory. We keep hammering away all the time, and there is no peace, inside or outside of Atlanta. To-day General Schofield got round the line which was assaulted yesterday by General Reilly's brigade, turned it and gained the ground where the assault had been made, and got possession of all our dead and wounded. He continued to press on that flank, and brought on a noisy but not a bloody battle. He drove the enemy behind his main breastworks, which cover the railroad from Atlanta to East Point, and captured a good many of the skirmishers, who are of his best troops—for the militia hug the breastworks close. I do not deem it prudent to extend any more to the right, but will push forward daily by parallels, and make the inside of Atlanta too hot to be endured. I have sent back to Chattanooga for two thirty-pound Parrotts, with which we can pick out almost any house in town. I am too impatient for a siege, and don't know but this is as good a place to fight it out on, as farther inland. One thing is certain, whether we get inside of Atlanta or not, it will be a used-up community when we are done with it.

In Schofield's extension on the 5th, General Reilly's brigade had struck an outwork, which he promptly attacked, but, as usual, got entangled in the trees and bushes which had been felled, and lost about five hundred men, in killed and wounded; but, as above reported, this outwork was found abandoned the next day, and we could see from it that the rebels were extending their lines, parallel with the railroad, about as fast as we could add to our line of investment. On the 10th of August the Parrott thirty-pounders were received and placed in position; for a couple of days we kept up a sharp fire from all our batteries converging on Atlanta, and at every available point we advanced our infantry-lines, thereby shortening and strengthening the investment; but I was not willing to order a direct assault, unless some accident or positive neglect on the part of our antagonist should reveal an opening. However, it was manifest that no such opening was intended by Hood, who felt secure behind his strong defenses. He had repelled our cavalry attacks on his railroad and had damaged us seriously thereby, so I expected that he would attempt the same game against our rear. Therefore I made extraordinary exertions to recompose our cavalry divisions, which were so essential, for both defense and offense. Kilpatrick was given that on our right rear, in support of Schofield's exposed flank; Garrard retained that on our general left; and McCook's division was held somewhat in reserve about Marietta and the railroad. On the 10th, having occasion to telegraph to General Grant, then in Washington, I used this language:

Since July 28th Hood has not attempted to meet us outside his parapets. In order to possess and destroy effectually his communications, I may have to leave a corps at the railroad-bridge, well intrenched, and cut loose with the balance to make a circle of desolation around Atlanta. I do not propose to assault the works, which are too strong, nor to proceed by regular approaches. I have lost a good many regiments, and will lose more, by the expiration of service; and this is the only reason why I want reenforcements. We have killed, crippled, and captured more of the enemy than we have lost by his acts.

Near Atlanta, Georgia
August 15th, 1864

Dearest Ellen,

I have just received your letter of August 9th, and though I intended to write to Lizzie tonight have concluded to write you again though I have written often of late. I think all your letters have reached me, and I have certainly written often enough though I can well imagine my thoughts and [fears?] naturally run in a channel of little interest to you. You know the cares and troubles of a family of six under your very eyes: think of mine of over a hundred thousand, with all the wants and cares of children, scattered, too, all over the Mississippi country. Not only their wants but their hopes and fears, their ambitions and jealousies. But I will not perplex you with these things but assure you every word you write is interesting to me, and however heedless I may seem it is not lost. I do want you to get settled. I could feel more comfortable, the more so as my life is most precarious. Even as I write I hear the bullets whiz and shells burst, any one of which would kill me as quick as any common soldier. It is all folly about my being able to avoid the danger. I must see everything, ground and roads and [travel?] with the advance pickets. In an open country this would not be so necessary, but here it is amidst woods and ravines. Again, I want you to realize that soon money will cease to have value. Even now it will take more than two months of my pay to satisfy that debt to Mr. [unclear] for the expenses of Lizzie's lot and I don't believe we can make a deed that anybody in California will take. As I say money will become less and less valuable as the war progresses, and I suspect it is hardly begun, and then you will have real hard times. Then potatoes, flour and meal will be the articles of real value and I had hoped you would make some arrangement about these on the farm, or get it as interest out of the farm note. I am perfectly willing you should go to South Bend if you can take all the family and live on our pay. But I would have some hopes of seeing the war coming to a pause or conclusion were it not that all facts public look as though the North would avoid the draft, by buying up Negroes and vagabonds. These won't fight as we must fight to win, and the old soldiers will gradually draw out if they see their fellows at the

North dodging. If Grant's army and mine could be kept up and also another ready to go up the Alabama, as soon as Mobile is taken, we could compress the war into a comparatively small space, but with Grant I suppose it is the same as with me—our three-year men are all going home and my army is falling away at the very time it should be strongest. These facts which the public do not and should not know are the causes of delay and failure which you cannot account for.

I sent you a check for $950 and will continue to send all I can spare and want you to feel as much at ease as possible, but neither you or Phil give weight enough to the causes which move me in my argument, viz. the fact that with each month money will become less and less valuable and whereas at the South it ceases to have any value at all. The nearer you are all together the better. If I were near I would have gone further to so manage his farm that a large share of the products should come into the family. Chase nor Fremantle can alter the laws of finances and when the volume of money out is greater than the ability of government to pay, it becomes less and less valuable till all despair of payment when it ceases to be of any value. But my pay will always be in that sort, for so vast are the necessary expenses of our government that it cannot do better, and yet the war must go on. No human power, not even the Copperheads or Peace Men, or Lincoln or Congress, or Jeff Davis, can stop it. The causes all lie beyond their control. Give my love to all and write me often and freely, for I assure you I need your letters now more than ever.

Yours truly,
W. T. Sherman

On the 12th of August I heard of the success of Admiral Farragut in entering Mobile Bay, which was regarded as a most valuable auxiliary to our operations at Atlanta; and learned that I had been commissioned a major-general in the regular army. These did not change the fact that we were held in check by the stubborn defense of Atlanta, and a conviction was forced on my mind that our enemy would hold fast, even though every house in the town should be battered down by our artillery. It was evident that we must decoy him out to fight us on something like equal terms or else, with the whole army, raise the siege and attack his communications. Accordingly, on the 13th of August, I gave general orders for the Twentieth Corps to draw back to the railroad-bridge at the Chattahoochee, to protect our trains, hospitals, spare artillery, and the railroad-depot, while the rest of the army should move bodily to some point on the Macon Railroad below East Point.

Luckily, I learned just then that the enemy's cavalry, under General Wheeler, had made a wide circuit around our left flank and had actually reached our railroad at Tilton Station, above Resaca, captured a drove of one thousand of our beef cattle and was strong enough to appear before Dalton and demand of its commander, Colonel Raum, the surrender of the place. General John E. Smith, who was at Kingston, collected together a couple of thousand men and proceeded in cars to the relief of Dalton, when Wheeler retreated northward toward Cleveland. On the 16th another detachment of the enemy's cavalry appeared in force about Allatoona and the Etowah bridge, when I became fully convinced that Hood had sent *all* of his cavalry to raid upon our railroads. For some days our communication with Nashville was interrupted by the destruction of the telegraph-lines, as well as railroad. I at once ordered strong reconnoissances forward from our flanks on the left by Garrard, and on the right by Kilpatrick. The former moved with so much caution that I was displeased; but Kilpatrick, on the contrary, displayed so much zeal and activity that I was attracted to him at once. He reached Fairburn Station on the West Point road and tore it up, returning safely to his position on our right flank. I summoned him to me and was so pleased with his spirit and confidence, that I concluded to suspend the general movement of the main army and to send him with his small division of cavalry to break up the Macon road about Jonesboro, in the hopes that it would force Hood to evacuate Atlanta, and that I should thereby not only secure possession of the city itself, but probably could catch Hood in the confusion of retreat; and, further to increase the chances of success, I ordered General Thomas to detach two brigades of Garrard's division of cavalry from the left to the right rear, to act as a reserve in support of General Kilpatrick. Meantime, also, the utmost activity was ordered along our whole front by the infantry and artillery. Kilpatrick got off during the night of the 18th and returned to us on the 22d, having made the complete circuit of Atlanta. He reported that he had destroyed three miles of the railroad about Jonesboro, which he reckoned would take ten days to repair; that he had encountered a division of infantry and a brigade of cavalry; that he had captured a battery and destroyed three of its guns, bringing one in as a trophy, and he also brought in three battle-flags and seventy prisoners. On the 23d, however, we saw trains coming into Atlanta from the south, when I became more than ever convinced that cavalry could not or would not work hard enough to disable a railroad properly and therefore resolved at once to proceed to the execution of my original plan. Meantime, the damage done to our own railroad and telegraph by Wheeler about Resaca and Dalton had been repaired, and Wheeler himself was too far away to be

98

of any service to his own army and where he could not do us much harm, up about the Hiawassee. On the 24th I rode down to the Chattahoochee bridge, to see in person that it could be properly defended by the single corps proposed to be left there for that purpose and found that the rebel works, which had been built by Johnston to resist us, could be easily utilized against themselves; and on returning to my camp, at 7:15 p.m. that same evening, I telegraphed to General Halleck as follows:

> Heavy fires in Atlanta all day, caused by our artillery. I will be all ready, and will commence the movement around Atlanta by the south, tomorrow night, and for some time you will hear little of us. I will keep open a courier line back to the Chattahoochee bridge, by way of Sandtown. The Twentieth Corps will hold the railroad-bridge, and I will move with the balance of the army, provisioned for twenty days.

Meantime General Dodge, commanding the Sixteenth Corps, had been wounded in the forehead, had gone to the rear, and his two divisions were distributed to the Fifteenth and Seventeenth Corps. The real movement commenced on the 25th at night. The Twentieth Corps drew back and took post at the railroad-bridge, and the Fourth Corps moved to his right rear, closing up with the Fourteenth Corps near Utoy Creek; at the same time Garrard's cavalry, leaving their horses out of sight, occupied the vacant trenches, so that the enemy did not detect the change at all. The next night, the 26th, the Fifteenth and Seventeenth Corps, composing the Army of the Tennessee, drew out of their trenches, made a wide circuit, and came up on the extreme right of the Fourth and Fourteenth Corps of the Army of the Cumberland along Utoy Creek, facing south. The enemy seemed to suspect something that night, using his artillery pretty freely; but I think he supposed we were going to retreat altogether. An artillery-shot, fired at random, killed one man and wounded another, and the next morning some of his infantry came out of Atlanta and found our camps abandoned. It was afterward related that there was great rejoicing in Atlanta "that the Yankees were gone;" the fact was telegraphed all over the South, and several trains of cars with ladies came up from Macon to assist in the celebration of their grand victory.

On the 28th, making a general left-wheel, pivoting on Schofield, both Thomas and Howard reached the West Point Railroad, extending from East Point to Red-Oak Station and Fairburn, where we spent the next day, the 29th, in breaking it up thoroughly. The track was heaved up in sections the length of a regiment, then separated rail by rail; bonfires were made of the ties and of fence-rails on which the rails were heated, carried to trees or telegraph-poles, wrapped around and left to cool. Such rails could not be used again; and, to be still more certain, we filled up many deep cuts with trees, brush, and earth, and commingled with them loaded shells, so arranged that they would explode on an attempt to haul out the bushes. The explosion of one such shell would have demoralized a gang of Negroes, and thus would have prevented even the attempt to clear the road.

Meantime Schofield, with the Twenty-third Corps, presented a bold front toward East Point, daring and inviting the enemy to sally out to attack him in position. His first movement was on the 30th, to Mount Gilead Church, then to Morrow's Mills, facing Rough and Ready. Thomas was on his right, within easy support, moving by cross-roads from Red Oak to the Fayetteville road, extending from Couch's to Renfrew's; and Howard was aiming for Jonesboro.

I was with General Thomas that day, which was hot but otherwise very pleasant. We stopped for a short noon-rest near a little church, marked on our maps as Shoal-Creek Church, which stood back about a hundred yards from the road in a grove of native oaks. The infantry column had halted in the road, stacked their arms, and the men were scattered about—some lying in the shade of the trees, and others were bringing corn-stalks from a large corn-field across the road to feed our horses, while still others had arms full of the roasting-ears, then in their prime. Hundreds of fires were soon started with the fence-rails, and the men were busy roasting the ears. Thomas and I were walking up and down the road which led to the church, discussing the chances of the movement, which he thought were extra-hazardous, and our path carried us by a fire at which a soldier was roasting his corn. The fire was built artistically; the man was stripping the ears of their husks, standing them in front of his fire, watching them carefully, and turning each ear little by little, so as to roast it nicely. He was down on his knees intent on his business, paying little heed to the stately and serious deliberations of his leaders. Thomas's mind was running on the fact that we had cut loose from our base of supplies, and that seventy thousand men were then dependent for their food on the chance supplies of the country (already impoverished by the requisitions of the enemy), and on the contents of our wagons. Between Thomas and his men there existed a most kindly relation, and he frequently talked with them in the most familiar way. Pausing awhile, and watching the operations of this man roasting his corn, he said, "What are you doing?" The man looked up smilingly: "Why, general, I am laying in a supply of provisions." "That is right, my man, but don't waste your provisions." As we resumed our walk, the man remarked, in a sort of musing way, but loud enough for me to hear: "There he goes, there goes the old man, economizing as usual." "Economizing" with corn, which cost only the labor of gathering and roasting!

As we walked, we could hear General Howard's guns at intervals; away off to our right front, but an ominous silence continued toward our left, where I was expecting at each moment to hear the sound of battle. That night we reached Renfrew's, and had reports from left to right from General Schofield, about Morrow's Mills, to General Howard, within a couple of miles of Jonesboro. The next morning, August 31st, all moved straight for the railroad. Schofield reached it near Rough and Ready, and Thomas at two points between there and Jonesboro. Howard found an intrenched foe, Hardee's corps, covering Jonesboro, and his men began at once to dig their accustomed rifle-pits. Orders were sent to Generals Thomas and Schofield to turn straight for Jonesboro, tearing up the railroad-track as they advanced. About 3 p.m. the enemy sallied from Jonesboro against the Fifteenth Corps, but was easily repulsed, and driven back within his lines. All hands were kept busy tearing up the railroad, and it was not until toward evening of the 1st day of September that Davis's Fourteenth Corps closed down on the north front of Jonesboro, connecting on his right with Howard, and his left reaching the railroad, along which General Stanley was moving, followed by Schofield. General Davis formed his divisions in line about 4 p.m., swept forward over some old cotton-fields in full view, and went over the rebel parapet handsomely, capturing the whole of Govan's brigade, with two field-batteries of ten guns. Being on the spot, I checked Davis's movement, and ordered General Howard to send the two divisions of Blair's Seventeenth Corps round by his right rear, to get below Jonesboro, and to reach the railroad, so as to cut off retreat in that direction. I also dispatched orders after orders to hurry forward Stanley, so as to lap around Jonesboro on the east, hoping thus to capture the whole of Hardee's corps. I sent first Captain Audenried (aide-de-camp), then Colonel Poe, of the Engineers, and lastly General Thomas himself. And that is the only time during the campaign I can recall seeing General Thomas urge his horse into a gallop. Night was approaching, and the country on the farther side of the railroad was densely wooded. General Stanley had come up on the left of Davis, and was deploying, though there could not have been on his front more than a skirmish-line. Had he moved straight on by the flank, or by a slight circuit to his left, he would have inclosed the whole ground occupied by Hardee's corps, and that corps could not have escaped us; but night came on, and Hardee did escape.

Meantime General Slocum had reached his corps, stationed at the Chattahoochee bridge, had relieved General A. S. Williams in command, and orders had been sent back to him to feel forward occasionally toward Atlanta, to observe the effect when we had reached the railroad. That night I was so restless and impatient that I could not sleep, and about midnight there arose toward Atlanta sounds of shells exploding, and other sounds like that of musketry. I walked to the house of a farmer close by my bivouac, called him out to listen to the reverberations which came from the direction of Atlanta twenty miles to the north of us, and inquired of him if he had resided there long. He said he had, and that these sounds were just like those of a battle. An interval of quiet then ensued, when again, about 4 a.m., arose other similar explosions, but I still remained in doubt whether the enemy was engaged in blowing up his own magazines, or whether General Slocum had not felt forward, and become engaged in a real battle.

The next morning General Hardee was gone, and we all pushed forward along the railroad south, in close pursuit, till we ran up against his lines at a point just above Lovejoy's Station. While bringing forward troops and feeling the new position of our adversary, rumors came from the rear that the enemy had evacuated Atlanta, and that General Slocum was in the city. Later in the day I received a note in Slocum's own handwriting, stating that he had heard during the night the very sounds that I have referred to; that he had moved rapidly up from the bridge about daylight, and had entered Atlanta unopposed. His letter was dated inside the city, so there was no doubt of the fact. General Thomas's bivouac was but a short distance from mine, and, before giving notice to the army in general orders, I sent one of my staff-officers to show him the note. In a few minutes the officer returned, soon followed by Thomas himself, who again examined the note, so as to be perfectly certain that it was genuine. The news seemed to him too good to be true. He snapped his fingers, whistled, and almost danced, and, as the news spread to the army, the shouts that arose from our men, the wild hallooing and glorious laughter, were to us a full recompense for the labor and toils and hardships through which we had passed in the previous three months.

26 miles south of Atlanta
September 3rd, 1864

Dearest Ellen,

My movement has been perfectly successful, and the corps I left at the Bridge are now in Atlanta, which was abandoned by the enemy the moment I made a good [attack?] on the Macon road. We have had some fighting at Jonesboro, where we beat Hardee's Corps bad. We now confront the Rebel army and we are studying the possibilities. I am very well. You doubtless hear of us through the papers oftener than I can write.

We are in a country rich in corn and our supplies are ample.

Yours ever,
W. T. Sherman

A courier-line was at once organized, messages were sent back and forth from our camp at Lovejoy's to Atlanta, and to our telegraph-station at the Chattahoochee bridge. Of course, the glad tidings flew on the wings of electricity to all parts of the North, where the people had patiently awaited news of their husbands, sons, and brothers, away down in "Dixie Land;" and congratulations came pouring back full of good-will and patriotism. This victory was most opportune; Mr. Lincoln himself told me afterward that even he had previously felt in doubt, for the summer was fast passing away; that General Grant seemed to be checkmated about Richmond and Petersburg, and my army seemed to have run up against an impassable barrier, when, suddenly and unexpectedly, came the news that "Atlanta was ours, and fairly won." A presidential election then agitated the North. Mr. Lincoln represented the national cause, and General McClellan had accepted the nomination of the Democratic party, whose platform was that the war was a failure, and that it was better to allow the South to go free to establish a separate government, whose corner-stone should be slavery. Success to our arms at that instant was therefore a political necessity; and it was all-important that something startling in our interest should occur before the election in November. The brilliant success at Atlanta filled that requirement and made the election of Mr. Lincoln certain. Among the many letters of congratulation received, those of Mr. Lincoln and General Grant seem most important:

EXECUTIVE MANSION,
WASHINGTON, D. C., *September 3, 1864.*

The national thanks are rendered by the President to Major-General W. T. Sherman and the gallant officers and soldiers of his command before Atlanta, for the distinguished ability and perseverance displayed in the campaign in Georgia, which, under Divine favor, has resulted in the capture of Atlanta. The marches, battles, sieges, and other military operations, that have signalized the campaign, must render it famous in the annals of war, and have entitled those who have participated therein to the applause and thanks of the nation.

ABRAHAM LINCOLN
President of the United States.

CITY POINT, VIRGINIA, *September 4, 1864*—9 p.m.

Major-General SHERMAN:

I have just received your dispatch announcing the capture of Atlanta. In honor of your great victory, I have ordered a salute to be fired with *shotted* guns from every battery bearing upon the enemy. The salute will be fired within an hour, amid great rejoicing.

U. S. GRANT, *Lieutenant-General.*

These dispatches were communicated to the army in general orders, and we all felt duly encouraged and elated by the praise of those competent to bestow it.

The army still remained where the news of success had first found us, Lovejoy's; but, after due reflection, I resolved not to attempt at that time a further pursuit of Hood's army, but slowly and deliberately to move back, occupy Atlanta, enjoy a short period of rest, and to think well over the next step required in the progress of events. Orders for this movement were made on the 5th September, and three days were given for each army to reach the place assigned it: the Army of the Cumberland in and about Atlanta; the Army of the Tennessee at East Point; and the Army of the Ohio at Decatur.

Personally I rode back to Jonesboro on the 6th and there inspected the rebel hospital, full of wounded officers and men left by Hardee in his retreat. The next night we stopped at Rough and Ready, and on the 8th of September we rode into Atlanta, then occupied by the Twentieth Corps. In the Court-House Square was encamped a brigade, embracing the Massachusetts Second

and Thirty-third Regiments, which had two of the finest bands of the army, and their music was to us all a source of infinite pleasure during our sojourn in that city. I took up my headquarters in the house of Judge Lyons, which stood opposite one corner of the Court-House Square, and at once set about a measure already ordered, of which I had thought much and long, to remove the entire civil population and to deny to all civilians from the rear the expected profits of civil trade. Hundreds of sutlers and traders were waiting at Nashville and Chattanooga, greedy to reach Atlanta with their wares and goods, with which to drive a profitable trade with the inhabitants. I gave positive orders that none of these traders, except three (one for each separate army), should be permitted to come nearer than Chattanooga; and, moreover, I peremptorily required that all the citizens and families resident in Atlanta should go away, giving to each the option to go south or north, as their interests or feelings dictated. I was resolved to make Atlanta a pure military garrison or depot, with no civil population to influence military measures. I had seen Memphis, Vicksburg, Natchez, and New Orleans, all captured from the enemy, and each at once was garrisoned by a full division of troops, if not more; so that success was actually crippling our armies in the field by detachments to guard and protect the interests of a hostile population.

I gave notice of this purpose, as early as the 4th of September, to General Halleck, in a letter concluding with these words:

> If the people raise a howl against my barbarity and cruelty, I will answer that war is war, and not popularity-seeking. If they want peace, they and their relatives must stop the war.

I knew, of course, that such a measure would be strongly criticised, but made up my mind to do it with the absolute certainty of its justness and that time would sanction its wisdom. I knew that the people of the South would read in this measure two important conclusions: one, that we were in earnest; and the other, if they were sincere in their common and popular clamor "to die in the last ditch," that the opportunity would soon come.

Soon after our reaching Atlanta, General Hood had sent in by a flag of truce a proposition, offering a general exchange of prisoners, saying that he was authorized to make such an exchange by the Richmond authorities, out of the vast number of our men then held captive at Andersonville, the same whom General Stoneman had hoped to rescue at the time of his raid. Some of these prisoners had already escaped and got in, had described the pitiable condition of the remainder, and, although I felt a sympathy for their hardships and sufferings as deeply as any man could, yet as nearly all the prisoners who had been captured by us during the campaign had been sent, as fast as taken, to the usual depots North, they were then beyond my control. There were still about two thousand, mostly captured at Jonesboro, who had been sent back by cars, but had not passed Chattanooga. These I ordered back and offered General Hood to exchange them for Stoneman, Buell, and such of my own army as would make up the equivalent; but I would not exchange for his prisoners *generally*, because I knew these would have to be sent to their own regiments, away from my army, whereas all we could give him could at once be put to duty in his immediate army. Quite an angry correspondence grew up between us, which is given here, as illustrative of the events referred to, and of the feelings of the actors in the game of war at that particular crisis:

HEADQUARTERS MILITARY DIVISION OF THE MISSISSIPPI, }
IN THE FIELD, ATLANTA, GEORGIA, *September* 7, 1864. }

General HOOD, *commanding Confederate Army*.

GENERAL: I have deemed it to the interest of the United States that the citizens now residing in Atlanta should remove, those who prefer it to go south, and the rest north. For the latter I can provide food and transportation to points of their election in Tennessee, Kentucky, or farther north. For the former I can provide transportation by cars as far as Rough and Ready, and also wagons; but, that their removal may be made with as little discomfort as possible, it will be necessary for you to help the families from Rough and Ready to the cars at Lovejoy's. If you consent, I will undertake to remove all the families in Atlanta who prefer to go south to Rough and Ready, with all their movable effects, viz., clothing, trunks, reasonable furniture, bedding, etc., with their servants, white and black, with the proviso that no force shall be used toward the blacks, one way or the other. If they want to go with their masters or mistresses, they may do so; otherwise they will be sent away, unless they be men, when they may be employed by our quartermaster. Atlanta is no place for families or non-combatants, and I have no desire to send them north if you will assist in conveying them south. If this proposition meets your views, I will consent to a truce in the neighborhood of Rough and Ready, stipulating that any wagons, horses, animals, or persons sent there for the purposes herein stated, shall in no manner be harmed or molested; you in your turn agreeing that any cars, wagons, or carriages, persons or animals sent to the same

106

point, shall not be interfered with. Each of us might send a guard of, say, one hundred men, to maintain order, and limit the truce to, say, two days after a certain time appointed.

I have authorized the mayor to choose two citizens to convey to you this letter, with such documents as the mayor may forward in explanation, and shall await your reply. I have the honor to be your obedient servant,

W. T. Sherman, *Major-General commanding.*

Headquarters Army of Tennessee, }
Office Chief of Staff, *September 9, 1864.* }

Major-General W. T. Sherman, *commanding United States Forces in Georgia.*

General: Your letter of yesterday's date, borne by James M. Ball and James R. Crew, citizens of Atlanta, is received. You say therein, "I deem it to be to the interest of the United States that the citizens now residing in Atlanta should remove," etc. I do not consider that I have any alternative in this matter. I therefore accept your proposition to declare a truce of two days, or such time as may be necessary to accomplish the purpose mentioned, and shall render all assistance in my power to expedite the transportation of citizens in this direction. I suggest that a staff-officer be appointed by you to superintend the removal from the city to Rough and Ready, while I appoint a like officer to control their removal farther south; that a guard of one hundred men be sent by either party as you propose, to maintain order at that place, and that the removal begin on Monday next.

And now, sir, permit me to say that the unprecedented measure you propose transcends, in studied and ingenious cruelty, all acts ever before brought to my attention in the dark history of war.

In the name of God and humanity, I protest, believing that you will find that you are expelling from their homes and firesides the wives and children of a brave people. I am, general, very respectfully, your obedient servant,

J. B. Hood, *General.*

Headquarters Military Division of the Mississippi, }
in the field, Atlanta, Georgia, *September 10, 1864.* }

General J. B. Hood, *commanding Army of Tennessee, Confederate Army.*

General: I have the honor to acknowledge the receipt of your letter of this date, at the hands of Messrs. Ball and Crew, consenting to the arrangements I had proposed to facilitate the removal south of the people of Atlanta, who prefer to go in that direction. I inclose you a copy of my orders, which will, I am satisfied, accomplish my purpose perfectly.

You style the measures proposed "unprecedented," and appeal to the dark history of war for a parallel, as an act of "studied and ingenious cruelty." It is not unprecedented; for General Johnston himself very wisely and properly removed the families all the way from Dalton down, and I see no reason why Atlanta should be excepted. Nor is it necessary to appeal to the dark history of war, when recent and modern examples are so handy. You yourself burned dwelling-houses along your parapet, and I have seen to-day fifty houses that you have rendered uninhabitable because they stood in the way of your forts and men. You defended Atlanta on a line so close to town that every cannon-shot and many musket-shots from our line of investment, that overshot their mark, went into the habitations of women and children. General Hardee did the same at Jonesboro, and General Johnston did the same, last summer, at Jackson, Mississippi. I have not accused you of heartless cruelty, but merely instance these cases of very recent occurrence, and could go on and enumerate hundreds of others, and challenge any fair man to judge which of us has the heart of pity for the families of a "brave people."

I say that it is kindness to these families of Atlanta to remove them now, at once, from scenes that women and children should not be exposed to, and the "brave people" should scorn to commit their wives and children to the rude barbarians who thus, as you say, violate the laws of war, as illustrated in the pages of its dark history.

In the name of common-sense, I ask you not to appeal to a just God in such a sacrilegious manner. You who, in the midst of peace and prosperity, have plunged a nation into war—dark and cruel war—who dared and badgered us to battle, insulted our flag, seized our arsenals and forts that were left in the honorable custody of peaceful ordnance-sergeants, seized and made "prisoners of war" the very garrisons sent to protect your people against Negroes and Indians, long before any overt act was committed by the (to you) hated Lincoln Government; tried to force Kentucky and Missouri into rebellion, spite of themselves; falsified the vote of Louisiana; turned loose your privateers to plunder unarmed ships; expelled Union families by the thousands, burned their houses, and declared, by an act of your Congress, the confiscation of all debts due Northern men for goods had and received! Talk thus to the marines, but not to me, who have seen these things, and who will this day make as much sacrifice for the peace and honor of the South as the best-born Southerner among you! If we must be enemies, let us be men, and fight it out as we propose to do, and not deal in such hypocritical appeals to God and humanity. God will judge us in due time, and he will pronounce whether it be more humane to fight with a town full of women and the families of a brave people at our back, or to remove them in time to places of safety among their own friends and people. I am, very respectfully, your obedient servant,

W. T. SHERMAN, *Major-General commanding.*

HEADQUARTERS ARMY OF TENNESSEE, ⎱
September 12, 1864. ⎰

Major-General W. T. SHERMAN, *commanding Military Division of the Mississippi.*

GENERAL: I have the honor to acknowledge the receipt of your letter of the 9th inst., with its inclosure in reference to the women, children, and others, whom you have thought proper to expel from their homes in the city of Atlanta. Had you seen proper to let the matter rest there, I would gladly have allowed your letter to close this correspondence, and, without your expressing it in words, would have been willing to believe that, while "the interests of the United States," in your opinion, compelled you to an act of barbarous cruelty, you regretted the necessity, and we would have dropped the subject; but you have chosen to indulge in statements which I feel compelled to notice, at least so far as to signify my dissent, and not allow silence in regard to them to be construed as acquiescence.

I see nothing in your communication which induces me to modify the language of condemnation with which I characterized your order. It but strengthens me in the opinion that it stands "preeminent in the dark history of war for studied and ingenious cruelty." Your original order was stripped of all pretenses; you announced the edict for the sole reason that it was "to the interest of the United States." This alone you offered to us and the civilized world as an all-sufficient reason for disregarding the laws of God and man. You say that "General Johnston himself very wisely and properly removed the families all the way from Dalton down." It is due to that gallant soldier and gentleman to say that no act of his distinguished career gives the least color to your unfounded aspersions upon his conduct. He depopulated no villages, nor towns, nor cities, either friendly or hostile. He offered and extended friendly aid to his unfortunate fellow-citizens who desired to flee from your fraternal embraces. You are equally unfortunate in your attempt to find a justification for this act of cruelty, either in the defense of Jonesboro, by General Hardee, or of Atlanta, by myself. General Hardee defended his position in front of Jonesboro at the expense of injury to the houses; an ordinary, proper, and justifiable act of war. I defended Atlanta at the same risk and cost. If there was any fault in either case, it was your own, in not giving notice, especially in the case of Atlanta, of your purpose to shell the town, which is usual in war among civilized nations. No inhabitant was expelled from his home and fireside by the orders of General Hardee or myself, and therefore your recent order can find no support from the conduct of either of us. I feel no other emotion other than pain in reading that portion of your letter which attempts to justify your shelling Atlanta without notice under pretense that I defended Atlanta upon a line so close to town that every cannon-shot and many musket-balls from your line of investment, that overshot their mark, went into the habitations of women and children. I made no complaint of your firing into Atlanta in any way you thought proper. I make none now, but there are a hundred thousand witnesses that you fired into the habitations of women and children for weeks, firing far above and miles beyond my line of defense. I have too good an opinion, founded both upon observation and experience, of the skill of your artillerists, to credit the insinuation that they for several weeks unintentionally fired too high for my modest field-works, and slaughtered women and children by accident and want of skill.

The residue of your letter is rather discussion. It opens a wide field for the discussion of questions which I do not feel are committed to me. I am only a general of one of the armies of the Confederate States, charged with military operations in the field, under the direction of my superior officers, and I am not called upon to discuss with you the causes of the present war, or the political questions which led to or resulted from it. These grave and important questions have been committed to far abler hands than mine, and I shall only refer to them so far as to repel any unjust conclusion which might be drawn from my silence. You charge my country with "daring and badgering you to battle." The truth is, we sent commissioners to you, respectfully offering a peaceful separation, before the first gun was fired on either side. You say we insulted your flag. The truth is, we fired upon it, and those who fought under it, when you came to our doors upon the mission of subjugation. You say we seized upon your forts and arsenals, and made prisoners of the garrisons sent to protect us against Negroes and Indians. The truth is, we, by force of arms, drove out insolent intruders and took possession of our own forts and arsenals, to resist your claims to dominion over masters, slaves, and Indians, all of whom are to this day, with a unanimity unexampled in the history of the world, warring against your attempts to become their masters. You say that we tried to force Missouri and Kentucky into rebellion in spite of themselves. The truth is, my Government, from the beginning of this struggle to this hour, has again and again offered, before the whole world, to leave it to the unbiased will of these States, and all others, to determine for themselves whether they will cast their destiny with your Government or ours; and your Government has resisted this fundamental principle of free institutions with the bayonet, and labors daily, by force and fraud, to fasten its hateful tyranny upon the unfortunate freemen of these States. You say we falsified the vote of Louisiana. The truth is, Louisiana not only separated herself from your Government by nearly a unanimous vote of her people, but has vindicated the act upon every battle-field from Gettysburg to the Sabine, and has exhibited an heroic devotion to her decision which challenges the admiration and respect of every man capable of feeling sympathy for the oppressed or admiration for heroic valor. You say that we turned loose pirates to plunder your unarmed ships. The truth is, when you robbed us of our part of the navy, we built and bought a few vessels, hoisted the flag of our country, and swept the seas, in defiance of your navy, around the whole circumference of the globe. You say we have expelled Union families by thousands. The truth is, not a single family has been expelled from the Confederate States, that I am aware of; but, on the contrary, the moderation of our Government toward traitors has been a fruitful theme of denunciation by its enemies and well-meaning friends of our cause. You say my Government, by acts of Congress, has confiscated "all debts due Northern men for goods sold and delivered." The truth is, our Congress gave due and ample time to your merchants and traders to depart from our shores with their ships, goods, and effects, and only sequestrated the property of our enemies in retaliation for their acts—declaring us traitors, and confiscating our property wherever their power extended, either in their country or our own. Such are your accusations, and such are the facts known of all men to be true.

You order into exile the whole population of a city; drive men, women, and children from their homes at the point of the bayonet, under the plea that it is to the interest of your Government, and on the claim that it is an act of "kindness to these families of Atlanta." Butler only banished from New Orleans the registered enemies of his Government, and acknowledged that he did it as a punishment. You issue a sweeping edict, covering all the inhabitants of a city, and add insult to the injury heaped upon the defenseless by assuming that you have done them a kindness. This you follow by the assertion that you will "make as much sacrifice for the peace and honor of the South as the best-born Southerner." And, because I characterize what you call a kindness as being real cruelty, you presume to sit in judgment between me and my God; and you decide that my earnest prayer to the Almighty Father to save our women and children from what you call kindness, is a "sacrilegious, hypocritical appeal."

You came into our country with your army, avowedly for the purpose of subjugating free white men, women, and children, and not only intend to rule over them, but you make Negroes your allies, and desire to place over us an inferior race, which we have raised from barbarism to its present position, which is the highest ever attained by that race, in any country, in all time. I must, therefore, decline to

111

accept your statements in reference to your kindness toward the people of Atlanta, and your willingness to sacrifice every thing for the peace and honor of the South, and refuse to be governed by your decision in regard to matters between myself, my country, and my God.

You say, "Let us fight it out like men." To this my reply is—for myself, and I believe for all the true men, ay, and women and children, in my country—we will fight you to the death! Better die a thousand deaths than submit to live under you or your Government and your Negro allies!

Having answered the points forced upon me by your letter of the 9th of September, I close this correspondence with you; and, notwithstanding your comments upon my appeal to God in the cause of humanity, I again humbly and reverently invoke his almighty aid in defense of justice and right.   Respectfully, your obedient servant,

J. B. HOOD, *General.*

HEADQUARTERS MILITARY DIVISION OF THE MISSISSIPPI, }
IN THE FIELD, ATLANTA, GEORGIA, *September* 14, 1864. }

General J. B. HOOD, *commanding Army of the Tennessee, Confederate Army.*

GENERAL: Yours of September 12th is received, and has been carefully perused. I agree with you that this discussion by two soldiers is out of place, and profitless; but you must admit that you began the controversy by characterizing an official act of mine in unfair and improper terms. I reiterate my former answer, and to the only new matter contained in your rejoinder add: We have no "Negro allies" in this army; not a single Negro soldier left Chattanooga with this army, or is with it now. There are a few guarding Chattanooga, which General Steedman sent at one time to drive Wheeler out of Dalton.

I was not bound by the laws of war to give notice of the shelling of Atlanta, a "fortified town, with magazines, arsenals, foundries, and public stores;" you were bound to take notice. See the books.

This is the conclusion of our correspondence, which I did not begin, and terminate with satisfaction.   I am, with respect, your obedient servant,

W. T. SHERMAN, *Major-General commanding.*

Atlanta, Georgia
September 17th, 1864

Dearest Ellen,

I have many letters from you of late, some of which seem by an unexplained cause to have laid at Nashville or Chattanooga, but I think the series is complete up to and including your visit to the school at South Bend. I got last night also Minnie's letter which you seem to have carried to Lancaster and mailed from there. I have telegraphed you and written short hasty letters to you, to your father and Tommy and cannot add much if anything of interest not involved in my orginal telegraph. Atlanta is ours and fairly won. I have had some sharp correspondence with Hood about expelling the poor families of a brave people, which correspondence in due time will become public and I take the ground that Atlanta is a conquered place and I propose to use it purely for our own military purposes, which are inconsistent with its habitation by the families of a brave people. I am shipping them all, and by next Wednesday the town will be a real military town with no women boring me every order I give. Hood no doubt thought he would make capital out of the barbarity, etc., but I rather think he will change his mind before he is done. I beat him on the strategy and fighting and if my troops had only been as smart as my old Tennessee Army I could have bagged all of Hardee's Corps at Jonesboro. Still on the whole the campaign is the best, cleanest and most satisfactory of this war. I have received the most fulsome praise of all from the President down, but I fear the world will jump to the wrong conclusion that because I am in Atlanta the work is done. Far from it. We must kill these three hundred thousand I have told you of so often, and the further they run the harder for us to get them.

I will send you the rough notes of my report as soon as copied in my letter book and you can read it to your father who will be more interested than you.

Do you remember when I was at Bellefonte in 1844 I boarded with a man named Martin. Some months ago he found out I was the same and wrote me asking me to enable him to gather his corn and some hogs. Of course I did so and wrote him very kindly. I send you his answer. It is a gem in its way. I send you a letter from a Mrs. Biddle also as a sample of the many that come to me and I really have not time to answer. I already write so hastily and badly that no one but my regular clerks can make it out. Dayton does much of my writing but the truth is I can write a dozen letters before he can one. I find it about as quick work to write as to tell what to write and modify and correct after.

Hill's time was out July 19th, but he stayed till the day before yesterday when he went to Illinois to see his mother who has charge of some cows, calves, mares and colts. I paid him up and had a grand settlement, paying him in full $292. He was honest and faithful to the last. I have two Negroes to take care of my horses, one a boy who now makes up my bed, blacks my shoes and sweeps out the room under the mastery of a very *good orderly who succeeded Rowyer, so that the machinery of my household works smooth as possible. We occupy a fine house, that of Judge Lyons, and have a good mess. I enclose you a letter to mail to Mr. Cassidy, asking him to sell that lot. I told Hill to write to you when he got home and you would send him a deed to a lot in Leavenworth, but I gave him to understand I would not be responsible for the consequences. He promised to come back to me before the winter campaign and I think he will. He turned over to his successor a minute account of [unclear] with orders on all. Love to all,*

Yours ever,
W. T. Sherman

In order to effect the exchange of prisoners, to facilitate the exodus of the people of Atlanta, and to keep open communication with the South, we established a neutral camp, at and about the railroad-station next south of Atlanta, known as "Rough and Ready," to which point I dispatched Lieutenant-Colonel Willard Warner, of my staff, with a guard of one hundred men, and General Hood sent Colonel Clare, of his staff, with a similar guard; these officers and men harmonized perfectly and parted good friends when their work was done. In the meantime I also had reconnoitred the entire rebel lines about Atlanta, which were well built, but were entirely too extensive to be held by a single corps or division of troops, so I instructed Colonel Poe, United States Engineers, on my staff, to lay off an inner and shorter line, susceptible of defense by a smaller garrison.

By the middle of September all these matters were in progress, the reports of the past campaign were written up and dispatched to Washington, and our thoughts began to turn toward the future. Admiral Farragut had boldly and successfully run the forts at the entrance to Mobile Bay, which resulted in the capture of Fort Morgan, so that General Canby was enabled to begin his regular operations against Mobile City, with a view to open the Alabama River to navigation. My first thoughts were to concert operations with him, either by way of Montgomery, Alabama, or by the Appalachicola; but so long a line, to be used as a base for further operations eastward, was not advisable, and I concluded to await the initiative of the enemy, supposing that he would be forced to resort to some desperate campaign by the clamor raised at the South on account of the great loss to them of the city of Atlanta.

General Thomas occupied a house on Marietta Street, which had a veranda with high pillars. We were sitting there one evening, talking about things generally, when General Thomas asked leave to send his trains back to Chattanooga, for the convenience and economy of forage. I inquired of him if he supposed we would be allowed much rest at Atlanta, and he said he thought we would, or that at all events it would not be prudent for us to go much farther into Georgia because of our already long line of communication, three hundred miles from Nashville. This was true; but there we were, and we could not afford to remain on the defensive, simply holding Atlanta and fighting for the safety of its railroad. I insisted on his retaining all trains, and on keeping all his divisions ready to move at a moment's warning. All the army, officers and men, seemed to relax more or less, and sink into a condition of idleness. General Schofield was permitted to go to Knoxville to look after matters in his Department of the Ohio; and Generals Blair and Logan went home to look after politics. Many of the regiments were entitled to and claimed their discharge, by reason of the expiration of their term of service; so that with victory and success came also many causes of disintegration.

The rebel General Wheeler was still in Middle Tennessee, threatening our railroads, and rumors came that Forrest was on his way from Mississippi to the same theatre, for the avowed purpose of breaking up our railroads and compelling us to fall back from our conquest. To prepare for this or any other emergency I ordered Newton's division of the Fourth Corps back to Chattanooga, and Corse's division of the Seventeenth Corps to Rome and instructed General Rousseau at Nashville, Granger at Decatur, and Steadman at Chattanooga, to adopt the most active measures to protect and insure the safety of our roads.

Hood still remained about Lovejoy's Station, and, up to the 15th of September, had given no signs of his future plans; so that with this date I close the campaign of Atlanta with the following review of our relative losses during the months of August and September, with a summary of those for the whole campaign, beginning May 6 and ending September 15, 1864. The losses for August and September are added together, so as to include those about Jonesboro:

Killed and missing	1,408
Wounded	3,731
Total	5,139

Hood's losses, reported for the same period:

Killed	482
Wounded	3,223
Captured	3,738
Total	7,443

On recapitulating the entire losses of each army during the entire campaign, from May to September, we have in the Union army:

Killed	4,423
Wounded	22,822
Missing	4,442
Total	31,687

In the Southern army:

Killed	3,044
Wounded	18,952
Captured	12,983
Total	34,979

ATLANTA AND AFTER

By the middle of September, matters and things had settled down in Atlanta, so that we felt perfectly at home. The telegraph and railroads were repaired, and we had uninterrupted communication to the rear. The trains arrived with regularity and dispatch and brought us ample supplies. General Wheeler had been driven out of Middle Tennessee, escaping south across the Tennessee River at Bainbridge; and things looked as though we were to have a period of repose.

One day, two citizens, Messrs. Hill and Nelson, came into our lines at Decatur and were sent to my headquarters. They represented themselves as former members of Congress and particular friends of my brother John Sherman; that Mr. Hill had a son killed in the rebel army as it fell back before us somewhere near Cassville, and they wanted to obtain the body, having learned from a comrade where it was buried. I gave them permission to go by rail to the rear, with a note to the commanding officer, General John E. Smith at Cartersville requiring him to furnish them an escort and an ambulance for the purpose. I invited them to take dinner with our mess, and we naturally ran into a general conversation about politics and the devastation and ruin caused by the war. They had seen a part of the country over which the army had passed and could easily apply its measure of desolation to the remainder of the State, if necessity should compel us to go ahead.

Mr. Hill resided at Madison, on the main road to Augusta, and seemed to realize fully the danger; said that further resistance on the part of the South was madness, that he hoped Governor

Brown of Georgia would so proclaim it and withdraw his people from the rebellion, in pursuance of what was known as the policy of "separate State action." I told him, if he saw Governor Brown, to describe to him fully what he had seen and to say that if he remained inert, I would be compelled to go ahead, devastating the State in its whole length and breadth; that there was no adequate force to stop us, etc.; but if he would issue his proclamation withdrawing his State troops from the armies of the Confederacy, I would spare the State, and in our passage across it confine the troops to the main roads and would, moreover, pay for all the corn and food we needed. I also told Mr. Hill that he might, in my name, invite Governor Brown to visit Atlanta; that I would give him a safeguard, and that if he wanted to make a speech, I would guarantee him as full and respectable an audience as any he had ever spoken to. I believe that Mr. Hill, after reaching his home at Madison, went to Milledgeville, the capital of the State, and delivered the message to Governor Brown. On the 15th of September I telegraphed to General Halleck as follows:

> My report is done, and will be forwarded as soon as I get in a few more of the subordinate reports. I am awaiting a courier from General Grant. All well; the troops are in good, healthy camps, and supplies are coming forward finely. Governor Brown has disbanded his militia, to gather the corn and sorghum of the State. I have reason to believe that he and Stephens want to visit me, and have sent them a hearty invitation. I will exchange two thousand prisoners with Hood, but no more.

Governor Brown's action at that time is fully explained by the following letter, since made public, which was then only known to us in part by hearsay:

> EXECUTIVE DEPARTMENT, }
> MILLEDGEVILLE, GEORGIA, *September* 10, 1864. }
>
> *General* J. B. HOOD, *commanding Army of Tennessee.*
>
> GENERAL: As the militia of the State were called out for the defense of Atlanta during the campaign against it, which has terminated by the fall of the city into the hands of the enemy, and as many of these left their homes without preparation (expecting to be gone but a few weeks), who have remained in service over three months (most of the time in the trenches), justice requires that they be permitted, while the enemy are preparing for the winter campaign, to return to their homes, and look for a time after important interests, and prepare themselves for such ser-

118

vice as may be required when another campaign commences against other important points in the State. I therefore hereby withdraw said organization from your command....

JOSEPH E. BROWN.

This militia had composed a division under command of Major-General Gustavus W. Smith and were thus dispersed to their homes, to gather the corn and sorghum, then ripe and ready for the harvesters.

On the 17th I received by telegraph from President Lincoln this dispatch:

WASHINGTON, D. C., September 17, 1864 — 10 a.m.

Major-General SHERMAN:

I feel great interest in the subjects of your dispatch, mentioning corn and sorghum, and the contemplated visit to you.

A. LINCOLN, President of the United States.

I replied at once:

HEADQUARTERS MILITARY DIVISION OF THE MISSISSIPPI, }
IN THE FIELD, ATLANTA, GEORGIA, September 17, 1864. }

President LINCOLN, *Washington, D. C.*:

I will keep the department fully advised of all developments connected with the subject in which you feel interested.

Mr. Wright, former member of Congress from Rome, Georgia, and Mr. King, of Marietta, are now going between Governor Brown and myself. I have said to them that some of the people of Georgia are engaged in rebellion, begun in error and perpetuated in pride, but that Georgia can now save herself from the devastations of war preparing for her, only by withdrawing her quota out of the Confederate Army, and aiding me to expel Hood from the borders of the State; in which event, instead of desolating the land as we progress, I will keep our men to the high-roads and commons, and pay for the corn and meat we need and take.

I am fully conscious of the delicate nature of such assertions, but it would be a magnificent stroke of policy if we could, without surrendering principle or a foot of ground, arouse the latent enmity of Georgia against Davis.

The people do not hesitate to say that Mr. Stephens was and is a Union man at heart; and they say that Davis will not trust him or let him have a share in his Government.

W. T. SHERMAN, Major-General.

I have not the least doubt that Governor Brown at that time seriously entertained the proposition; but he hardly felt ready to act and simply gave a furlough to the militia and called a special session of the Legislature, to meet at Milledgeville, to take into consideration the critical condition of affairs in the State.

About this time we detected signs of activity on the part of the enemy. On the 21st Hood shifted his army across from the Macon road at Lovejoy's to the West Point road at Palmetto Station, and his cavalry appeared on the west side of the Chattahoochee toward Powder Springs; thus, as it were, stepping aside, and opening wide the door for us to enter Central Georgia. I inferred, however, that his real purpose was to assume the offensive against our railroads, and on the 24th a heavy force of cavalry from Mississippi, under General Forrest, made its appearance at Athens, Alabama, and captured its garrison.

General Newton's division and Corse's were sent back by rail, the former to Chattanooga and the latter to Rome. On the 25th I telegraphed to General Halleck:

> Hood seems to be moving, as it were, to the Alabama line, leaving open the road to Macon, as also to Augusta; but his cavalry is busy on all our roads. A force, number estimated as high as eight thousand, are reported to have captured Athens, Alabama; and a regiment of three hundred and fifty men sent to its relief. I have sent Newton's division up to Chattanooga in cars, and will send another division to Rome. If I were sure that Savannah would soon be in our possession, I should be tempted to march for Milledgeville and Augusta; but I must first secure what I have. Jeff Davis is at Macon.
>
> W. T. Sherman, *Major-General.*

On the next day I telegraphed further that Jefferson Davis was with Hood at Palmetto Station. One of our spies was there at the time, who came in the next night, and reported to me the substance of his speech to the soldiers. It was a repetition of those he had made at Columbia, South Carolina, and Macon, Georgia, on his way out, which I had seen in the newspapers. Davis seemed to be perfectly upset by the fall of Atlanta, and to have lost all sense and reason. He denounced General Joseph Johnston and Governor Brown as little better than traitors; attributed to them personally the many misfortunes which had befallen their cause and informed the soldiers that now the tables were to be turned; that General Forrest was already on our roads in Middle Tennessee; and that Hood's army would soon be there. He asserted that the Yankee army would

120

have to retreat or starve, and that the retreat would prove more disastrous than was that of Napoleon from Moscow. He promised his Tennessee and Kentucky soldiers that their feet should soon tread their "native soil." He made no concealment of these vainglorious boasts, and thus gave us the full key to his future designs. To be forewarned was to be forearmed, and I think we took full advantage of the occasion.

On the 26th I received this dispatch:

> CITY POINT, VIRGINIA, *September* 26, 1864 — 10 a.m.
>
> *Major-General* SHERMAN, *Atlanta:*
>
> It will be better to drive Forrest out of Middle Tennessee as a first step, and do any thing else you may feel your force sufficient for. When a movement is made on any part of the sea-coast, I will advise you. If Hood goes to the Alabama line, will it not be impossible for him to subsist his army?
>
> U. S. GRANT, *Lieutenant-General.*

Answer:

> HEADQUARTERS MILITARY DIVISION OF THE MISSISSIPPI,
> IN THE FIELD, ATLANTA, GEORGIA, *September* 26, 1864.
>
> GENERAL: I have your dispatch of to-day. I have already sent one division (Newton's) to Chattanooga, and another (Corse's) to Rome.
>
> Our armies are much reduced, and if I send back any more, I will not be able to threaten Georgia much. There are men enough to the rear to whip Forrest, but they are necessarily scattered to defend the roads.
>
> Can you expedite the sending to Nashville of the recruits that are in Indiana and Ohio? They could occupy the forts.
>
> Hood is now on the West Point road, twenty-four miles south of this, and draws his supplies by that road. Jefferson Davis is there to-day, and superhuman efforts will be made to break my road.
>
> Forrest is now lieutenant-general, and commands all the enemy's cavalry.
>
> W. T. Sherman, *Major-General.*

All this time Hood and I were carrying on the foregoing correspondence relating to the exchange of prisoners, the removal of the people from Atlanta, and the relief of our prisoners of war at Andersonville. Notwithstanding the severity of their imprisonment, some of these men escaped from Andersonville and got to me at Atlanta. They described their sad condition: more than twenty-five thousand prisoners confined in a stockade designed for only ten thousand; debarred the privilege of gathering wood out of which to make huts; deprived of sufficient healthy food, and the little stream that ran through their prison-pen poisoned and polluted by the offal from their cooking and butchering houses above. On the 22d of September I wrote to General Hood, describing the condition of our men at Andersonville, purposely refraining from casting odium on him or his associates for the treatment of these men, but asking his consent for me to procure from our generous friends at the North the articles of clothing and comfort which they wanted, under-clothing, soap, combs, scissors, etc.—all needed to keep them in health—and to send these stores with a train and an officer to issue them. General Hood, on the 24th, promptly consented, and I telegraphed to my friend Mr. James E. Yeatman, Vice-President of the Sanitary Commission at St. Louis, to send us all the under-clothing and soap he could spare, specifying twelve hundred fine-tooth combs and four hundred pairs of shears to cut hair. These articles indicate the plague that most afflicted our prisoners at Andersonville.

Mr. Yeatman promptly responded to my request, expressed the articles, but they did not reach Andersonville in time, for the prisoners were soon after removed; these supplies did, however, finally overtake them at Jacksonville, Florida, just before the war closed.

On the 28th I received from General Grant two dispatches:

CITY POINT, VIRGINIA, *September 27, 1864—8:30 a.m.*
Major-General SHERMAN:

It is evident, from the tone of the Richmond press and from other sources of information, that the enemy intend making a desperate effort to drive you from where you are. I have directed all new troops from the West, and from the East too, if necessary, in case none are ready in the West, to be sent to you. If General Burbridge is not too far on his way to Abingdon, I think he had better be recalled and his surplus troops sent into Tennessee.

U. S. GRANT, *Lieutenant-General.*

CITY POINT, VIRGINIA, *September 27, 1864—10:30 a.m.*
Major-General SHERMAN:

I have directed all recruits and new troops from all the Western States to be sent to Nashville, to receive their further orders from you. I was mistaken about Jeff. Davis being in Richmond on Thursday last. He was then on his way to Macon.

U. S. GRANT, *Lieutenant-General.*

Forrest having already made his appearance in Middle Tennessee, and Hood evidently edging off in that direction, satisfied me that the general movement against our roads had begun. I therefore determined to send General Thomas back to Chattanooga, with another division, to meet the danger in Tennessee. General Thomas went up on the 29th, and Morgan's division followed the same day, also by rail. And I telegraphed to General Halleck:

> I take it for granted that Forrest will cut our road, but think we can prevent him from making a serious lodgment. His cavalry will travel a hundred miles where ours will ten. I have sent two divisions up to Chattanooga and one to Rome, and General Thomas started to-day to drive Forrest out of Tennessee. Our roads should be watched from the rear, and I am glad that General Grant has ordered reserves to Nashville. I prefer for the future to make the movement on Milledgeville, Millen, and Savannah. Hood now rests twenty-four miles south, on the Chattahoochee, with his right on the West Point road. He is removing the iron of the Macon road. I can whip his infantry, but his cavalry is to be feared.

There was great difficulty in obtaining correct information about Hood's movements from Palmetto Station. I could not get spies to penetrate his camps, but on the 1st of October I was satisfied that the bulk of his infantry was at and across the Chattahoochee River near Campbellton and that his cavalry was on the west side at Powder Springs. On that day I telegraphed to General Grant:

> Hood is evidently across the Chattahoochee, below Sweetwater. If he tries to get on our road, this side of the Etowah, I shall attack him; but if he goes to the Selma & Talladega road, why will it not do to leave Tennessee to the forces which Thomas has, and the reserves soon to come to Nashville, and for me to destroy Atlanta and march across Georgia to Savannah or Charleston, breaking roads and doing irreparable damage? We cannot remain on the defensive.

Orders were at once made for the Twentieth Corps to hold Atlanta and the bridges of the Chattahoochee, and the other corps were put in motion for Marietta.

We had strong railroad guards at Marietta and Kennesaw, Allatoona, Etowah Bridge, Kingston, Rome, Resaca, Dalton, Ringgold, and Chattanooga. All the important bridges were likewise protected by good block-houses, admirably constructed, and capable of a strong defense against cavalry or infantry; and at nearly all the regular railroad-stations we had smaller detachments intrenched. I had little fear of the enemy's cavalry damaging our roads seriously, for they rarely made a break which could not be repaired in a few days; but it was absolutely necessary to keep General Hood's infantry off our main route of communication and supply. Forrest had with him in Middle Tennessee about eight thousand cavalry, and Hood's army was estimated at from thirty-five to forty thousand men, infantry and artillery, including Wheeler's cavalry, then about three thousand strong.

We crossed the Chattahoochee River during the 3d and 4th of October, rendezvoused at the old battle-field of Smyrna Camp, and the next day reached Marietta and Kennesaw. The telegraph-wires had been cut above Marietta, and learning that heavy masses of infantry, artillery, and cavalry, had been seen from Kennesaw, marching north, I inferred that Allatoona was their objective point; and on the 4th of October I signaled from Vining's Station to Kennesaw, and from Kennesaw to Allatoona, over the heads of the enemy, a message for General Corse at Rome to hurry back to the assistance of the garrison at Allatoona. Allatoona was held by a small brigade, commanded by Lieutenant-Colonel Tourtellotte, my present aide-de-camp. He had two small redoubts on either side of the railroad, overlooking the village of Allatoona, and the warehouses, in which were stored over a million rations of bread.

Reaching Kennesaw Mountain about 8 a.m. of October 5th, a beautiful day, I had a superb view of the vast panorama to the north and west. To the southwest, about Dallas, could be seen the smoke of camp-fires, indicating the presence of a large force of the enemy, and the whole line of railroad from Big Shanty up to Allatoona (full fifteen miles) was marked by the fires of the burning railroad. We could plainly see the smoke of battle about Allatoona, and hear the faint reverberation of the cannon.

From Kennesaw I ordered the Twenty-third Corps to march due west on the Burnt Hickory road and to burn houses or piles of brush as it progressed, to indicate the head of column, hoping to interpose this corps between Hood's main army at Dallas and the detachment then assailing Allatoona. The rest of the army was directed straight for Allatoona, northwest, distant eighteen miles. The signal-officer on Kennesaw reported that since daylight he had failed to obtain any answer to his call for Allatoona; but, while I was with him, he caught a faint glimpse of the tell-tale flag through an embrasure, and after much time he made out these letters—"C.," "R.," "S.," "E.," "H.," "E.," "R.," and translated the message—"Corse is here." It was a source of great relief, for it gave me the first assurance that General Corse had received his orders and that the place was adequately garrisoned.

I watched with painful suspense the indications of the battle raging there and was dreadfully impatient at the slow progress of the relieving column, whose advance was marked by the smokes which were made according to orders, but about 2 p.m. I noticed with satisfaction that the smoke of battle about Allatoona grew less and less and ceased altogether about 4 p.m. For a time I attributed this result to the effect of General Cox's march, but later in the afternoon the signal-flag announced the welcome tidings that the attack had been fairly repulsed, but that General Corse was wounded. The next day my aide, Colonel Dayton, received this characteristic dispatch:

ALLATOONA, GEORGIA, *October* 6, 1864 — 2 p.m.
Captain L. M. DAYTON, *Aide-de-Camp:*

I am short a cheek-bone and an ear, but am able to whip all hell yet! My losses are very heavy. A force moving from Stilesboro to Kingston gives me some anxiety. Tell me where Sherman is.

JOHN M. CORSE, *Brigadier-General.*

Inasmuch as the enemy had retreated southwest, and would probably next appear at Rome, I answered General Corse with orders to get back to Rome with his troops as quickly as possible.

General Corse's report of this fight at Allatoona is very full and graphic. It is dated Rome, October 27, 1864; recites the fact that he received his orders by signal to go to the assistance of Allatoona on the 4th, when he telegraphed to Kingston for cars, and a train of thirty empty cars was started for him, but about ten of them got off the track and caused delay. By 7 p.m. he had at Rome a train of twenty cars, which he loaded up with Colonel Rowett's brigade, and part of the Twelfth Illinois Infantry; started at 8 p.m., reached Allatoona (distant thirty-five miles) at 1 a.m. of the 5th, and sent the train back for more men; but the road was in bad order, and no more men came in time. He found Colonel Tourtellotte's garrison composed of eight hundred and ninety men; his reenforcement was one thousand and fifty-four: total for the defense, nineteen hundred and forty-four. The outposts were already engaged, and as soon as daylight came he drew back the men from the village to the ridge on which the redoubts were built.

The enemy was composed of French's division of three brigades, variously reported from

125

four to five thousand strong. This force gradually surrounded the place by 8 a.m., when General French sent in by flag of truce this note:

AROUND ALLATOONA, *October 5, 1864.*
Commanding Officer, United States Forces, Allatoona:

I have placed the forces under my command in such positions that you are surrounded, and to avoid a needless effusion of blood I call on you to surrender your forces at once, and unconditionally.

Five minutes will be allowed you to decide. Should you accede to this, you will be treated in the most honorable manner as prisoners of war.

I have the honor to be, very respectfully yours,

S. G. FRENCH,
Major-General commanding forces Confederate States.

General Corse answered immediately:

HEADQUARTERS FOURTH DIVISION, FIFTEENTH CORPS, }
ALLATOONA, GEORGIA, 8.30 A. M., *October 5, 1864.* }

Major-General S. G. FRENCH, *Confederate States, etc.:*

Your communication demanding surrender of my command I acknowledge receipt of, and respectfully reply that we are prepared for the "needless effusion of blood" whenever it is agreeable to you.

I am, very respectfully, your obedient servant,

JOHN M. CORSE,
Brigadier-General commanding forces United States.

Of course the attack began at once, coming from front, flank, and rear. There were two small redoubts, with slight parapets and ditches, one on each side of the deep railroad-cut. These redoubts had been located by Colonel Poe, United States Engineers, at the time of our advance on Kennesaw, the previous June. Each redoubt overlooked the storehouses close by the railroad, and each could aid the other defensively by catching in flank the attacking force of the other. Our troops at first endeavored to hold some ground outside the redoubts, but were soon driven inside, when the enemy made repeated assaults, but were always driven back. About 11 a.m. Colonel Redfield of the Thirty-ninth Iowa was killed, and Colonel Rowett was wounded, but never ceased to fight and encourage his men. Colonel Tourtellotte was shot through the hips, but continued to command. General Corse was, at 1 p.m., shot across the face, the ball cutting his ear,

126

which stunned him, but he continued to encourage his men and to give orders. About 1:30 p.m. the enemy made a last and desperate effort to carry one of the redoubts, but was badly cut to pieces by the artillery and infantry fire from the other, when he began to draw off, leaving his dead and wounded on the ground.

Before finally withdrawing, General French converged a heavy fire of his cannon on the block-house at Allatoona Creek, about two miles from the depot, set it on fire, and captured its garrison, consisting of four officers and eighty-five men. By 4 p.m. he was in full retreat south, on the Dallas road and got by before the head of General Cox's column had reached it; still several ambulances and stragglers were picked up by this command on that road. General Corse reported two hundred and thirty-one rebel dead, four hundred and eleven prisoners, three regimental colors, and eight hundred muskets captured.

Among the prisoners was a Brigadier-General Young, who thought that French's aggregate loss would reach two thousand. Colonel Tourtellotte says that, for days after General Corse had returned to Rome, his men found and buried at least a hundred more dead rebels, who had doubtless been wounded, and died in the woods near Allatoona. I know that when I reached Allatoona, on the 9th, I saw a good many dead men, who had been collected for burial. Corse's entire loss, officially reported, was 142 killed, 353 wounded, 212 missing.

I esteemed this defense of Allatoona so handsome and important that I made it the subject of a general order, No. 86, of October 7, 1864:

> The general commanding avails himself of the opportunity, in the handsome defense made of Allatoona, to illustrate the most important principle in war, that fortified posts should be defended to the last, regardless of the relative numbers of the party attacking and attacked. . . . The thanks of this army are due and are hereby accorded to General Corse, Colonel Tourtellotte, Colonel Rowett, officers, and men, for their determined and gallant defense of Allatoona, and it is made an example to illustrate the importance of preparing in time, and meeting the danger, when present, boldly, manfully, and well.
>
> Commanders and garrisons of the posts along our railroads are hereby instructed that they must hold their posts to the last minute, sure that the time gained is valuable and necessary to their comrades at the front.
>
> By order of Major-General W. T. Sherman,
>
> L. M. DAYTON, *Aide-de-Camp*.

The rebels had struck our railroad a heavy blow, burning every tie, bending the rails for eight miles, from Big Shanty to above Acworth, so that the estimate for repairs called for thirty-five thousand new ties and six miles of iron. Ten thousand men were distributed along the break to replace the ties and to prepare the road-bed, while the regular repair-party, under Colonel W. W. Wright, came down from Chattanooga with iron, spikes, etc., and in about seven days the road was all right again. It was by such acts of extraordinary energy that we discouraged our adversaries, for the rebel soldiers felt that it was a waste of labor for them to march hurriedly, on wide circuits, day and night, to burn a bridge and tear up a mile or so of track, when they knew that we could lay it back so quickly. They supposed that we had men and money without limit and that we always kept on hand, distributed along the road, duplicates of every bridge and culvert of any importance.

A good story is told of one who was on Kennesaw Mountain during our advance in the previous June or July. A group of rebels lay in the shade of a tree, one hot day, overlooking our camps about Big Shanty. One soldier remarked to his fellows:

"Well, the Yanks will have to git up and git now, for I heard General Johnston himself say that General Wheeler had blown up *the tunnel* near Dalton, and that the Yanks would have to retreat, because they could get no more rations."

"Oh, hell!" said a listener, "don't you know that old Sherman carries a *duplicate* tunnel along?"

After the war was over, General Johnston inquired of me who was our chief railroad-engineer. When I told him that it was Colonel W. W. Wright, a civilian, he was much surprised, said that our feats of bridge-building and repairs of roads had excited his admiration; and he instanced the occasion at Kennesaw in June, when an officer from Wheeler's cavalry had reported to him in person that he had come from General Wheeler, who had made a bad break in our road about Tilton Station, which he said would take at least a fortnight to repair; and, while they were talking, a train was seen coming down the road, which had passed that very break and had reached me at Big Shanty as soon as the fleet horseman had reached General Johnston at Marietta!

In person I reached Allatoona on the 9th of October, still in doubt as to Hood's immediate intentions. Our cavalry could do little against his infantry in the rough and wooded country about Dallas, which masked the enemy's movements; but General Corse at Rome with Spencer's

First Alabama Cavlry and a mounted regiment of Illinois Infantry, could feel the country south of Rome about Cedartown and Villa Rica; and reported the enemy to be in force at both places. On the 9th I telegraphed to General Thomas at Nashville as follows:

> I came up here to relieve our road. The Twentieth Corps remains at Atlanta. Hood reached the road and broke it up between Big Shanty and Acworth. He attacked Allatoona, but was repulsed. We have plenty of bread and meat, but forage is scarce. I want to destroy all the road below Chattanooga, including Atlanta, and to make for the sea-coast. We cannot defend this long line of road.

And on the same day I telegraphed to General Grant, at City Point:

> It will be a physical impossibility to protect the roads, now that Hood, Forrest, Wheeler, and the whole batch of devils, are turned loose without home or habitation. I think Hood's movements indicate a diversion to the end of the Selma & Talladega road, at Blue Mountain, about sixty miles southwest of Rome, from which he will threaten Kingston, Bridgeport, and Decatur, Alabama. I propose that we break up the railroad from Chattanooga forward, and that we strike out with our wagons for Milledgeville, Millen, and Savannah. Until we can repopulate Georgia, it is useless for us to occupy it; but the utter destruction of its roads, houses, and people, will cripple their military resources. By attempting to hold the roads, we will lose a thousand men each month, and will gain no result. I can make this march, and make Georgia howl! We have on hand over eight thousand head of cattle and three million rations of bread, but no corn. We can find plenty of forage in the interior of the State.

Atlanta, Georgia
October 11th, 1864

Dearest Ellen,

We are all well. Forrest is threatening our road in Tennessee, but I think ample steps are in progress to meet and defeat him. Should he temporarily disturb our roads we are well prepared with accumulated supplies here, and our repair parties are so distributed that breaks can be speedily repaired. Should Hood's main army attempt our rear I think we can make him suffer. Georgia is now open to me, and steps are being perfected at other and distant points that will increase the value of my position here.

The telegraph brings me word that Grant is not idle about Richmond. I know his perseverance and have no apprehensions that in the end he will bring Lee out. Sheridan's success up the Valley of the Shenandoah will again threaten Lee's line of supply, which is by Gordonsville and Lynchburg. Also that same road is being attacked at a point further west from another quarter. I am in advance of all the other columns and therefore shall not be in a hurry, but if the enemy is restless I may go ahead. Our men are now well clad and fed, well rested and ready to go wherever I lead.

The people of the South have made a big howl at my moving the families of Atlanta, but I would have been a silly fool to take a town at such cost, and left it in the occupation of a helpless and hostile people. The War Department has simply been silent, has not committed itself one way or the other, so that the whole measure rests on me, but I am used to such things. Some of the correspondence between Hood and myself has been published, and the whole has been sent to Washington, where at some day it also will be published and I think General Hood will have no reason to glorify. I have letters of thanks from the Mayor of Atlanta and Colonel Clare who was the Confederate officer appointed to receive the families and transport them to the south. Instead of robbing them, not an article was taken away, not even their Negro servants who were willing to go along, and we even bought their provisions which I knew to have been Confederate stores distributed to the people at the last moment and were really our captured property.

Charley tells me he writes to you often, but I think he means to do so and wants you to take the will for the deed. I sent you a few days ago some photographs, one of which [unclear] was very fair. He stood like a gentleman for his portrait, and I like it better than any I ever had taken.

I have two large groups of all my staff, which I will send you if an opportunity offers. They are very fair. I have not heard from you for some time, but of course you have got [unclear] the bundle I sent by Colonel [Moore?]. They will prove interesting and will answer for reading a long time. I want to see the critiques of the English military press on my campaign. They seem to study the principles and really are the only persons that caught the true spirit of the Chattanooga and Knoxville campaigns. As to the Cincinnati papers and Catholic Telegraph I have the most profound contempt. Their praise or censure is alike puerile. If they would confine their observations to illicit nuisances and religious picnics they would better fill their offices. They have no more knowledge or appreciation of military men or measures than the children of a Sunday school. If you get a chance let Bishop Powell convey to his brother this my opinion. I hope Master Charley is again well, and that the rest of our flock are progressing well.

Yours ever,
W. T. Sherman

Dearest Ellen,

I owe you several letters but our mails have been so much interrupted that I would not write save in cypher, for a private letter of mine, written with however much caution, would contain much an enemy should not know. I have yours of the 11th. The monument should not be changed from the original design of the donors. You might order a hood or shelter of white pine of the design of the artist but if superadded of marble it would so change the original that the contributors would construe it into a reflection upon the design, in other words they would infer "theirs" imperfect to the extent of the additions. Hood is afraid to fight me on open ground and therefore he tries to break up the railroad which supplies my army. First, Forrest got across the Tennessee but never reached the Chattanooga road. Next, Hood with three corps, about 40,000 men, swung round by Dallas and broke the road at Big Shanty to Kennesaw. He stole a march on me of one day, and his men, disencumbered of baggage, move faster than we can. I have labored hard to cut down wagons, but [in] spite of all I can do, officers surround me. All the campaign I slept without a tent, and yet doctors and teamsters and clerks and staff officers on one pretext or another get tents and baggage, and now we can hardly move. I'll stop this or dispense with doctors, clerks and staff officers as "useless in war." Hood got up as far as the tunnel before I could head him off, but at Resaca I broke through the gap and he at once commenced to move south, and is now beyond my reach. He may now try to enter Tennessee by way of Decatur. I shall make proper dispositions and if seconded can keep him south, but I cannot get anybody to move as quick as they should, save some of my old favorites. Corse saved Allatoona by obeying promptly a message sent him by signals over the head of Hood's army. Mower is also coming to me and when I move south I shall have some smart columns. I am not going to stand on the defensive and you will soon hear of me on a bigger road than that to Meridian. Unless things take a turn not anticipated, you will have to get used to being without letters from me for some years, as it will be impossible to keep up mails much further. As to Charley being a Major General it is simple folly to think of it till he commands a regiment and a brigade in battle. I will give a recommendation to no one unless he has fulfilled the above conditions. You know that I did not want him to have a staff position but recommended he should seek the command of a regiment and work his way up. But he would come on my staff [in] spite of my advice and now I cannot, as a way out because he is my brother. You know that. There has been too much of this during the war, and the consequence is two-thirds of the brigadiers are best home. But he need not be uneasy. The war will last all his life, and he will have ample chances to become Lieutenant General if he has the industry. [letter unclear and breaks off]

On the 19th of October I telegraphed to General Halleck, at Washington:

> Hood has retreated rapidly by all the roads leading south. Our advance columns are now at Alpine and Melville Post-Office. I shall pursue him as far as Gaylesville. The enemy will not venture toward Tennessee except around by Decatur. I propose to send the Fourth Corps back to General Thomas, and leave him, with that corps, the garrisons, and new troops, to defend the line of the Tennessee River; and with the rest I will push into the heart of Georgia and come out at Savannah, destroying all the railroads of the State. The break in our railroad at Big Shanty is almost repaired, and that about Dalton should be done in ten days. We find abundance of forage in the country.

On the same day I telegraphed to General L. C. Easton, chief-quartermaster at Chattanooga:

> Go in person to superintend the repairs of the railroad, and make all orders in my name that will expedite its completion. I want it finished, to bring back from Atlanta to Chattanooga the sick and wounded men and surplus stores. On the 1st of November I want nothing in front of Chattanooga except what we can use as food and clothing and haul in our wagons. There is plenty of corn in the country, and we only want forage for the posts. I allow ten days for all this to be done, by which time I expect to be at or near Atlanta.

I telegraphed also to General Amos Beckwith, chief-commissary in Atlanta, who was acting as chief-quartermaster during the absence of General Easton:

> Hood will escape me. I want to prepare for my big raid. On the 1st of November I want nothing in Atlanta but what is necessary for war. Send all trash to the rear at once, and have on hand thirty days' food and but little forage. I propose to abandon Atlanta, and the railroad back to Chattanooga, to sally forth to ruin Georgia and bring up on the sea-shore. Make all dispositions accordingly. I will go down the Coosa until I am sure that Hood has gone to Blue Mountain.

On the 10th of October the enemy appeared south of the Etowah River at Rome, when I ordered all the armies to march to Kingston, rode myself to Cartersville with the Twenty-third Corps and telegraphed from there to General Grant at City Point:

Hood is now crossing the Coosa, twelve miles below Rome, bound west. If he passes over to the Mobile & Ohio Railroad, had I not better execute the plan of my letter sent you by Colonel Porter, and leave General Thomas, with the troops now in Tennessee, to defend the State? He will have an ample force when the reenforcements ordered reach Nashville.

From General Corse, at Rome, I learned that Hood's army had disappeared, but in what direction he was still in doubt; and I was so strongly convinced of the wisdom of my proposition to change the whole tactics of the campaign, to leave Hood to General Thomas and to march across Georgia for Savannah or Charleston, that I again telegraphed to General Grant:

We cannot now remain on the defensive. With twenty-five thousand infantry and the bold cavalry he has, Hood can constantly break my road. I would infinitely prefer to make a wreck of the road and of the country from Chattanooga to Atlanta, including the latter city; send back all my wounded and unserviceable men, and with my effective army move through Georgia, smashing things to the sea. Hood may turn into Tennessee and Kentucky, but I believe he will be forced to follow me. Instead of being on the defensive, I will be on the offensive. Instead of my guessing at what he means to do, he will have to guess at my plans. The difference in war would be fully twenty-five per cent. I can make Savannah, Charleston, or the mouth of the Chattahoochee (Appalachicola). Answer quick, as I know we will not have the telegraph long.

I received no answer to this at the time. Neither General Grant nor General Thomas heartily favored my proposed plan of campaign. On October 17th, I wrote to General Schofield at Chattanooga:

Hood is not at Dear Head Cove. We occupy Ship's Gap and Lafayette. Hood is moving south *via* Summerville, Alpine, and Gadsden. If he enters Tennessee, it will be to the west of Huntsville, but I think he has given up all such idea. I want the road repaired to Atlanta; the sick and wounded men sent north of the Tennessee; my army recomposed; and I will then make the interior of Georgia feel the weight of war. It is folly for us to be moving our armies on the reports of scouts and citizens. We must maintain the offensive. Your first move on Trenton and Valley Head was right—the move to defend Caperton's Ferry is wrong. Notify General Thomas of these my views. We must follow Hood till he is beyond the reach of mischief, and then resume the offensive.

133

On the 26th of October I learned that Hood's whole army had made its appearance about Decatur, Alabama, and at once caused a strong reconnoissance to be made down the Coosa to near Gadsden, which revealed the truth that the enemy was gone, except a small force of cavalry, commanded by General Wheeler, which had been left to watch us. I then finally resolved on my future course, which was to leave Hood to be encountered by General Thomas, while I should carry into full effect the long-contemplated project of marching for the sea-coast, and thence to operate toward Richmond.

Gaylesville, Alabama
October 21st, 1864

Dearest Ellen,

I enclose a bill of Brooks Brothers showing me in debt $12. This I honestly believe is the only debt I have in the world, so pay it off. I have some money in my pocket and have two months' pay nearly due, so I can promise you $1000 before I take my final departure for the pine woods. Since I have become famous for taking Atlanta and writing impudent letters I get the most wonderful medley that you can conceive of from all parts of the world. Some are amusing but all breathe the utmost respect and cannot be disregarded. Some I toss in the camp fire and some I answer, but usually in a very hasty, imperfect manner; but it seems that my letters now even are sought after like hot cakes. As long as I am not a candidate I hope more will be published as samples of literary composition. You can read my letters and guess at the meaning, but judging from my copy clerks, some readers would make an awful jumble of my letters, written usually in the small hours of the night by a single candle on a box. Actually, one man wrote that it was seriously contemplated even to put me up for President! That was cruel and unkind. You remember when the solemn committee waited on me at San Francisco to tender the Regular Democratic nomination for Treasurer my answer was that I was ineligible because I had not graduated at the "Penitentiary." If a similar committee should be rash enough to venture the other nomination I fear I should proceed to personal violence, for I would receive a sentence to be hung and damned with infinitely more composure than to be the Executive of this nation. I send you a few letters that may interest you as samples.

Hood escaped south down the valley of the Chattooga to Gadsden and is en route for Blue Mountain, ten miles south of Jacksonville, the end of the Selma road, where he hopes to threaten my road and Tennessee to keep me out of Georgia. Maybe he will and maybe he won't. If a reasonable number of the drafted men reached me, I think he won't.

This army is now ready to march to Mobile, Savannah or Charleston, and I am practising them in the art of foraging and they take to it like ducks to water. They like pigs, sheep, chicken, calves and sweet potatoes better than rations. We won't starve in Georgia. Our mules are doing better in the corn fields than on the bagged corn brought by the railroads.

Love to all, in haste as usual. Charley reiterates he writes all the time.

Yours ever,
W. T. Sherman

Gaylesville, Alabama
October 27th, 1864

Dearest Ellen,

I have just received your letter of the 16th and as I have more leisure at this moment than I will likely again for a long time I will write at length. I have written not often but certainly as often as possible, consistent with my manifold duties and the fear of my letters, unless in cypher, falling into wrong hands. Hood has swung over towards [unclear] and may and probably will attempt to enter Tennessee about Huntsville, but I think there are troops enough in Tennessee, but we are expected to defend so many points that our difficulties grow exactly in proportion to our advances and the Rebels gain proportionately. I expect very soon now to attempt another feat in which I think I shall succeed, but it is hazardous and you will not hear from me for months. The War Department will know my whereabouts, and the Rebels and you will be able to guess. Charley went to Nashville to have his teeth fixed. I told him he would be left behind, but he knew he would get back in time. I think not and suppose I understand the chances better. He is always provoked when I, after each letter, tell him you say he does not write to you. He uses even strong language and seems offended. One thing is certain: he says he writes very often. I know he gets all your letters, for I hand them to him. As to his being Brigadier General he must first be colonel of a regiment and then must command it in battle. This will take time and all chance of promotion was and is cut off by his accepting a staff place. I told him so at the time and a hundred times since, and I am not going to commit the folly of recommending for a general one who has not demonstrated his fitness. Mr. Lincoln says he used to be very careless about such appointments, but now it is very difficult. There are many colonels who have commanded brigades for three years, and done it well who are not promoted. What would they say of me who would recommend a brother-in-law that had not even had a regiment. As to Dayton he has not resigned. I have no vacancies on my staff and, had I, would be disposed to leave them, for every staff officer must have a wagon and tent. I can get along with a fly [tent] and blanket, but there is a staff [in] spite of all I can do. Tents and wagons multiply. I am about to order the abolishment of all headquarters except that of the doctors and team-

sters. *Hood can march all round me and laugh, whilst I drag along with a wagon train. This wagon train in the end will defeat me. Soldiers get along well enough, but we are borne down with generals, headquarters and staff. I have been making some sweeping reforms but yet there is wide room for improvement. I might be a hundred miles further in my journey were it not for the excess of wagons and artillery, but I am sending it back. The break in our railroad will be done tonight and if the Rebels let it alone for a few days, I will get back the worthless and sick and baggage and then cut loose. However, I expect next to hear of Hood between here and Nashville. You ask my opinion of McClellan. I have been much amused at similar inquiries of John and others in answer to a news paragraph that I pledged ninety-nine votes of the hundred to Mc-Clellan. Of course this is the invention of some knave. I never said such thing. I will vote for nobody, because I am not entitled to vote. Of the two, with the inferences to be drawn at home and abroad, I would prefer Lincoln, though I know that McClellan, Vallandingham or even Jeff Davis if President of the United States would prosecute the war, and no one with more vigor than the latter. But at the time the howl was raised against McClellan I knew it was in a measure unjust, for he was charged with delinquencies that the American people are chargeable for. Thus, how unjust to blame me for any misfortune now when all the authorities and people are conspiring to heat up the army till the election is over. Our armies vanish before our eyes and it is useless to complain because the election is more important than the war. Our armies are merely paper armies. I have 40,000 cavalry on paper but less than 5000 in fact. A like measure runs through the whole, and so it was with McClellan. He had to fight partly with figures. Still I admit he never manifested the simple courage and manliness of Grant, and he had too much staff, too many toadies and looked too much to no one. When I was in Kentucky he would not heed my counsels and never wrote me once, but since I have gained some notoriety at Atlanta and the papers announced, as usual falsely, that I was for him, he has written me twice and that has depreciated him more in my estimation than all else. He cannot be elected. Mr. Lincoln will be, but I hope it will be done quick, that voters may come to their regiments and not give the Rebs the advantage they know so well to take. I believe McClellan to be an honest man as to money, of good habits, descent and of far more than average intelligence and therefore I never have joined in the hue and cry against him. In revolutions men fall and rise. Long before this war is over, much as you hear me praised now, you may hear me cursed and insulted. Read history. Read* Coriolanus *and you will see the true measure of popular applause. Grant, Sheridan and I are now the popular favorites, but neither of us will survive this war. Some other must rise greater than either of us, and he has not yet manifested himself.*

Some of my best officers are those whom I favored at Big [Shanty?]. Corse, Mower, [unclear], Wood, Warren, etc. Corse saved us Allatoona and Mower saved Bank's command up Red River. Still, they are not great leaders but rather soldiers in training. I hardly look for any real developments of military talents on our side for two years yet. Congress, instead of providing an army, has legislated it out of existence. In twelve months we will have no army and Jeff will walk on the track without an opponent, unless some one rises this winter. The old men have gone out, and the officers, disgusted at new ones coming over their heads, have retired. We are now getting one-year men who will be discharged before they know how to post a guard, so that I see more trouble ahead than ever. I am satisfied the people of the United States will rise to the occasion if they are only told the truth, but everybody tells them the Rebels are played out, starved out, tired of the war, etc., when if they were just to think they would see guerillas in sight of Washington, Louisville and St. Louis today. When we concentrate our energies to any one point as Vicksburg, Mobile or Atlanta we can take it, but the trouble is the country at large. We should as a people declare that we would have peace and submission to authority [even] if we had to devastate every acre and should proceed to do it. A merciless conscription should fill our ranks, and we should mark out our lines and go ahead leaving nothing behind, not one column but six, eight or ten. We can now live on the corn of the South, some salt and beef on the hoof, but it discourages our men to be compelled to turn back to attend to what others in our rear should. I would make every man North a soldier till the war is over, and then he might go home and not before. I think at the rate we are now going it will take more than my thirty years, so you can begin to school even the young Charley.

I am glad to hear such good accounts of the children. I have not heard from Minnie or Lizzie for some time, but have no doubt they are progressing well. As to Tom, he will need much of your attention for he is solitary and will need boys' company. As to Elly and Rachel the [unclear], they will gather shells and flowers for many years yet and still be children. Master Charley must now begin to assume the human form and to manifest some of his future self. I would like to see him as a curiosity but have not the remotest chance this year.

I cannot tell much of things hereabout. Hill is not with me, but his successor and a couple of black boys fill my household as well as I expect. My horses are all well groomed and come at my bidding. We have about the same old mess out of doors, and I sleep on the ground with a comforter, pillows, pair of blankets and spread. It has been cold, and I have no winter socks or flannels. Those you sent from Cincinnati have not come, I have telegraphed for some out of my trunk at Nashville, but have pretty much made up my mind to get away with what I have. Our railroad is broken so often and the difficulties of the trip so great that I think somebody else gets my consignments. I suppose I will have to appeal to the Sanitary or Christian Commission. Paymasters are afraid to come down, and the army has not been paid for ten months. This is a long letter and not *much in it, but there is not much here that can interest you. The town of Gaylesville that was is now among the rest, and is converted into soldiers' huts soon to be abandoned. We have foraged close, and guerillas and armies won't follow this road. That was one object of my coming.*

Yours ever,
W. T. Sherman

Rome, Georgia
October 29th, 1864

Dearest Ellen,

I wrote you a very long letter two days ago at my camp at Gaylesville, but since then I have two more from you. I again think Willy's monument should be an [unclear], just as the donors present it. The inscription on the vacant tablets proposed are very good. All words seem so inadequate to my sense of the loss that I could offer none. Today his image in my mind is as ever, and I can think of him now as during my long absences when memory alone told me of my family. But when I think of myself do I most grieve, for he seemed so wrapt up in me. So selfish was I in my power and station, yet I miss in him [now] the only pride I could have in fame or success. Now I have no such incentive. To see his full eye dilate and brighten when he heard that his Papa was a great general would be to me now more grateful than the clamor of the millions. Why I cannot tell I do not think that Tommy or anyone else would feel in me one bit of the pride that Willy did. He seemed to know me better than anybody else, and realized the truth that if I labored it was for him. He knew or seemed to know that all I have was his, whether of money or property or fame. I may be in error, but with him died in me all real ambition and what has come to me since is unsought, unsolicited. But as to the monument, the canopy you describe and of which I have a drawing is very fine and might be made separate of wood, and large enough to protect the marble. Even large enough to sit beneath. Yesterday I had Willy's death brought before me in painful reality. General Ransom, one of our youngest and best generals, McPherson's favorite, and who shared with us all the Mississippi campaigns, took sick on this march and neglected himself till too late. He gave up and yesterday I saw him on the road, borne on a litter on the shoulders of [his] men, alive, but with that look I can never forget—the same that Willy had for two days before he died. Ransom was still alive and his doctors said he might still recover, but I say soon he will die and may now be dead. He was twenty miles from here and may arrive tomorrow, but if alive I will be surprised. I cannot tell you much of the present in the future, as the guerillas so infest our roads that they might capture one of my [hiatus] military men can easily interpret a paragraph, but events will develop fast enough. Hood appears to be in a hurry and so will I be when all is ready. The enemy has shifted over to Decatur, Alabama, and contemplates the invasion of Tennessee from that quarter. Charley has gone to Nashville to have his teeth fixed. Dayton has not resigned and I don't think he will. I have never heard from [unclear] about Captain [unclear]. I have never seen him. He is a captain and cannot be detailed as [unclear] without a vacancy and appointment by the President. I endorse you a slip of paper which, if sent back with his own letter to him and presented at Leavenworth, would I think secure him employment, though I have no right to command it. Down here he would not like to come, as our whereabouts is too uncertain. Hill got back last night and brought me some flannels. I needed them and have now a pair on my shoulder for the cold on the ground.

Yours ever,
[W. T. Sherman]

On the 1st of November I telegraphed very fully to General Grant, at City Point, who must have been disturbed by the wild rumors that filled the country, and on the 2d of November received at Rome this dispatch:

CITY POINT, *November* 1, 1864—6 p.m.

Major-General SHERMAN:

Do you not think it advisable, now that Hood has gone so far north, to entirely ruin him before starting on your proposed campaign? With Hood's army destroyed, you can go where you please with impunity. I believed and still believe, if you had started south while Hood was in the neighborhood of you, he would have been forced to go after you. Now that he is far away he might look upon the chase as useless, and he will go in one direction while you are pushing in the other. If you can see a chance of destroying Hood's army, attend to that first, and make your other move secondary.

U. S. GRANT, *Lieutenant-General.*

My answer is dated—

ROME GEORGIA, *November* 2, 1864.

Lieutenant-General U. S. GRANT, *City Point, Virginia:*

Your dispatch is received. If I could hope to overhaul Hood, I would turn against him with my whole force; then he would retreat to the southwest, drawing me as a decoy away from Georgia, which is his chief object. If he ventures north of the Tennessee River, I may turn in that direction, and endeavor to get below him on his line of retreat; but thus far he has not gone above the Tennessee River. Gen-

139

eral Thomas will have a force strong enough to prevent his reaching any country in which we have an interest; and he has orders, if Hood turns to follow me, to push for Selma, Alabama. No single army can catch Hood, and I am convinced the best results will follow from our defeating Jeff. Davis's cherished plan of making me leave Georgia by manœuvring. Thus far I have confined my efforts to thwart this plan, and have reduced baggage so that I can pick up and start in any direction; but I regard the pursuit of Hood as useless. Still, if he attempts to invade Middle Tennessee, I will hold Decatur, and be prepared to move in that direction; but, unless I let go of Atlanta, my force will not be equal to his.

W. T. SHERMAN, Major-General.

By this date, under the intelligent and energetic action of Colonel W. W. Wright, and with the labor of fifteen hundred men, the railroad break of fifteen miles about Dalton was repaired so far as to admit of the passage of cars, and I transferred my headquarters to Kingston as more central; and from that place, on the same day again telegraphed to General Grant.

KINGSTON, GEORGIA, November 2, 1864.

Lieutenant-General U. S. GRANT, *City Point, Virginia:*

If I turn back, the whole effect of my campaign will be lost. By my movements I have thrown Beauregard (Hood) well to the west, and Thomas will have ample time and sufficient troops to hold him until the reenforcements from Missouri reach him. We have now ample supplies at Chattanooga and Atlanta, and can stand a month's interruption to our communications. I do not believe the Confederate army can reach our railroad-lines except by cavalry-raids, and Wilson will have cavalry enough to checkmate them. I am clearly of opinion that the best results will follow my contemplated movements through Georgia.

W. T. SHERMAN, Major-General.

That same day I received, in answer to the Rome dispatch, the following:

CITY POINT, VIRGINIA, November 2, 1864—11:30 a.m.

Major-General SHERMAN:

Your dispatch of 9 a.m. yesterday is just received. I dispatched you the same date, advising that Hood's army, now that it had worked so far north, ought to be looked upon now as the "object." With the force, however, that you have left with General Thomas, he must be able to take care of Hood and destroy him.

I do not see that you can withdraw from where you are to follow Hood, without giving up all we have gained in territory. I say, then, go on as you propose.

U. S. GRANT, *Lieutenant-General.*

I have often been asked, by well-meaning friends, when the thought of that march first entered my mind. I knew that an army which had penetrated Georgia as far as Atlanta could not turn back. It must go ahead, but when, how, and where, depended on many considerations. As soon as Hood had shifted across from Lovejoy's to Palmetto, I saw the move in my "mind's eye;" and, after Jeff Davis's speech at Palmetto, of September 26th, I was more positive in my conviction, but was in doubt as to the time and manner. When General Hood first struck our railroad above Marietta, we were not ready, and I was forced to watch his movements further, till he had "caromed" off to the west of Decatur. Then I was perfectly convinced, and had no longer a shadow of doubt. The only possible question was as to Thomas's strength and ability to meet Hood in the open field. I did not suppose that General Hood, though rash, would venture to attack fortified places like Allatoona, Resaca, Decatur, and Nashville; but he did so, and in so doing he played into our hands perfectly.

On the 2d of November I was at Kingston, Georgia, and my four corps, with one division of cavalry, were strung from Rome to Atlanta. Our railroads and telegraph had been repaired, and I deliberately prepared for the march to Savannah, distant three hundred miles from Atlanta. All the sick and wounded men had been sent back by rail to Chattanooga; all our wagon-trains had been carefully overhauled and loaded, so as to be ready to start on an hour's notice, and there was no serious enemy in our front.

General Hood remained still at Florence, Alabama, occupying both banks of the Tennessee River, busy in collecting shoes and clothing for his men and the necessary ammunition and stores with which to invade Tennessee, most of which had to come from Mobile, Selma, and Montgomery, Alabama, over railroads that were still broken. Beauregard was at Corinth, hastening forward these necessary preparations.

On the 6th of November, at Kingston, I wrote and telegraphed to General Grant, reviewing the whole situation, gave him my full plan of action, stated that I was ready to march as soon as the election was over, and appointed November 10th as the day for starting. On the 8th I received this dispatch:

141

Major-General SHERMAN:

Your dispatch of this evening received. I see no present reason for changing your plan. Should any arise, you will see it, or if I do I will inform you. I think every thing here is favorable now. Great good fortune attend you! I believe you will be eminently successful, and, at worst, can only make a march less fruitful of results than hoped for.

U. S. GRANT, *Lieutenant-General.*

Meantime trains of cars were whirling by, carrying to the rear an immense amount of stores which had accumulated at Atlanta and at the other stations along the railroad; and General Steedman had come down to Kingston, to take charge of the final evacuation and withdrawal of the several garrisons below Chattanooga.

On the 10th of November the movement may be said to have fairly begun. All the troops designed for the campaign were ordered to march for Atlanta, and General Corse, before evacuating his post at Rome, was ordered to burn all the mills, factories, etc., etc., that could be useful to the enemy, should he undertake to pursue us, or resume military possession of the country. On the 12th, with a full staff, I started from Kingston for Atlanta; and about noon of that day we reached Cartersville, and sat on the edge of a porch to rest, when the telegraph operator, Mr. Van Valkenburg, or Eddy, got the wire down from the poles to his lap, in which he held a small pocket instrument. About that instant of time, some of our men burnt a bridge, which severed the telegraph-wire, and all communication with the rear ceased thenceforth.

As we rode on toward Atlanta that night, I remember the railroad-trains going to the rear with a furious speed; the engineers and the few men about the trains waving us an affectionate adieu. It surely was a strange event—two hostile armies marching in opposite directions, each in the full belief that it was achieving a final and conclusive result in a great war; and I was strongly inspired with the feeling that the movement on our part was a direct attack upon the rebel army and the rebel capital at Richmond, though a full thousand miles of hostile country intervened, and that, for better or worse, it would end the war.

FROM ATLANTA TO SAVANNAH

On the 12th of November the railroad and telegraph communications with the rear were broken, and the army stood detached from all friends, dependent on its own resources and supplies. No time was to be lost; all the detachments were ordered to march rapidly for Atlanta, breaking up the railroad *en route*, and generally to so damage the country as to make it untenable to the enemy. By the 14th all the troops had arrived at or near Atlanta, and were, according to orders, grouped into two wings, the right and left, commanded respectively by Major-Generals O. O. Howard and H. W. Slocum, both comparatively young men, but educated and experienced officers, fully competent to their command.

The strength of the army was an aggregate of fifty-five thousand three hundred and twenty-nine infantry, five thousand and sixty-three cavalry, and eighteen hundred and twelve artillery—in all, sixty-two thousand two hundred and four officers and men. The most extraordinary efforts had been made to purge this army of non-combatants and of sick men, for we knew well that there was to be no place of safety save with the army itself; our wagons were loaded with ammunition, provisions, and forage, and we could ill afford to haul even sick men in the ambulances, so that all on this exhibit may be assumed to have been able-bodied, experienced soldiers, well armed, well equipped and provided, as far as human foresight could, with all the essentials of life, strength, and vigorous action.

The two general orders made for this march appear to me, even at this late day, so clear, emphatic, and well-digested, that no account of that historic event is perfect without them, and I give them entire, even at the seeming appearance of repetition; and, though they called for great sacrifice and labor on the part of the officers and men, I insist that these orders were obeyed as well as any similar orders ever were, by an army operating wholly in an enemy's country, and dispersed, as we necessarily were, during the subsequent period of nearly six months.

HEADQUARTERS MILITARY DIVISION OF THE MISSISSIPPI, }
IN THE FIELD, KINGSTON, GEORGIA, *November* 8, 1864. }

The general commanding deems it proper at this time to inform the officers and men of the Fourteenth, Fifteenth, Seventeenth, and Twentieth Corps, that he has organized them into an army for a special purpose, well known to the War Department and to General Grant. It is sufficient for you to know that it involves a departure from our present base, and a long and difficult march to a new one. All the chances of war have been considered and provided for, as far as human sagacity can. All he asks of you is to maintain that discipline, patience, and courage, which have characterized you in the past; and he hopes, through you, to strike a blow at our enemy that will have a material effect in producing what we all so much desire, his complete overthrow. Of all things, the most important is, that the men, during marches and in camp, keep their places and do not scatter about as stragglers or foragers, to be picked up by a hostile people in detail. It is also of the utmost importance that our wagons should not be loaded with any thing but provisions and ammunition. All surplus servants, non-combatants, and refugees, should now go to the rear, and none should be encouraged to encumber us on the march. At some future time we will be able to provide for the poor whites and blacks who seek to escape the bondage under which they are now suffering. With these few simple cautions, he hopes to lead you to achievements equal in importance to those of the past.

By order of Major-General W. T. Sherman,

L. M. DAYTON, *Aide-de-Camp*.

HEADQUARTERS MILITARY DIVISION OF THE MISSISSIPPI, }
IN THE FIELD, KINGSTON, GEORGIA, *November* 9, 1864. }

1. For the purpose of military operations, this army is divided into two wings, viz.:

The right wing, Major-General O. O. Howard commanding, composed of the Fifteenth and Seventeenth Corps; the left wing, Major-General H. W. Slocum commanding, composed of the Fourteenth and Twentieth Corps.

2. The habitual order of march will be, wherever practicable, by four roads,

as nearly parallel as possible, and converging at points hereafter to be indicated in orders. The cavalry, Brigadier-General Kilpatrick commanding, will receive special orders from the commander-in-chief.

3. There will be no general train of supplies, but each corps will have its ammunition-train and provision-train, distributed habitually as follows: Behind each regiment should follow one wagon and one ambulance; behind each brigade should follow a due proportion of ammunition-wagons, provision-wagons, and ambulances. In case of danger, each corps commander should change this order of march, by having his advance and rear brigades unencumbered by wheels. The separate columns will start habitually at 7 a.m., and make about fifteen miles per day, unless otherwise fixed in orders.

4. The army will forage liberally on the country during the march. To this end, each brigade commander will organize a good and sufficient foraging party, under the command of one or more discreet officers, who will gather, near the route traveled, corn or forage of any kind, meat of any kind, vegetables, corn-meal, or whatever is needed by the command, aiming at all times to keep in the wagons at least ten days' provisions for his command, and three days' forage. Soldiers must not enter the dwellings of the inhabitants, or commit any trespass; but, during a halt or camp, they may be permitted to gather turnips, potatoes, and other vegetables, and to drive in stock in sight of their camp. To regular foraging-parties must be intrusted the gathering of provisions and forage, at any distance from the road traveled.

5. To corps commanders alone is intrusted the power to destroy mills, houses, cotton-gins, etc.; and for them this general principle is laid down: In districts and neighborhoods where the army is unmolested, no destruction of such property should be permitted; but should guerrillas or bushwhackers molest our march, or should the inhabitants burn bridges, obstruct roads, or otherwise manifest local hostility, then army commanders should order and enforce a devastation more or less relentless, according to the measure of such hostility.

6. As for horses, mules, wagons, etc., belonging to the inhabitants, the cavalry and artillery may appropriate freely and without limit; discriminating, however, between the rich, who are usually hostile, and the poor and industrious, usually neutral or friendly. Foraging-parties may also take mules or horses, to replace the jaded animals of their trains, or to serve as pack-mules for the regiments of brigades. In all foraging, of whatever kind, the parties engaged will refrain from abusive or threatening language, and may, where the officer in command thinks proper, give written certificates of the facts, but no receipts; and they will endeavor to leave with each family a reasonable portion for their maintenance.

7. Negroes who are able-bodied and can be of service to the several columns may be taken along; but each army commander will bear in mind that the question of supplies is a very important one, and that his first duty is to see to those who bear arms.

8. The organization, at once, of a good pioneer battalion for each army corps, composed if possible of Negroes, should be attended to. This battalion should follow the advance-guard, repair roads and double them if possible, so that the columns will not be delayed after reaching bad places. Also, army commanders should practise the habit of giving the artillery and wagons the road, marching their troops on one side, and instruct their troops to assist wagons at steep hills or bad crossings of streams.

9. Captain O. M. Poe, chief-engineer, will assign to each wing of the army a pontoon-train, fully equipped and organized; and the commanders thereof will see to their being properly protected at all times.

By order of Major-General W. T. Sherman,

L. M. DAYTON, *Aide-de-Camp.*

The greatest possible attention had been given to the artillery and wagon trains. The number of guns had been reduced to sixty-five, or about one gun to each thousand men, and these were generally in batteries of four guns each.

Each gun, caisson, and forge was drawn by four teams of horses. We had in all about twenty-five hundred wagons, with teams of six mules to each, and six hundred ambulances, with two horses to each. The loads were made comparatively light, about twenty-five hundred pounds net; each wagon carrying in addition the forage needed by its own team. Each soldier carried on his person forty rounds of ammunition, and in the wagons were enough cartridges to make up about two hundred rounds per man, and in like manner two hundred rounds of assorted ammunition were carried for each gun.

The wagon-trains were divided equally between the four corps, so that each had about eight hundred wagons, and these usually on the march occupied five miles or more of road. Each corps commander managed his own train; and habitually the artillery and wagons had the road, while the men, with the exception of the advance and rear guards, pursued paths improvised by the side of the wagons, unless they were forced to use a bridge or causeway in common.

I reached Atlanta during the afternoon of the 14th, and found that all preparations had been

146

made—Colonel Beckwith, chief commissary, reporting one million two hundred thousand rations in possession of the troops, which was about twenty days' supply, and he had on hand a good supply of beef cattle to be driven along on the hoof. Of forage, the supply was limited, being of oats and corn enough for five days, but I knew that within that time we would reach a country well stocked with corn, which had been gathered and stored in cribs, seemingly for our use, by Governor Brown's militia.

Colonel Poe, United States Engineers, of my staff, had been busy in his special task of destruction. He had a large force at work, had leveled the great depot, round-house, and the machine-shops of the Georgia Railroad, and had applied fire to the wreck. One of these machine-shops had been used by the rebels as an arsenal, and in it were stored piles of shot and shell, some of which proved to be loaded, and that night was made hideous by the bursting of shells, whose fragments came uncomfortably near Judge Lyon's house, in which I was quartered. The fire also reached the block of stores near the depot, and the heart of the city was in flames all night, but the fire did not reach the parts of Atlanta where the court-house was or the great mass of dwelling-houses.

The march from Atlanta began on the morning of November 15th, the right wing and cavalry following the railroad southeast toward Jonesboro and General Slocum with the Twentieth Corps leading off to the east by Decatur and Stone Mountain, toward Madison. These were divergent lines, designed to threaten both Macon and Augusta at the same time, so as to prevent a concentration at our intended destination, Milledgeville, the capital of Georgia, distant southeast about one hundred miles. The time allowed each column for reaching Milledgeville was seven days. I remained in Atlanta during the 15th with the Fourteenth Corps, and the rear-guard of the right wing, to complete the loading of the trains and the destruction of the buildings of Atlanta which could be converted to hostile uses, and on the morning of the 16th started with my personal staff, a company of Alabama cavalry, commanded by Lieutenant Snelling, and an infantry company, commanded by Lieutenant McCrory, which guarded our small train of wagons.

My staff was then composed of Major L. M. Dayton, aide-de-camp and acting adjutant-general, Major J. C. McCoy, and Major J. C. Audenried, aides. Major Ward Nichols had joined some weeks before at Gaylesville, Alabama, and was attached as an acting aide-de-camp. Also Major Henry Hitchcock had joined at the same time as judge-advocate. Colonel Charles Ewing was inspector-general and Surgeon John Moore medical director. These constituted our mess. We had no tents, only the flies, with which we nightly made bivouacs with the assistance of the abundant pine-boughs, which made excellent shelter, as well as beds.

About 7 a.m. of November 16th we rode out of Atlanta by the Decatur road, filled by the marching troops and wagons of the Fourteenth Corps; and reaching the hill, just outside of the old rebel works, we naturally paused to look back upon the scenes of our past battles. We stood upon the very ground whereon was fought the bloody battle of July 22d and could see the copse of wood where McPherson fell. Behind us lay Atlanta, smouldering and in ruins, the black smoke rising high in air and hanging like a pall over the ruined city. Away off in the distance, on the McDonough road, was the rear of Howard's column, the gun-barrels glistening in the sun, the white-topped wagons stretching away to the south; and right before us the Fourteenth Corps, marching steadily and rapidly, with a cheery look and swinging pace, that made light of the thousand miles that lay between us and Richmond. Some band, by accident, struck up the anthem of "John Brown's soul goes marching on;" the men caught up the strain, and never before or since have I heard the chorus of "Glory, glory, hallelujah!" done with more spirit, or in better harmony of time and place.

Then we turned our horses' heads to the east; Atlanta was soon lost behind the screen of trees, and became a thing of the past. Around it clings many a thought of desperate battle, of hope and fear, that now seem like the memory of a dream. The day was extremely beautiful, clear sunlight, with bracing air, and an unusual feeling of exhilaration seemed to pervade all minds—a feeling of something to come, vague and undefined, still full of venture and intense interest. Even the common soldiers caught the inspiration, and many a group called out to me as I worked my way past them, "Uncle Billy, I guess Grant is waiting for us at Richmond!" Indeed, the general sentiment was that we were marching for Richmond, and that there we should end the war, but how and when they seemed to care not; nor did they measure the distance or count the cost in life or bother their brains about the great rivers to be crossed and the food required for man and beast that had to be gathered by the way. There was a "devil-may-care" feeling pervading officers and men that made me feel the full load of responsibility, for success would be accepted as a matter of course, whereas, should we fail, this "march" would be adjudged the wild adventure of a crazy fool. I had no purpose to march direct for Richmond by way of Augusta and Charlotte,

148

but always designed to reach the sea-coast first at Savannah or Port Royal, South Carolina, and even kept in mind the alternative of Pensacola.

The first night out we camped by the road-side near Lithonia. Stone Mountain, a mass of granite, was in plain view, cut out in clear outline against the blue sky; the whole horizon was lurid with the bonfires of rail-ties, and groups of men all night were carrying the heated rails to the nearest trees and bending them around the trunks. Colonel Poe had provided tools for ripping up the rails and twisting them when hot; but the best and easiest way is the one I have described, of heating the middle of the iron-rails on bonfires made of the cross-ties and then winding them around a telegraph-pole or the trunk of some convenient sapling. I attached much importance to this destruction of the railroad, gave it my own personal attention, and made reiterated orders to others on the subject.

The next day we passed through the handsome town of Covington, the soldiers closing up their ranks, the color-bearers unfurling their flags, and the bands striking up patriotic airs. The white people came out of their houses to behold the sight, in spite of their deep hatred of the invaders, and the Negroes were simply frantic with joy. Whenever they heard my name, they clustered about my horse, shouted and prayed in their peculiar style, which had a natural eloquence that would have moved a stone. I have witnessed hundreds, if not thousands, of such scenes; and can now see a poor girl, in the very ecstasy of the Methodist "shout," hugging the banner of one of the regiments, and jumping up to the "feet of Jesus."

I remember, when riding around by a by-street in Covington, to avoid the crowd that followed the marching column, that some one brought me an invitation to dine with a sister of Samuel Anderson, who was a cadet at West Point with me; but the messenger reached me after we had passed the main part of the town. I asked to be excused and rode on to a place designated for camp at the crossing of the Ulcofauhachee River about four miles to the east of the town. Here we made our bivouac, and I walked up to a plantation-house close by, where were assembled many Negroes, among them an old, gray-haired man, of as fine a head as I ever saw. I asked him if he understood about the war and its progress. He said he did; that he had been looking for the "angel of the Lord" ever since he was knee-high, and, though we professed to be fighting for the Union, he supposed that slavery was the cause and that our success was to be his freedom. I asked him if all the Negro slaves comprehended this fact, and he said they surely did. I then explained

149

to him that we wanted the slaves to remain where they were and not to load us down with useless mouths, which would eat up the food needed for our fighting-men; that our success was their assured freedom; that we could receive a few of their young, hearty men as pioneers; but that, if they followed us in swarms of old and young, feeble and helpless, it would simply load us down and cripple us in our great task. It was at this very plantation that a soldier passed me with a ham on his musket, a jug of sorghum-molasses under his arm, and a big piece of honey in his hand, from which he was eating, and, catching my eye, he remarked *sotto voce* and carelessly to a comrade, "Forage liberally on the country," quoting from my general orders. On this occasion, as on many others that fell under my personal observation, I reproved the man, explained that foraging must be limited to the regular parties properly detailed and that all provisions thus obtained must be delivered to the regular commissaries, to be fairly distributed to the men who kept their ranks.

From Covington the Fourteenth Corps, with which I was traveling, turned to the right for Milledgeville, *via* Shady Dale. General Slocum was ahead at Madison, with the Twentieth Corps, having torn up the railroad as far as that place, and thence had sent Geary's division on to the Oconee, to burn the bridges across that stream, when this corps turned south by Eatonton, for Milledgeville, the common objective for the first stage of the march. We found abundance of corn, molasses, meal, bacon, and sweet-potatoes. We also took a good many cows and oxen and a large number of mules. In all these the country was quite rich, never before having been visited by a hostile army; the recent crop had been excellent, had been just gathered and laid by for the winter. As a rule, we destroyed none, but kept our wagons full, and fed our teams bountifully.

The skill and success of the men in collecting forage was one of the features of this march. Each brigade commander had authority to detail a company of foragers, usually about fifty men, with one or two commissioned officers selected for their boldness and enterprise. This party would be dispatched before daylight with a knowledge of the intended day's march and camp; would proceed on foot five or six miles from the route traveled by their brigade and then visit every plantation and farm within range. They would usually procure a wagon or family carriage, load it with bacon, corn-meal, turkeys, chickens, ducks, and every thing that could be used as food or forage and would then regain the main road, usually in advance of their train. When this came up, they would deliver to the brigade commissary the supplies thus gathered by the way. Often would I pass these foraging-parties at the road-side, waiting for their wagons to come up,

150

and was amused at their strange collections—mules, horses, even cattle, packed with old saddles and loaded with hams, bacon, bags of corn-meal, and poultry of every character and description. Although this foraging was attended with great danger and hard work, there seemed to be a charm about it that attracted the soldiers, and it was a privilege to be detailed on such a party. Daily they returned mounted on all sorts of beasts, which were at once taken from them and appropriated to the general use; but the next day they would start out again on foot, only to repeat the experience of the day before. No doubt, many acts of pillage, robbery, and violence, were committed by these parties of foragers, usually called "bummers;" for I have since heard of jewelry taken from women and the plunder of articles that never reached the commissary. But I never heard of any cases of murder or rape; and no army could have carried along sufficient food and forage for a march of three hundred miles; so that foraging in some shape was necessary. The country was sparsely settled, with no magistrates or civil authorities who could respond to requisitions, as is done in all the wars of Europe; so that this system of foraging was simply indispensable to our success. By it our men were well supplied with all the essentials of life and health, while the wagons retained enough in case of unexpected delay and our animals were well fed. Indeed, when we reached Savannah, the trains were pronounced by experts to be the finest in flesh and appearance ever seen with any army.

Habitually each corps followed some main road, and the foragers, being kept out on the exposed flank, served all the military uses of flankers. The main columns gathered, by the roads traveled, much forage and food, chiefly meat, corn, and sweet-potatoes, and it was the duty of each division and brigade quartermaster to fill his wagons as fast as the contents were issued to the troops. The wagon-trains had the right to the road *always*, but each wagon was required to keep closed up, so as to leave no gaps in the column. If for any purpose any wagon or group of wagons dropped out of place, they had to wait for the rear. And this was always dreaded, for each brigade commander wanted his train up at camp as soon after reaching it with his men as possible.

I have seen much skill and industry displayed by these quartermasters on the march, in trying to load their wagons with corn and fodder by the way without losing their place in column. They would, while marching, shift the loads of wagons, so as to have six or ten of them empty. Then, riding well ahead, they would secure possession of certain stacks of fodder near the road, or cribs of corn, leave some men in charge, then open fences and a road back for a couple of miles, return to their trains, divert the empty wagons out of column, and conduct them rapidly to their forage, load up and regain their place in column without losing distance. On one occasion I remember to have seen ten or a dozen wagons thus loaded with corn from two or three full cribs, almost without halting. These cribs were built of logs and roofed. The train-guard, by a lever, had raised the whole side of the crib a foot or two; the wagons drove close alongside, and the men in the cribs, lying on their backs, kicked out a wagon-load of corn in the time I have taken to describe it.

In a well-ordered and well-disciplined army, these things might be deemed irregular, but I am convinced that the ingenuity of these younger officers accomplished many things far better than I could have ordered, and the marches were thus made, and the distances were accomplished, in the most admirable way. Habitually we started from camp at the earliest break of dawn and usually reached camp soon after noon. The marches varied from ten to fifteen miles a day, though sometimes on extreme flanks it was necessary to make as much as twenty, but the rate of travel was regulated by the wagons; and, considering the nature of the roads, fifteen miles per day was deemed the limit.

The pontoon-trains were in like manner distributed in about equal proportions to the four corps, giving each a section of about nine hundred feet. The pontoons were of the skeleton pattern, with cotton-canvas covers, each boat, with its proportion of balks and chesses, constituting a load for one wagon. By uniting two such sections together, we could make a bridge of eighteen hundred feet, enough for any river we had to traverse; but habitually the leading brigade would, out of the abundant timber, improvise a bridge before the pontoon-train could come up, unless in the cases of rivers of considerable magnitude, such as the Ocmulgee, Oconee, Ogeechee, Savannah, etc.

On the 20th of November I was still with the Fourteenth Corps, near Eatonton Factory, waiting to hear of the Twentieth Corps; and on the 21st we camped near the house of a man named Vann; the next day, about 4 p.m., General Davis had halted his head of column on a wooded ridge, overlooking an extensive slope of cultivated country, about ten miles short of Milledgeville, and was deploying his troops for camp when I got up. There was a high, raw wind blowing, and I asked him why he had chosen so cold and bleak a position. He explained that he had accomplished his full distance for the day and had there an abundance of wood and water.

Thunderbolt Battery looking down the River – Wis – Waud

TURN OVER – sketch on back –

REAR OF
THUNDERBOLT BATTERY

He explained further that his advance-guard was a mile or so ahead; so I rode on, asking him to let his rear division, as it came up, move some distance ahead into the depression or valley beyond. Riding on some distance to the border of a plantation, I turned out of the main road into a cluster of wild-plum bushes, that broke the force of the cold November wind, dismounted, and instructed the staff to pick out the place for our camp.

The afternoon was unusually raw and cold. My orderly was at hand with his invariable saddle-bags, which contained a change of under-clothing, my maps, a flask of whiskey, and bunch of cigars. Taking a drink and lighting a cigar, I walked to a row of Negro-huts close by, entered one and found a soldier or two warming themselves by a wood-fire. I took their place by the fire, intending to wait there till our wagons had got up, and a camp made for the night. I was talking to the old Negro woman, when some one came and explained to me that, if I would come farther down the road, I could find a better place. So I started on foot, and found on the main road a good double-hewed-log house, in one room of which Colonel Poe, Dr. Moore, and others, had started a fire. I sent back orders to the plum-bushes to bring our horses and saddles up to this house, and an orderly to conduct our headquarter wagons to the same place. In looking around the room, I saw a small box, like a candle-box, marked "Howell Cobb," and, on inquiring of a Negro, found that we were at the plantation of General Howell Cobb, of Georgia, one of the leading rebels of the South, then a general in the Southern army, and who had been Secretary of the United States Treasury in Mr. Buchanan's time. Of course, we confiscated his property, and found it rich in corn, beans, pea-nuts, and sorghum-molasses. Extensive fields were all round the house; I sent word back to General Davis to explain whose plantation it was and instructed him to spare nothing. That night huge bonfires consumed the fence-rails, kept our soldiers warm, and the teamsters and men, as well as the slaves, carried off an immense quantity of corn and provisions of all sorts.

In due season the headquarter wagons came up, and we got supper. After supper I sat on a chair astride, with my back to a good fire, musing, and became conscious that an old Negro, with a tallow-candle in his hand, was scanning my face closely. I inquired, "What do you want, old man?" He answered, "Dey say you is Massa Sherman." I answered that such was the case, and inquired what he wanted. He only wanted to look at me and kept muttering, "Dis Nigger can't sleep dis night." I asked him why he trembled so, and he said that he wanted to be sure that we

153

were in fact "Yankees," for on a former occasion some rebel cavalry had put on light-blue over-coats, personating Yankee troops, and many of the Negroes were deceived thereby, himself among the number—had shown them sympathy, and had in consequence been unmercifully beaten therefor. This time he wanted to be certain before committing himself; so I told him to go out on the porch, from which he could see the whole horizon lit up with camp-fires, and he could then judge whether he had ever seen any thing like it before. The old man became convinced that the "Yankees" had come at last, about whom he had been dreaming all his life; and some of the staff-officers gave him a strong drink of whiskey, which set his tongue going. Lieutenant Snelling, who commanded my escort, was a Georgian, and recognized in this old Negro a favorite slave of his uncle, who resided about six miles off; but the old slave did not at first recognize his young mas-ter in our uniform. One of my staff-officers asked him what had become of his young master, George. He did not know, only that he had gone off to the war, and he supposed him killed, as a matter of course. His attention was then drawn to Snelling's face, when he fell on his knees and thanked God that he had found his young master alive and along with the Yankees. Snelling in-quired all about his uncle and the family, asked my permission to go and pay his uncle a visit, which I granted, of course, and the next morning he described to me his visit. The uncle was not cordial, by any means, to find his nephew in the ranks of the host that was desolating the land, and Snelling came back, having exchanged his tired horse for a fresher one out of his uncle's stables, explaining that surely some of the "bummers" would have got the horse had he not.

The next morning, November 23d, we rode into Milledgeville, the capital of the State, whither the Twentieth Corps had preceded us; and during that day the left wing was all united, in and around Milledgeville. From the inhabitants we learned that some of Kilpatrick's cavalry had preceded us by a couple of days and that all of the right wing was at and near Gordon, twelve miles off, at the place where the branch railroad came to Milledgeville from the Macon & Savannah road. The first stage of the journey was, therefore, complete, and absolutely successful.

The people of Milledgeville remained at home, except Governor Brown, the State officers, and Legislature, who had fled, in the utmost disorder and confusion; standing not on the order of their going, but going at once—some by rail, some by carriages, and many on foot. Some of the citizens who remained behind described this flight of the "brave and patriotic" Governor Brown. He had occupied a public building known as the "Governor's Mansion," and had hastily stripped it of carpets, curtains, and furniture of all sorts, which were removed to a train of freight-cars, which carried away these things—even the cabbages and vegetables from his kitchen and cellar—leaving behind muskets, ammunition, and the public archives. On arrival at Milledgeville I occupied the same public mansion and was soon overwhelmed with appeals for protection. General Slocum had previously arrived with the Twentieth Corps, had taken up his quarters at the Milledgeville Hotel, established a good provost-guard, and excellent order was maintained. The most frantic appeals had been made by the Governor and Legislature for help from every quarter, and the people of the State had been called *en masse* to resist and destroy the invaders of their homes and firesides. Even the prisoners and convicts of the penitentiary were released on condition of serving as soldiers, and the cadets were taken from their military college for the same purpose. These constituted a small battalion, under General Harry Wayne, a former officer of the United States Army, and son of the then Justice Wayne of the Supreme Court. But these hastily retreated east across the Oconee River, leaving us a good bridge, which we promptly secured.

At Milledgeville we found newspapers from all the South, and learned the consternation which had filled the Southern mind at our temerity; many charging that we were actually fleeing for our lives and seeking safety at the hands of our fleet on the sea-coast. All demanded that we should be assailed, "front, flank, and rear;" that provisions should be destroyed in advance, so that we would starve; that bridges should be burned, roads obstructed, and no mercy shown us. Judging from the tone of the Southern press of that day, the outside world must have supposed us ruined and lost.

Of course, we were rather amused than alarmed at these threats and made light of the feeble opposition offered to our progress. Some of the officers, in the spirit of mischief, gathered together in the vacant hall of Representatives, elected a Speaker, and constituted themselves the Legislature of the State of Georgia! A proposition was made to repeal the ordinance of secession, which was well debated, and resulted in its repeal by a fair vote! I was not present at these frolics, but heard of them at the time and enjoyed the joke.

Meantime orders were made for the total destruction of the arsenal and its contents and of such public buildings as could be easily converted to hostile uses. But little or no damage was done to private property, and General Slocum, with my approval, spared several mills and many thousands of bales of cotton, taking what he knew to be worthless bonds, that the cotton should not be used for the Confederacy. Meantime the right wing continued its movement along the railroad toward Savannah, tearing up the track and destroying its iron. At the Oconee was met a feeble resistance from Harry Wayne's troops, but soon the pontoon-bridge was laid, and that wing crossed over. Kilpatrick's cavalry was brought into Milledgeville and crossed the Oconee by the bridge near the town; and on the 23d I made the general orders for the next stage of the march as far as Millen. These were, substantially, for the right wing to follow the Savannah Railroad, by roads on its south; the left wing was to move to Sandersville, by Davisboro and Louisville, while the cavalry was ordered by a circuit to the north and to march rapidly for Millen, to rescue our prisoners of war confined there. The distance was about a hundred miles.

On the 24th we renewed the march, and I accompanied the Twentieth Corps, which took the direct road to Sandersville, which we reached simultaneously with the Fourteenth Corps, on the 26th. A brigade of rebel cavalry was deployed before the town and was driven in and through it by our skirmish-line. I myself saw the rebel cavalry apply fire to stacks of fodder standing in the fields at Sandersville and gave orders to burn some unoccupied dwellings close by. On entering the town, I told citizens that, if the enemy attempted to carry out their threat to burn their food, corn, and fodder, in our route, I would most undoubtedly execute to the letter the general orders of devastation made at the outset of the campaign. With this exception, and one or two minor cases near Savannah, the people did not destroy food, for they saw clearly that it would be ruin to themselves.

At Sandersville I halted the left wing until I heard that the right wing was abreast of us on the railroad. During the evening a Negro was brought to me, who had that day been to Tennille station, about six miles south of the town. I inquired of him if there were any Yankees there, and he answered, "Yes." He described in his own way what he had seen. "First, there come along some cavalry-men, and they burned the depot; then come along some infantry-men, and they tore up the track, and burned it;" and just before he left they had "sot fire to the well!"

The next morning, the 27th, I rode down to the station, and found General Corse's division engaged in destroying the railroad and saw the well which my Negro informant had seen "burnt." It was a square pit about twenty-five feet deep, boarded up, with wooden steps leading to the bottom, wherein was a fine copper pump, to lift the water to a tank above. The soldiers had broken up the pump, heaved in the steps and lining, and set fire to the mass of lumber in the bottom of the well, which corroborated the Negro's description.

From this point Blair's Seventeenth Corps took up the work of destroying the railroad, the Fifteenth Corps following another road leading eastward, farther to the south of the railroad. While the left wing was marching toward Louisville, north of the railroad, General Kilpatrick had, with his cavalry division, moved rapidly toward Waynesboro, on the branch railroad leading from Millen to Augusta. He found Wheeler's division of rebel cavalry there, and had considerable skirmishing with it; but, learning that our prisoners had been removed two days before from Millen, he returned to Louisville on the 29th, where he found the left wing. Here he remained a couple of days to rest his horses, and, receiving orders from me to engage Wheeler and give him all the fighting he wanted, he procured from General Slocum the assistance of the infantry division of General Baird, and moved back for Waynesboro on the 2d of December, the remainder of the left wing continuing its march on toward Millen. Near Waynesboro Wheeler was again encountered and driven through the town and beyond Brier Creek, toward Augusta, thus keeping up the delusion that the main army was moving toward Augusta. General Kilpatrick's fighting and movements about Waynesboro and Brier Creek were spirited and produced a good effect by relieving the infantry column and the wagon-trains of all molestation during their march on Millen. Having thus covered that flank, he turned south and followed the movement of the Fourteenth Corps to Buckhead Church, north of Millen and near it.

On the 3d of December I entered Millen with the Seventeenth Corps and there paused one day, to communicate with all parts of the army. General Howard was south of the Ogeechee River, with the Fifteenth Corps, opposite Scarboro. General Slocum was at Buckhead Church, four miles north of Millen, with the Twentieth Corps. The Fourteenth was at Lumpkin's Station, on the Augusta road, about ten miles north of Millen, and the cavalry division was within easy support of this wing. Thus the whole army was in good position and in good condition. We had largely subsisted on the country; our wagons were full of forage and provisions; but, as we approached the sea-coast, the country became more sandy and barren, and food became more scarce; still, with little or no loss, we had traveled two-thirds of our distance, and I concluded to push on for Savannah. At Millen I learned that General Bragg was in Augusta, and that General Wade Hampton had been ordered there from Richmond, to organize a large cavalry force with which to resist our progress.

General Hardee was ahead, between us and Savannah, with McLaw's division, and other irregular troops, that could not, I felt assured, exceed ten thousand men. I caused the fine depot at Millen to be destroyed and other damage done and then resumed the march directly on Savannah, by the four main roads. The Seventeenth Corps followed substantially the railroad, and, along with it on the 5th of December, I reached Ogeechee Church, about fifty miles from Savannah, and found there fresh earthworks, which had been thrown up by McLaw's division; but he must have seen that both his flanks were being turned and prudently retreated to Savannah without a fight. All the columns then pursued leisurely their march toward Savannah, corn and forage becoming more and more scarce, but rice-fields beginning to occur along the Savannah and Ogeechee Rivers, which proved a good substitute, both as food and forage. The weather was fine, the roads good, and every thing seemed to favor us. Never do I recall a more agreeable sensation than the sight of our camps by night, lit up by the fires of fragrant pine-knots. The trains were all in good order, and the men seemed to march their fifteen miles a day as though it were nothing. No enemy opposed us, and we could only occasionally hear the faint reverberation of a gun to our left rear, where we knew that General Kilpatrick was skirmishing with Wheeler's cavalry, which persistently followed him. But the infantry columns had met with no opposition whatsoever. McLaw's division was falling back before us, and we occasionally picked up a few of his men as prisoners, who insisted that we would meet with strong opposition at Savannah.

On the 8th, as I rode along, I found the column turned out of the main road, marching through the fields. Close by, in the corner of a fence, was a group of men standing around a handsome young officer, whose foot had been blown to pieces by a torpedo planted in the road. He was waiting for a surgeon to amputate his leg and told me that he was riding along with the rest of his brigade-staff of the Seventeenth Corps, when a torpedo trodden on by his horse had exploded, killing the horse and literally blowing off all the flesh from one of his legs. I saw the terrible wound, and made full inquiry into the facts. There had been no resistance at that point, nothing to give warning of danger, and the rebels had planted eight-inch shells in the road, with friction-matches to explode them by being trodden on. This was not war, but murder, and it made me very angry. I immediately ordered a lot of rebel prisoners to be brought from the provost-guard, armed with picks and spades, and made them march in close order along the road, so as to explode their own torpedoes, or to discover and dig them up. They begged hard, but I reiterated the order, and could hardly help laughing at their stepping so gingerly along the road, where it was supposed sunken torpedoes might explode at each step, but they found no other torpedoes till near Fort McAllister. That night we reached Pooler's Station, eight miles from Savannah, and during the next two days, December 9th and 10th, the several corps reached the defenses of Savannah—the Fourteenth Corps on the left, touching the river; the Twentieth Corps next; then the Seventeenth; and the Fifteenth on the extreme right; thus completely investing the city. Wishing to reconnoitre the place in person, I rode forward by the Louisville road, into a dense wood of oak, pine, and cypress, left the horses, and walked down to the railroad-track, at a place where there was a side-track, and a cut about four feet deep. From that point the railroad was straight, leading into Savannah, and about eight hundred yards off were a rebel parapet and battery. I could see the cannoneers preparing to fire and cautioned the officers near me to scatter, as we would likely attract a shot. Very soon I saw the white puff of smoke and, watching close, caught sight of the ball as it rose in its flight, and, finding it coming pretty straight, I stepped a short distance to one side, but noticed a Negro very near me in the act of crossing the track at right angles. Some one called to him to look out; but, before the poor fellow understood his danger, the ball (a thirty-two-pound round shot) struck the ground, and rose in its first ricochet, caught the Negro under the right jaw, and literally carried away his head, scattering blood and brains about. A soldier close by spread an overcoat over the body, and we all concluded to get out of that railroad-cut. Meantime, General Mower's division of the Seventeenth Corps had crossed the canal to the right of the Louisville road and had found the line of parapet continuous; so at Savannah we had again run up against the old familiar parapet, with its deep ditches, canals, and bayous, full of water; and it looked as though another siege was inevitable. I accordingly made a camp or bivouac near the Louisville road, about five miles from Savannah, and proceeded to invest the place closely, pushing forward reconnoissances at every available point.

As soon as it was demonstrated that Savannah was well fortified, with a good garrison, commanded by General William J. Hardee, a competent soldier, I saw that the first step was to open communication with our fleet, supposed to be waiting for us with supplies and clothing in Ossabaw Sound.

General Howard had, some nights previously, sent one of his best scouts, Captain Duncan, with two men in a canoe to drift past Fort McAllister and to convey to the fleet a knowledge of our approach. General Kilpatrick's cavalry had also been transferred to the south bank of the Ogeechee, with orders to open communication with the fleet. Leaving orders with General Slocum to press the siege, I instructed General Howard to send a division with all his engineers to King's Bridge, fourteen and a half miles southwest from Savannah, to rebuild it. On the evening of the 12th I rode over myself, and spent the night at Mr. King's house, where I found General Howard, with General Hazen's division of the Fifteenth Corps. His engineers were hard at work on the bridge, which they finished that night, and at sunrise Hazen's division passed over. I gave General Hazen, in person, his orders to march rapidly down the right bank of the Ogeechee and without hesitation to assault and carry Fort McAllister by storm. I knew it to be strong in heavy artillery, as against an approach from the sea, but believed it open and weak to the rear. I explained to General Hazen fully that on his action depended the safety of the whole army and the success of the campaign. Kilpatrick had already felt the fort, and had gone farther down the coast to Kilkenny Bluff or St. Catharine's Sound where, on the same day, he had communication with a vessel belonging to the blockading fleet; but, at the time, I was not aware of this fact and trusted entirely to General Hazen and his division of infantry, the same old division which I had commanded at Shiloh and Vicksburg, in which I felt a special pride and confidence.

Having seen General Hazen fairly off, accompanied by General Howard, I rode with my staff down the left bank of the Ogeechee, ten miles to the rice-plantation of a Mr. Cheeves, where General Howard had established a signal-station to overlook the lower river, and to watch for any vessel of the blockading squadron, which the Negroes reported to be expecting us, because they nightly sent up rockets, and daily dispatched a steamboat up the Ogeechee as near to Fort McAllister as it was safe.

On reaching the rice-mill at Cheeves's, I found a guard and a couple of twenty-pound Parrott guns, of De Gres's battery, which fired an occasional shot toward Fort McAllister, plainly seen over the salt-marsh, about three miles distant. Fort McAllister had the rebel flag flying and occasionally sent a heavy shot back across the marsh to where we were, but otherwise every thing about the place looked as peaceable and quiet as on the Sabbath.

The signal-officer had built a platform on the ridge-pole of the rice-mill. Leaving our horses behind the stacks of rice-straw, we all got on the roof of a shed attached to the mill, wherefrom I could communicate with the signal-officer above and at the same time look out toward Ossabaw

160

Sound and across the Ogeechee River at Fort McAllister. About 2 p.m. we observed signs of commotion in the fort and noticed one or two guns fired inland and some musket-skirmishing in the woods close by.

This betokened the approach of Hazen's division, which had been anxiously expected, and soon thereafter the signal-officer discovered about three miles above the fort a signal-flag, with which he conversed, and found it to belong to General Hazen, who was preparing to assault the fort and wanted to know if I were there. On being assured of this fact and that I expected the fort to be carried before night, I received by signal the assurance of General Hazen that he was making his preparations and would soon attempt the assault. The sun was rapidly declining, and I was dreadfully impatient. At that very moment some one discovered a faint cloud of smoke and an object gliding, as it were, along the horizon above the tops of the sedge toward the sea, which little by little grew till it was pronounced to be the smoke-stack of a steamer coming up the river. "It must be one of our squadron!" Soon the flag of the United States was plainly visible, and our attention was divided between this approaching steamer and the expected assault. When the sun was about an hour high, another signal-message came from General Hazen that he was all ready, and I replied to go ahead, as a friendly steamer was approaching from below. Soon we made out a group of officers on the deck of this vessel, signaling with a flag, "Who are you?" The answer went back promptly, "General Sherman." Then followed the question, "Is Fort McAllister taken?" "Not yet, but it will be in a minute!" Almost at that instant of time, we saw Hazen's troops come out of the dark fringe of woods that encompassed the fort, the lines dressed as on parade, with colors flying, and moving forward with quick, steady pace. Fort McAllister was then all alive, its big guns belching forth dense clouds of smoke, which soon enveloped our assaulting lines. One color went down, but was up in a moment. As the lines advanced, faintly seen in the white sulphurous smoke, there was a pause, a cessation of fire; the smoke cleared away, and the parapets were blue with our men, who fired their muskets in the air and shouted so that we actually heard them, or felt that we did. Fort McAllister was taken, and the good news was instantly sent by the signal-officer to our navy friends on the approaching gunboat, for a point of timber had shut out Fort McAllister from their view, and they had not seen the action at all, but must have heard the cannonading.

During the progress of the assault, our little group on Cheeves's mill hardly breathed; but no sooner did we see our flags on the parapet than I exclaimed, in the language of the poor Negro at Cobb's plantation, "This nigger will have no sleep this night!"

I was resolved to communicate with our fleet that night, which happened to be a beautiful moonlight one. At the wharf belonging to Cheeves's mill was a small skiff, that had been used by our men in fishing or in gathering oysters. I was there in a minute, called for a volunteer crew, when several young officers, Nichols and Merritt among the number, said they were good oarsmen, and volunteered to pull the boat down to Fort McAllister. General Howard asked to accompany me; so we took seats in the stern of the boat, and our crew of officers pulled out with a will. The tide was setting in strong, and they had a hard pull, for, though the distance was but three miles in an air-line, the river was so crooked that the actual distance was fully six miles. On the way down we passed the wreck of a steamer which had been sunk some years before, during a naval attack on Fort McAllister.

Night had fairly set in when we discovered a soldier on the beach. I hailed him and inquired if he knew where General Hazen was. He answered that the general was at the house of the overseer of the McAllister plantation and that he could guide me to it. We accordingly landed, tied our boat to a drift-log, and followed our guide through bushes to a frame-house, standing in a grove of live-oaks, near a row of Negro quarters. General Hazen was there with his staff, in the act of getting supper; he invited us to join them, which we accepted promptly, for we were really very hungry. Of course, I congratulated Hazen most heartily on his brilliant success and praised its execution very highly, as it deserved, and he explained to me more in detail the exact results. The fort was an inclosed work, and its land-front was in the nature of a bastion and curtains, with good parapet, ditch, *fraise*, and *chevaux-de-frise*, made out of the large branches of live-oaks. Luckily, the rebels had left the larger and unwieldy trunks on the ground, which served as a good cover for the skirmish-line, which crept behind these logs, and from them kept the artillerists from loading and firing their guns accurately.

The assault had been made by three parties in line, one from below, one from above the fort, and the third directly in rear, along the capital. All were simultaneous and had to pass a good abatis and line of torpedoes, which actually killed more of the assailants than the heavy guns of the fort, which generally overshot the mark. Hazen's entire loss was reported, killed and wounded, ninety-two. Each party reached the parapet about the same time, and the garrison inside, of

162

about two hundred and fifty men (about fifty of them killed or wounded), were in his power. The commanding officer, Major Anderson, was at that moment a prisoner, and General Hazen invited him in to take supper with us, which he did.

Up to this time General Hazen did not know that a gunboat was in the river below the fort; for it was shut off from sight by a point of timber, and I was determined to board her that night, at whatever risk or cost, as I wanted some news of what was going on in the outer world. Accordngly, after supper, we all walked down to the fort, nearly a mile from the house where we had been, entered Fort McAllister, held by a regiment of Hazen's troops, and the sentinel cautioned us to be very careful, as the ground outside the fort was full of torpedoes. Indeed, while we were there, a torpedo exploded, tearing to pieces a poor fellow who was hunting for a dead comrade. Inside the fort lay the dead as they had fallen, and they could hardly be distinguished from their living comrades, sleeping soundly side by side in the pale moonlight. In the river, close by the fort, was a good yawl tied to a stake, but the tide was high, and it required some time to get it in to the bank; the commanding officer manned the boat with a good crew of his men, and, with General Howard, I entered, and pulled down-stream, regardless of the warnings of all about the torpedoes.

The night was unusually bright, and we expected to find the gunboat within a mile or so; but, after pulling down the river fully three miles and not seeing the gunboat, I began to think she had turned and gone back to the sound; but we kept on, following the bends of the river, and about six miles below McAllister we saw her light and soon were hailed by the vessel at anchor. Pulling alongside, we announced ourselves and were received with great warmth and enthusiasm on deck by half a dozen naval officers. She proved to be the *Dandelion*, a tender of the regular gunboat *Flag*, posted at the mouth of the Ogeechee. All sorts of questions were made and answered, and we learned that Captain Duncan had safely reached the squadron, had communicated the good news of our approach, and they had been expecting us for some days. They explained that Admiral Dahlgren commanded the South-Atlantic Squadron, which was then engaged in blockading the coast from Charleston south, and was on his flagship, *Harvest Moon*, lying in Wassaw Sound; that General J. G. Foster was in command of the Department of the South, with his headquaters at Hilton Head; and that several ships loaded with stores for the army were lying in Tybee Roads and in Port Royal Sound. From these officers I also learned that General Grant was still besieging Petersburg and Richmond and that matters and things generally remained pretty much the same as when we had left Atlanta. All thoughts seemed to have been turned to us in Georgia, cut off from all communication with our friends; and the rebel papers had reported us to be harassed, defeated, starving, and fleeing for safety to the coast. I then asked for pen and paper and wrote several hasty notes to General Foster, Admiral Dahlgren, General Grant, and the Secretary of War, giving in general terms the actual state of affairs, the fact of the capture of Fort McAllister, and of my desire that means should be taken to establish a line of supply from the vessels in port up the Ogeechee to the rear of the army. As a sample, I give one of these notes, addressed to the Secretary of War, intended for publication to relieve the anxiety of our friends at the North generally:

ON BOARD DANDELION, OSSABAW SOUND, *December* 13, 1864—11:50 p.m.

To Hon. E. M. STANTON, *Secretary of War, Washington, D. C.:*

To-day, at 5 p.m., General Hazen's division of the Fifteenth Corps carried Fort McAllister by assault, capturing its entire garrison and stores. This opened to us Ossabaw Sound, and I pushed down to this gunboat to communicate with the fleet. Before opening communication we had completely destroyed all the railroads leading into Savannah, and invested the city. The left of the army is on the Savannah River three miles above the city, and the right on the Ogeechee, at King's Bridge. The army is in splendid order, and equal to any thing. The weather has been fine, and supplies were abundant. Our march was most agreeable, and we were not at all molested by guerrillas.

We reached Savannah three days ago, but, owing to Fort McAllister, could not communicate; but, now that we have McAllister, we can go ahead.

We have already captured two boats on the Savannah River, and prevented their gunboats from coming down.

I estimate the population of Savannah at twenty-five thousand, and the garrison at fifteen thousand. General Hardee commands.

We have not lost a wagon on the trip; but have gathered a large supply of Negroes, mules, horses, etc., and our teams are in far better condition than when we started.

My first duty will be to clear the army of surplus Negroes, mules, and horses. We have utterly destroyed over two hundred miles of rails, and consumed stores and provisions that were essential to Lee's and Hood's armies.

The quick work made with McAllister, the opening of communication with our fleet, and our consequent independence as to supplies, dissipate all their boasted threats to head us off and starve the army.

I regard Savannah as already *gained*. Yours truly,

W. T. SHERMAN, *Major-General*.

By this time the night was well advanced, and the tide was running ebb-strong; so I asked Captain Williamson to tow us up as near Fort McAllister as he would venture for the torpedoes, of which the navy-officers had a wholesome dread. The *Dandelion* steamed up some three or four miles, till the lights of Fort McAllister could be seen, when she anchored, and we pulled to the fort in our own boat. General Howard and I then walked up to the McAllister House, where we found General Hazen and his officers asleep on the floor of one of the rooms. Lying down on the floor, I was soon fast asleep but shortly became conscious that some one in the room was inquiring for me among the sleepers. Calling out, I was told that an officer of General Foster's staff had just arrived from a steamboat anchored below McAllister; that the general was extremely anxious to see me on important business but that he was lame from an old Mexican-War wound and could not possibly come to me. I was extremely weary from the incessant labor of the day and night before, but got up and again walked down the sandy road to McAllister, where I found a boat awaiting us, which carried us some three miles down the river, to the steamer *W. W. Coit*, on board of which we found General Foster. He had just come from Port Royal, expecting to find Admiral Dahlgren in Ossabaw Sound, and, hearing of the capture of Fort McAllister, he had come up to see me. He described fully the condition of affairs with his own command in South Carolina. He had made several serious efforts to effect a lodgment on the railroad which connects Savannah with Charleston near Pocotaligo, but had not succeeded in reaching the railroad itself, though he had a full division of troops, strongly intrenched, near Broad River, within cannon-range of the railroad. He explained, moreover, that there were at Port Royal abundant supplies of bread and provisions, as well as of clothing, designed for our use. We still had in our wagons and in camp abundance of meat, but we needed bread, sugar, and coffee, and it was all-important that a route of supply should at once be opened, for which purpose the aid and assistance of the navy were indispensable. We accordingly steamed down the Ogeechee River to Ossabaw Sound, in hopes to meet Admiral Dahlgren, but he was not there, and we continued on by the inland channel to

Wassaw Sound, where we found the *Harvest Moon* and Admiral Dahlgren. I was not personally acquainted with him at the time, but he was so extremely kind and courteous that I was at once attracted to him. There was nothing in his power, he said, which he would not do to assist us, to make our campaign absolutely successful. He undertook at once to find vessels of light draught to carry our supplies from Port Royal to Cheeves's Mill or to King's Bridge, whence they could be hauled by wagons to our several camps; he offered to return with me to Fort McAllister, to super-intend the removal of the torpedoes, and to relieve me of all the details of this most difficult work. General Foster then concluded to go on to Port Royal, to send back to us six hundred thousand rations, and all the rifled guns of heavy calibre and ammunition on hand with which I thought we could reach the city of Savannah from the positions already secured. Admiral Dahlgren then returned with me in the *Harvest Moon* to Fort McAllister. This consumed all of the 14th of De-cember; and by the 15th I had again reached Cheeves's Mill, where my horse awaited me, and rode on to General Howard's headquarters at Anderson's plantation, on the plank-road, about eight miles back of Savannah. I reached this place about noon and immediately sent orders to my own headquarters on the Louisville road to have them brought over to the plank-road, as a place more central and convenient; gave written notice to Generals Slocum and Howard of all the steps taken and ordered them to get ready to receive the siege-guns, to put them in position to bombard Savannah, and to prepare for the general assault. The country back of Savannah is very low and intersected with innumerable salt-water creeks, swamps, and rice-fields. Fortunately the weather was good and the roads were passable, but, should the winter rains set in, I knew that we would be much embarrassed. Therefore, heavy details of men were at once put to work to prepare a wharf and depot at King's Bridge, and the roads leading thereto were corduroyed in advance. The Ogeechee Canal was also cleared out for use; and boats, such as were common on the river plantations, were collected, in which to float stores from our proposed base on the Ogeechee to the points most convenient to the several camps.

Fort McAllister was captured as described, late in the evening of December 13th, and by the 16th many steamboats had passed up as high as King's Bridge; among them one which General Grant had dispatched with the mails for the army, which had accumulated since our departure from Atlanta. These mails were most welcome to all the officers and soldiers of the army, which had been cut off from friends and the world for two months, and this prompt receipt of letters

166

from home had an excellent effect, making us feel that home was near. By this vessel also came Lieutenant Dunn, aide-de-camp, with the following letter of December 3d, from General Grant, and on the next day Colonel Babcock, United States Engineers, arrived with the letter of December 6th, both of which are in General Grant's own handwriting, and are given entire:

HEADQUARTERS ARMIES OF THE UNITED STATES, }
CITY POINT, VIRGINIA, *December 3, 1864.* }

Major-General W. T. SHERMAN, *commanding Armies near Savannah, Georgia.*

GENERAL: The little information gleaned from the Southern press indicating no great obstacle to your progress, I have directed your mails (which had been previously collected in Baltimore by Colonel Markland, special agent of the Post-Office Department) to be sent as far as the blockading squadron off Savannah, to be forwarded to you as soon as heard from on the coast.

Not liking to rejoice before the victory is assured, I abstain from congratulating you and those under your command, until bottom has been struck. I have never had a fear, however, for the result.

Since you left Atlanta no very great progress has been made here. The enemy has been closely watched, though, and prevented from detaching against you. I think not one man has gone from here, except some twelve or fifteen hundred dismounted cavalry. Bragg has gone from Wilmington. I am trying to take advantage of his absence to get possession of that place. Owing to some preparations Admiral Porter and General Butler are making to blow up Fort Fisher (which, while hoping for the best, I do not believe a particle in), there is a delay in getting this expedition off. I hope they will be ready to start by the 7th, and that Bragg will not have started back by that time.

In this letter I do not intend to give you any thing like directions for future action, but will state a general idea I have, and will get your views after you have established yourself on the sea-coast. With your veteran army I hope to get control of the only two through routes from east to west possessed by the enemy before the fall of Atlanta. The condition will be filled by holding Savannah and Augusta, or by holding any other port to the east of Savannah and Branchville. If Wilmington falls, a force from there can cooperate with you.

Thomas has got back into the defenses of Nashville, with Hood close upon him. Decatur has been abandoned, and so have all the roads, except the main one leading to Chattanooga. Part of this falling back was undoubtedly necessary, and all of it may have been. It did not look so, however, to me. In my opinion, Thomas far outnumbers Hood in infantry. In cavalry Hood has the advantage in *morale* and numbers. I hope yet that Hood will be badly crippled, if not destroyed. The general news you will learn from the papers better than I can give it.

After all becomes quiet, and roads become so bad up here that there is likely to be a week or two when nothing can be done, I will run down the coast to see you. If you desire it, I will ask Mrs. Sherman to go with me.

Yours truly,

U. S. GRANT, *Lieutenant-General.*

HEADQUARTERS ARMIES OF THE UNITED STATES, ⎫
CITY POINT, VIRGINIA, *December,* 6, 1864. ⎭

Major-General W. T. SHERMAN, *commanding Military Division of the Mississippi.*

GENERAL: On reflection since sending my letter by the hands of Lieutenant Dunn, I have concluded that the most important operation toward closing out the rebellion will be to close out Lee and his army.

You have now destroyed the roads of the South so that it will probably take them three months without interruption to reestablish a through line from east to west. In that time I think the job here will be effectually completed.

My idea now is that you establish a base on the sea-coast, fortify and leave in it all your artillery and cavalry, and enough infantry to protect them, and at the same time so threaten the interior that the militia of the South will have to be kept at home. With the balance of your command come here by water with all dispatch. Select yourself the officer to leave in command, but you I want in person. Unless you see objections to this plan which I cannot see, use every vessel going to you for purposes of transportation.

Hood has Thomas close in Nashville. I have said all I can to force him to attack, without giving the positive order until to-day. To-day, however, I could stand it no longer, and gave the order without any reserve. I think the battle will take place to-morrow. The result will probably be known in New York before Colonel Babcock (the bearer of this) will leave it. Colonel Babcock will give you full information of all operations now in progress. Very respectfully your obedient servant,

U. S. GRANT, *Lieutenant-General.*

The contents of these letters gave me great uneasiness, for I had set my heart on the capture of Savannah, which I believed to be practicable, and to be near; for me to embark for Virginia by sea was so complete a change from what I had supposed would be the course of events that I was very much concerned. I supposed, as a matter of course, that a fleet of vessels would soon pour in, ready to convey the army to Virginia, and as General Grant's orders contemplated my leaving the cavalry, trains, and artillery, behind, I judged Fort McAllister to be the best place for the purpose, and sent my chief-engineer, Colonel Poe, to that fort, to reconnoitre the ground, and to prepare it so as to make a fortified camp large enough to accommodate the vast herd of mules and horses that would thus be left behind. And as some time might be required to collect the necessary shipping, which I estimated at little less than a hundred steamers and sailing-vessels, I determined to push operations, in hopes to secure the city of Savannah before the necessary fleet could be available. All these ideas are given in my answer to General Grant's letters:

HEADQUARTERS MILITARY DIVISION OF THE MISSISSIPPI, }
IN THE FIELD, NEAR SAVANNAH, *December* 16, 1864. }

Lieutenant-General U. S. GRANT, *Commander-in-Chief, City Point, Virginia.*

GENERAL: I received, day before yesterday, at the hands of Lieutenant Dunn, your letter of December 3d, and last night, at the hands of Colonel Babcock, that of December 6th. I had previously made you a hasty scrawl from the tugboat *Dandelion*, in Ogeechee River, advising you that the army had reached the sea-coast, destroying all the railroads across the State of Georgia, investing closely the city of Savannah, and had made connection with the fleet.

Since writing that note, I have in person met and conferred with General Foster and Admiral Dahlgren, and made all the arrangements which were deemed essential for reducing the city of Savannah to our possession. But, since the receipt of yours of the 6th, I have initiated measures looking principally to coming to you with fifty or sixty thousand infantry, and incidentally to capture Savannah, if time will allow.

At the time we carried Fort McAllister by assault so handsomely, with its twenty-two guns and entire garrison, I was hardly aware of its importance; but, since passing down the river with General Foster and up with Admiral Dahlgren, I realize how admirably adapted are Ossabaw Sound and Ogeechee River to supply an army operating against Savannah. Sea-going vessels can easily come to King's Bridge, a point on Ogeechee River, fourteen and a half miles due west of Savannah, from which point we have roads leading to all our camps. The country is low and sandy, and cut up with marshes, which in wet weather will be very bad, but we have been so favored with weather that they are all now comparatively good, and heavy details are constantly employed in double-corduroying the marshes, so that

I have no fears even of bad weather. Fortunately, also, by liberal and judicious foraging, we reached the sea-coast abundantly supplied with forage and provisions, needing nothing on arrival except bread. Of this we started from Atlanta, with from eight to twenty days' supply per corps, and some of the troops only had one day's issue of bread during the trip of thirty days; yet they did not want, for sweet-potatoes were very abundant, as well as corn-meal, and our soldiers took to them naturally. We started with about five thousand head of cattle, and arrived with over ten thousand, of course consuming mostly turkeys, chickens, sheep, hogs, and the cattle of the country. As to our mules and horses, we left Atlanta with about twenty-five hundred wagons, many of which were drawn by mules which had not recovered from the Chattanooga starvation, all of which were replaced, the poor mules shot, and our transportation is now in superb condition. I have no doubt the State of Georgia has lost, by our operations, fifteen thousand first-rate mules. As to horses, Kilpatrick collected all his remounts, and it looks to me, in riding along our columns, as though every officer had three or four led horses, and each regiment seems to be followed by at least fifty Negroes and foot-sore soldiers, riding on horses and mules. The custom was for each brigade to send out daily a foraging-party of about fifty men, on foot, who invariably returned mounted, with several wagons loaded with poultry, potatoes, etc., and as the army is composed of about forty brigades, you can estimate approximately the number of horses collected. Great numbers of these were shot by my order, because of the disorganizing effect on our infantry of having too many idlers mounted. General Easton is now engaged in collecting statistics on this subject, but I know the Government will never receive full accounts of our captures, although the result aimed at was fully attained, viz., to deprive our enemy of them. All these animals I will have sent to Port Royal, or collected behind Fort McAllister, to be used by General Saxton in his farming operations, or by the Quartermaster's Department, after they are systematically accounted for. While General Easton is collecting transportation for my troops to James River, I will throw to Port Royal Island all our means of transportation I can, and collect the rest near Fort McAllister, covered by the Ogeechee River and intrenchments to be erected, and for which Captain Poe, my chief-engineer, is now reconnoitring the ground, but in the mean time will act as I have begun, as though the city of Savannah were my objective: namely, the troops will continue to invest Savannah closely, making attacks and feints wherever we have fair ground to stand upon, and I will place some thirty-pound Parrotts, which I have got from General Foster, in position, near enough to reach the centre of the city, and then will demand its surrender. If General Hardee is alarmed, or fears starvation, he may surrender; otherwise I will bombard the city, but not risk the lives of our men by assaults across the narrow causeways, by which alone I can now reach it.

If I had time, Savannah, with all its dependent fortifications, would surely fall into our possession, for we hold all its avenues of supply.

The enemy has made two desperate efforts to get boats from above to the city, in both of which he has been foiled — General Slocum (whose left flank rests on the river) capturing and burning the first boat, and in the second instance driving back two gunboats and capturing the steamer *Resolute*, with seven naval officers and a crew of twenty-five seamen. General Slocum occupies Argyle Island and the upper end of Hutchinson Island, and has a brigade on the South Carolina shore opposite, and is very urgent to pass one of his corps over to that shore. But, in view of the change of plan made necessary by your order of the 6th, I will maintain things *in statu quo* till I have got all my transportation to the rear and out of the way, and until I have sea-transportation for the troops you require at James River, which I will accompany and command in person. Of course, I will leave Kilpatrick, with his cavalry (say five thousand three hundred), and, it may be, a division of the Fifteenth Corps; but, before determining on this, I must see General Foster, and may arrange to shift his force (now over above the Charleston Railroad, at the head of Broad River) to the Ogeechee, where, in cooperation with Kilpatrick's cavalry, he can better threaten the State of Georgia than from the direction of Port Royal. Besides, I would much prefer not to detach from my regular corps any of its veteran divisions, and would even prefer that other less valuable troops should be sent to reenforce Foster from some other quarter. My four corps, full of experience and full of ardor, coming to you *en masse*, equal to sixty thousand fighting-men, will be a reenforcement that Lee cannot disregard. Indeed, with my present command, I had expected, after reducing Savannah, instantly to march to Columbia, South Carolina; thence to Raleigh, and thence to report to you. But this would consume, it may be, six weeks' time after the fall of Savannah; whereas, by sea, I can probably reach you with my men and arms before the middle of January.

I myself am somewhat astonished at the attitude of things in Tennessee. I purposely delayed at Kingston until General Thomas assured me that he was all ready, and my last dispatch from him of the 12th of November was full of confidence, in which he promised me that he would ruin Hood if he dared to advance from Florence, urging me to go ahead, and give myself no concern about Hood's army in Tennessee.

Why he did not turn on him at Franklin, after checking and discomfiting him, surpasses my understanding. Indeed, I do not approve of his evacuating Decatur, but think he should have assumed the offensive against Hood from Pulaski, in the direction of Waynesburg. I know full well that General Thomas is slow in mind and in action; but he is judicious and brave, and the troops feel great confidence in him. I still hope he will outmanœuvre and destroy Hood.

As to matters in the Southeast, I think Hardee, in Savannah, has good artillerists, some five or six thousand good infantry, and, it may be, a mongrel mass of eight to ten thousand militia. In all our marching through Georgia, he has not forced us to use any thing but a skirmish-line, though at several points he had erected fortifications and tried to alarm us by bombastic threats. In Savannah he has taken refuge in a line constructed behind swamps and overflowed rice-fields, extending from a point on the Savannah River about three miles above the city, around by a branch of the Little Ogeechee, which stream is impassable from its salt-marshes and boggy swamps, crossed only by narrow causeways or common corduroy-roads.

There must be twenty-five thousand citizens, men, women, and children, in Savannah, that must also be fed, and how he is to feed them beyond a few days I cannot imagine. I know that his requisitions for corn on the interior counties were not filled, and we are in possession of the rice-fields and mills, which could alone be of service to him in this neighborhood. He can draw nothing from South Carolina, save from a small corner down in the southeast, and that by a disused wagon-road. I could easily get possession of this, but hardly deem it worth the risk of making a detachment, which would be in danger by its isolation from the main army. Our whole army is in fine condition as to health, and the weather is splendid. For that reason alone I feel a personal dislike to turning northward. I will keep Lieutenant Dunn here until I know the result of my demand for the surrender of Savannah, but, whether successful or not, shall not delay my execution of your order of the 6th, which will depend alone upon the time it will require to obtain transportation by sea.

I am, with respect, etc., your obedient servant,

W. T. SHERMAN, *Major-General United States Army.*

Near Savannah, Georgia
December 16th, 1864

Dearest Ellen,

I have no doubt you have heard of my safe arrival on the coast. The fact is I never doubted the fact, but these southern Blatherskites have been bragging of all manner of things but have done nothing. We came right along living on turkeys, chickens, pigs, etc., bringing along our wagons loaded as we started with bread, etc. I suppose Jeff Davis will now have to feed the people of Georgia instead of collecting provisions of them

172

to feed his armies. We have destroyed nearly 200 miles of railroad and are not yet done. As I approached Savannah I found every river and outlet fortified. The Ogeechee River emptying into Ossabaw Sound was best adapted to our use, but it was guarded by Fort McAllister which has defied the navy for two years. I ordered Howard to carry it with one division. The detail fell on the Second Division of the Fifteenth Corps, and it was the handsomest thing I have seen in this war. The division is the same I commanded at Shiloh in which Buckland, Hildebrand, Cockerill and others were. And Cockerill's regiment was about the first to reach the interior and is now its garrison. But Cockerill is not in service now. As soon as we got the fort I pulled down the bay and opened communication. General Foster and Admiral Dahlgren received me, manned the yard [arm]s and cheered, the highest honor at sea. They had become really nervous as to our safety and were delighted at all I told them of our easy success. I can now starve out Savannah unless events call my army to Virginia. I would prefer to march through Columbia and Raleigh, but the time would be too long, and we may go by sea. I have letters from Grant of the 3rd and 6th. I never saw a more confident army. The soldiers think I know everything and that they can do anything. The strength of Savannah lies in its swamps, which can only be crossed by narrow causeways, all of which are swept by heavy artillery. I came near being hit the first day in approaching too near to reconnoiter. A Negro's head was shot off close by me. The weather is and has been all we could have asked. It is now warm and pleasant, and the live oaks are sublime, Japonicas in blossom in the open air, and the orange is but slightly touched by the frost. I expect rain soon and have heavy details at work corduroying the roads in anticipation of such an event. I have some heavy guns coming from Port Royal and as soon as they come I shall demand the surrender of Savannah, but will not assault, as a few days will starve out its garrison, about 15,000, and its people 25,000. I do not apprehend any army to attempt to relieve Savannah except Lee's, and if he gives up Richmond it will be the best piece of strategy ever made, to make him let go there. We have lived sumptuously—turkeys, chickens and sweet potatoes all the way, but the poor women and children will starve. All I could tell them was if Jeff Davis expects to found an empire on the ruins of the South, he ought to afford to feed the people. Charley promises to write fully. Dayton says he wrote yesterday and the newspaper and mischief mongers will give you gorgeous details of our march across Georgia. It was just thirty days from Atlanta till I was sitting with the admiral on a sea steamer at sea. Grant's letter of the 3rd proposed to bring you down to see me, but his of the 6th looked to my coming to James River. Await events and trust to fortune. I'll turn up where and when you least expect me. I should like to hear how you all are but suppose of course you are at South Bend. Write me care of Adjutant General, Washington, D.C. Love to all.

Yours ever,

W. T. Sherman

Having concluded all needful preparations, I rode from my headquarters, on the plank-road, over to General Slocum's headquarters, on the Macon road, and thence dispatched (by flag of truce) into Savannah, by the hands of Colonel Ewing, inspector-general, a demand for the surrender of the place. The following letters give the result. General Hardee refused to surrender, and I then resolved to make the attempt to break his line of defense at several places, trusting that some one would succeed.

HEADQUARTERS MILITARY DIVISION OF THE MISSISSIPPI,
IN THE FIELD, SAVANNAH, GEORGIA, *December* 17, 1864.

General WILLIAM J. HARDEE, *commanding Confederate Forces in Savannah.*

GENERAL: You have doubtless observed, from your station at Rosedew, that sea-going vessels now come through Ossabaw Sound and up the Ogeechee to the rear of my army, giving me abundant supplies of all kinds, and more especially heavy ordnance necessary for the reduction of Savannah. I have already received guns that can cast heavy and destructive shot as far as the heart of your city; also, I have for some days held and controlled every avenue by which the people and garrison of Savannah can be supplied, and I am therefore justified in demanding the surrender of the city of Savannah, and its dependent forts, and shall wait a reasonable time for your answer, before opening with heavy ordnance. Should you entertain the proposition, I am prepared to grant liberal terms to the inhabitants and garrison; but should I be forced to resort to assault, or the slower and surer process of starvation, I shall then feel justified in resorting to the harshest measures, and shall make little effort to restrain my army—burning to avenge the national wrong which they attach to Savannah and other large cities which have been so prominent in dragging our country into civil war. I inclose you a copy of General Hood's demand for the surrender of the town of Resaca, to be used by you for what it is worth.

I have the honor to be your obedient servant,

W. T. SHERMAN, *Major-General.*

HEADQUARTERS DEPARTMENT SOUTH CAROLINA, GEORGIA, AND FLORIDA,
SAVANNAH, GEORGIA, *December* 17, 1864.

Major-General W. T. SHERMAN, *commanding Federal Forces near Savannah, Georgia.*

GENERAL: I have to acknowledge the receipt of a communication from you of this date, in which you demand "the surrender of Savannah and its dependent forts," on the ground that you "have received guns that can cast heavy and destructive shot into the heart of the city," and for the further reason that you "have, for some days, held and controlled every avenue by which the people and garrison can be supplied." You add that, should you be "forced to resort to assault, or to the slower and surer process of starvation, you will then feel justified in resorting to the harshest measures, and will make little effort to restrain your army," etc., etc. The position of your forces (a half-mile beyond the outer line for the land-defense of Savannah) is, at the nearest point, at least four miles from the heart of the city. That and the interior line are both intact.

Your statement that you have, for some days, held and controlled every avenue by which the people and garrison can be supplied, is incorrect. I am in free and constant communication with my department.

Your demand for the surrender of Savannah and its dependent forts is refused.

With respect to the threats conveyed in the closing paragraphs of your letter (of what may be expected in case your demand is not complied with), I have to say that I have hitherto conducted the military operations intrusted to my direction in strict accordance with the rules of civilized warfare, and I should deeply regret the adoption of any course by you that may force me to deviate from them in future. I have the honor to be, very respectfully, your obedient servant,

W. J. Hardee, *Lieutenant-General.*

Headquarters Military Division of the Mississippi, }
in the Field, near Savannah, Georgia, *December* 18, 1864—8 p.m. }

Lieutenant-General U. S. Grant, *City Point, Virginia.*

General: I wrote you at length (by Colonel Babcock) on the 16th instant. As I therein explained my purpose, yesterday I made a demand on General Hardee for the surrender of the city of Savannah, and to-day received his answer—refusing; copies of both letters are herewith inclosed. You will notice that I claim that my lines are within easy cannon-range of the heart of Savannah; but General Hardee asserts that we are four and a half miles distant. But I myself have been to the intersection of the Charleston and Georgia Central Railroads, and the three-mile post is but a few yards beyond, within the line of our pickets. The enemy has no pickets outside of his fortified line (which is a full quarter of a mile within the three-mile post), and I have the evidence of Mr. R. R. Cuyler, President of the Georgia Central Railroad (who was a prisoner in our hands), that the mile-posts are measured from the Exchange, which is but two squares back from the river. By to-morrow morning I will have six thirty-pound Parrotts in position, and General Hardee will learn whether I am right or not. From the left of our line, which is on the Savannah River, the spires can be plainly seen; but the country is so densely wooded with pine and live-oak, and lies so flat, that we can see nothing from any other portion of our lines. General Slocum feels confident that he can make a successful assault at one or two points in front of General Davis's (Fourteenth) corps. All of General Howard's troops (the right wing) lie behind the Little Ogeechee, and I doubt if it can be passed by troops in the face of an enemy. Still, we can make strong feints, and if I can get a sufficient number of boats, I shall make a cooperative demonstration up Vernon River or Wassaw Sound. I should like very much indeed to take Savannah before coming to you; but, as I wrote to you before, I will do nothing rash or hasty, and will embark for the James River as soon as General Easton (who is gone to Port Royal for that purpose) reports to me that he has an approximate number of vessels for the transportation of the contemplated force. I fear even this will cost more delay than you anticipate, for already the movement of our transports and the gunboats has required more time than I had expected. We have had dense fogs; there are more mud-banks in the Ogeechee than were reported, and there are no pilots whatever. Admiral Dahlgren promised to have the channel buoyed and staked, but it is not done yet. We find only six feet of water up to King's Bridge at low tide, about ten feet up to the rice-mill, and sixteen to Fort McAllister. All these points may be used by us, and we have a good, strong bridge across Ogeechee at King's, by which our wagons can go to Fort McAllister, to which point I am sending all wagons not absolutely necessary for daily use, the Negroes, prisoners of war, sick, etc., *en route* for Port Royal. In relation to Savannah, you will remark that General Hardee refers to his still being in communication with his department. This language he thought would deceive me; but I am confirmed in the belief that the route to which he refers (the Union Plank-road on the South Carolina shore) is inadequate to feed his army and the people of Savannah, and General Foster assures me that he has his force on that very road, near the head of Broad River, so that cars no longer run between Charleston and Savannah. We hold this end of the Charleston Railroad, and have destroyed it from the three-mile post back to the bridge (about twelve miles). In anticipation of leaving this country, I am continuing the destruction of their railroads, and at this moment have two divisions and the cavalry at work breaking up the Gulf Railroad from the Ogeechee to the Altamaha; so that, even if I do not take Savannah, I will leave it in a bad way. But I still hope that events will give me time to take Savannah, even if I have to assault with some loss. I am satisfied that, unless we take it, the gunboats never will, for they can make no impression upon the batteries which guard every approach from the sea. I have a faint belief that, when Colonel Babcock reaches

you, you will delay operations long enough to enable me to succeed here. With Savannah in our possession, at some future time if not now, we can punish South Carolina as she deserves, and as thousands of the people in Georgia hoped we would do. I do sincerely believe that the whole United States, North and South, would rejoice to have this army turned loose on South Carolina, to devastate that State in the manner we have done in Georgia, and it would have a direct and immediate bearing on your campaign in Virginia.

I have the honor to be your obedient servant,

W. T. Sherman, *Major-General United States Army.*

On the 18th of December, at my camp by the side of the plank-road, eight miles back of Savannah, I received General Hardee's letter declining to surrender, when nothing remained but to assault. The ground was difficult, and, as all former assaults had proved so bloody, I concluded to make one more effort to completely surround Savannah on all sides, so as further to excite Hardee's fears, and, in case of success, to capture the whole of his army. We had already completely invested the place on the north, west, and south, but there remained to the enemy on the east the use of the old dike or plank-road leading into South Carolina, and I knew that Hardee would have a pontoon-bridge across the river. On examining my maps, I thought that the division of John P. Hatch, belonging to General Foster's command, might be moved from its then position at Broad River, by water, down to Bluffton, from which it could reach this plank-road, fortify and hold it—at some risk, of course, because Hardee could avail himself of his central position to fall on this detachment with his whole army. I did not want to make a mistake like "Ball's Bluff" at that period of the war; so, taking one or two of my personal staff, I rode back to King's Bridge, leaving with Generals Howard and Slocum orders to make all possible preparations, but not to attack, during my two or three days' absence; and there I took a boat for Wassaw Sound, whence Admiral Dahlgren conveyed me in his own boat, the *Harvest Moon*, to Hilton Head, where I represented the matter to General Foster, and he promptly agreed to give his personal attention to it. During the night of the 20th we started back, the wind blowing strong, Admiral Dahlgren ordered the pilot of the *Harvest Moon* to run into Tybee and to work his way through to Wassaw Sound and the Ogeechee River by the Romney Marshes. We were caught by a low tide and stuck in the mud. After laboring some time, the admiral ordered out his barge; in it we pulled through this intricate and shallow channel, and toward evening of December 21st we discovered, coming

177

toward us, a tug, called the *Red Legs*, with a staff-officer on board, bearing letters from Colonel Dayton to myself and the admiral, reporting that the city of Savannah had been found evacuated on the morning of December 21st and was then in our possession. General Hardee had crossed the Savannah River by a pontoon-bridge, carrying off his men and light artillery, blowing up his iron-clads and navy-yard, but leaving for us all the heavy guns, stores, cotton, railway-cars, steamboats, and an immense amount of public and private property. Admiral Dahlgren concluded to go toward a vessel of his blockading fleet, which lay at anchor near Beaulieu, and I transferred to the *Red Legs* and hastened up the Ogeechee River to King's Bridge, whence I rode to my camp that same night. I there learned that, early on the morning of December 21st, the skirmishers had detected the absence of the enemy, and had occupied his lines simultaneously along their whole extent.

Generals Slocum and Howard moved their headquarters at once into the city, leaving the bulk of their troops in camps outside. On the morning of December 22d I followed with my own headquarters and rode down Bull Street to the custom-house, from the roof of which we had an extensive view over the city, the river, and the vast extent of marsh and rice-fields on the South Carolina side. The navy-yard and the wreck of the iron-clad ram *Savannah* were still smouldering, but all else looked quiet enough. Turning back, we rode to the Pulaski Hotel, which I had known in years long gone and found it kept by a Vermont man with a lame leg, and I inquired about the capacity of his hotel for headquarters. He was very anxious to have us for boarders, but I soon explained to him that we had a full mess equipment along, and that we were not in the habit of paying board; that one wing of the building would suffice for our use, while I would allow him to keep an hotel for the accommodation of officers and gentlemen in the remainder. I then dispatched an officer to look around for a livery-stable that could accommodate our horses, and, while waiting there, an English gentleman, Mr. Charles Green, came and said that he had a fine house completely furnished, for which he had no use, and offered it as headquarters. He explained, moreover, that General Howard had informed him, the day before, that I would want his house for headquarters. At first I felt strongly disinclined to make use of any private dwelling, lest complaints should arise of damage and loss of furniture, and so expressed myself to Mr. Green; but, after riding about the city, and finding his house so spacious, so convenient, with large yard and stabling, I accepted his offer, and occupied that house during our stay in Savannah. He only reserved for himself the use of a couple of rooms above the dining-room, and we had all else, and a most excellent house it was in all respects.

I was disappointed that Hardee had escaped with his army, but on the whole we had reason to be content with the substantial fruits of victory. The Savannah River was found to be badly obstructed by torpedoes, and by log piers stretched across the channel below the city, which piers were filled with the cobble stones that formerly paved the streets. Admiral Dahlgren was extremely active, visited me repeatedly in the city, while his fleet still watched Charleston, and all the avenues, for the blockade-runners that infested the coast, which were notoriously owned and managed by Englishmen, who used the island of Nassau as a sort of entrepot. One of these small blockade-runners came into Savannah after we were in full possession, and the master did not discover his mistake till he came ashore to visit the custom-house. Of course his vessel fell a prize to the navy. A heavy force was at once set to work to remove the torpedoes and obstructions in the main channel of the river, and, from that time forth, Savannah became the great depot of supply for the troops operating in that quarter.

I only regarded the march from Atlanta to Savannah as a "shift of base," as the transfer of a strong army, which had no opponent, and had finished its then work, from the interior to a point on the sea-coast, from which it could achieve other important results. I considered this march as a means to an end, and not as an essential act of war. Still, then, as now, the march to the sea was generally regarded as something extraordinary, something anomalous, something out of the usual order of events; whereas, in fact, I simply moved from Atlanta to Savannah, as one step in the direction of Richmond, a movement that had to be met and defeated, or the war was necessarily at an end. Were I to express my measure of the relative importance of the march to the sea, and of that from Savannah northward, I would place the former at one, and the latter at ten, or the maximum:

The property captured consisted of horses and mules by the thousand, and of quantities of subsistence stores that aggregate very large, but may be measured with sufficient accuracy by assuming that sixty-five thousand men obtained abundant food for about forty days, and thirty-five thousand animals were fed for a like period, so as to reach Savannah in splendid flesh and condition.

SAVANNAH

THE city of Savannah was an old place and usually accounted a handsome one. Its houses were of brick or frame, with large yards, ornamented with shrubbery and flowers; its streets perfectly regular, crossing each other at right angles; and at many of the intersections were small inclosures in the nature of parks. These streets and parks were lined with the handsomest shade-trees of which I have knowledge, the willow-leaf live-oak, evergreens of exquisite beauty; and these certainly entitled Savannah to its reputation as a handsome town more than the houses, which, though comfortable, would hardly make a display on Fifth Avenue or the Boulevard Haussmann of Paris. The city was built on a plateau of sand about forty feet above the level of the sea, abutting against the river, leaving room along its margin for a street of stores and warehouses. The custom-house, court-house, post-office, etc., were on the plateau above. In rear of Savannah was a large park, with a fountain.

Within an hour of taking up my quarters in Mr. Green's house, Mr. A. G. Brown, of Salem, Massachusetts, United States Treasury agent for the Department of the South, made his appearance to claim possession, in the name of the Treasury Department, of all captured cotton, rice, buildings, etc. Having use for these articles ourselves and having fairly earned them, I did not feel inclined to surrender possession and explained to him that the quartermaster and commissary could manage them more to my liking than he; but I agreed, after the proper inventories had been prepared, if there remained any thing for which we had no special use, I would turn it over to him. It was then known that in the warehouses were stored at least twenty-five thousand bales of

180

cotton, and in the forts one hundred and fifty large, heavy sea-coast guns; although afterward, on a more careful count, there proved to be more than two hundred and fifty sea-coast or siege guns, and thirty-one thousand bales of cotton. At that interview Mr. Brown, who was a shrewd, clever Yankee, told me that a vessel was on the point of starting for Old Point Comfort, and, if she had good weather off Cape Hatteras, would reach Fortress Monroe by Christmas-day, and he suggested that I might make it the occasion of sending a welcome Christmas gift to the President, Mr. Lincoln, who peculiarly enjoyed such pleasantry. I accordingly sat down and wrote on a slip of paper, to be left at the telegraph-office at Fortress Monroe for transmission the following:

SAVANNAH, GEORGIA, *December* 22, 1864.
To His Excellency President LINCOLN, *Washington, D. C.:*

I beg to present you as a Christmas-gift the city of Savannah, with one hundred and fifty heavy guns and plenty of ammunition, also about twenty-five thousand bales of cotton.

W. T. SHERMAN, *Major-General.*

This message actually reached him on Christmas Eve, was extensively published in the newspapers, and made many a household unusually happy on that festive day.

On the 23d of December were made the following general orders for the disposition of the troops in and about Savannah:

HEADQUARTERS MILITARY DIVISION OF THE MISSISSIPPI, ⎱
IN THE FIELD, SAVANNAH, GEORGIA, *December* 23, 1864. ⎰

Savannah, being now in our possession, the river partially cleared out, and measures having been taken to remove all obstructions, will at once be made a grand depot for future operations:

1. The chief-quartermaster, General Easton, will, after giving the necessary orders touching the transports in Ogeechee River and Ossabaw Sound, come in person to Savannah, and take possession of all public buildings, vacant store-rooms, warehouses, etc., that may be now or hereafter needed for any department of the army. No rents will be paid by the Government of the United States during the war, and all buildings must be distributed according to the accustomed rules of the Quartermaster's Department, as though they were public property.

2. The chief commissary of subsistence, Colonel A. Beckwith, will transfer the grand depot of the army to the city of Savannah, secure possession of the needful

buildings and offices, and give the necessary orders, to the end that the army may be supplied abundantly and well.

3. The chief-engineer, Captain Poe, will at once direct which of the enemy's forts are to be retained for our use, and which dismantled and destroyed. The chief ordnance-officer, Captain Baylor, will in like manner take possession of all property pertaining to his department captured from the enemy, and cause the same to be collected and conveyed to points of security; all the heavy coast-guns will be dismounted and carried to Fort Pulaski.

4. The troops, for the present, will be grouped about the city of Savannah, looking to convenience of camps; General Slocum taking from the Savannah River around to the seven-mile post on the canal, and General Howard thence to the sea; General Kilpatrick will hold King's Bridge until Fort McAllister is dismantled, and the troops withdrawn from the south side of the Ogeechee, when he will take post about Anderson's plantation, on the plank-road, and picket all the roads leading from the north and west.

5. General Howard will keep a small guard at Forts Rosedale, Beaulieu, Wimberley, Thunderbolt, and Bonaventura, and he will cause that shore and Skidaway Island to be examined very closely, with a view to finding many and convenient points for the embarkation of troops and wagons on sea-going vessels.

By order of Major-General W. T. Sherman,

L. M. DAYTON, *Aide-de-Camp*.

HEADQUARTERS MILITARY DIVISION OF THE MISSISSIPPI, }
IN THE FIELD, SAVANNAH, GEORGIA, *December* 26, 1864. }

The city of Savannah and surrounding country will be held as a military post, and adapted to future military uses, but, as it contains a population of some twenty thousand people, who must be provided for, and as other citizens may come, it is proper to lay down certain general principles, that all within its military jurisdiction may understand their relative duties and obligations.

1. During war, the military is superior to civil authority, and, where interests clash, the civil must give way; yet, where there is no conflict, every encouragement should be given to well-disposed and peaceful inhabitants to resume their usual pursuits. Families should be disturbed as little as possible in their residences, and tradesmen allowed the free use of their shops, tools, etc.; churches, schools, and all places of amusement and recreation, should be encouraged, and streets and roads made perfectly safe to persons in their pursuits. Passes should not be exacted within the line of outer pickets, but if any person shall abuse these privileges by communicating with the enemy, or doing any act of hostility to the Government of

the United States, he or she will be punished with the utmost rigor of the law. Commerce with the outer world will be resumed to an extent commensurate with the wants of the citizens, governed by the restrictions and rules of the Treasury Department.

2. The chief quartermaster and commissary of the army may give suitable employment to the people, white and black, or transport them to such points as they may choose where employment can be had; and may extend temporary relief in the way of provisions and vacant houses to the worthy and needy, until such time as they can help themselves. They will select first the buildings for the necessary uses of the army; next, a sufficient number of stores, to be turned over to the Treasury agent for trade-stores. All vacant storehouses or dwellings, and all buildings belonging to absent rebels, will be construed and used as belonging to the United States, until such time as their titles can be settled by the courts of the United States.

3. The Mayor and City Council of Savannah will continue to exercise their functions, and will, in concert with the commanding officer of the post and the chief-quartermaster, see that the fire-companies are kept in organization, the streets cleaned and lighted, and keep up a good understanding between the citizens and soldiers. They will ascertain and report to the chief commissary of subsistence, as soon as possible, the names and number of worthy families that need assistance and support. The mayor will forthwith give public notice that the time has come when all must choose their course, viz., remain within our lines, and conduct themselves as good citizens, or depart in peace. He will ascertain the names of all who choose to leave Savannah, and report their names and residence to the chief-quartermaster, that measures may be taken to transport them beyond our lines.

4. Not more than two newspapers will be published in Savannah; their editors and proprietors will be held to the strictest accountability, and will be punished severely, in person and property, for any libelous publication, mischievous matter, premature news, exaggerated statements, or any comments whatever upon the acts of the constituted authorities; they will be held accountable for such articles, even though copied from other papers.

By order of Major-General W. T. Sherman,

L. M. DAYTON, *Aide-de-Camp.*

It was estimated that there were about twenty thousand inhabitants in Savannah, all of whom had participated more or less in the war, and had no special claims to our favor, but I regarded the war as rapidly drawing to a close, and it was becoming a political question as to what was to be done with the people of the South, both white and black, when the war was actually over. I concluded to give them the option to remain or to join their friends in Charleston or Augusta, and so announced in general orders. The mayor, Dr. Arnold, was completely "subjugated," and, after consulting with him, I authorized him to assemble his City Council to take charge generally of the interests of the people; but warned all who remained that they must be strictly subordinate to the military law and to the interests of the General Government. About two hundred persons, mostly the families of men in the Confederate army, prepared to follow the fortunes of their husbands and fathers, and these were sent in a steamboat under a flag of truce, in charge of my aide Captain Audenried, to Charleston harbor, and there delivered to an officer of the Confederate army. But the great bulk of the inhabitants chose to remain in Savannah, generally behaved with propriety, and good social relations at once arose between them and the army. Shortly after our occupation of Savannah, a lady was announced at my headquarters by the orderly or sentinel at the front-door, who was ushered into the parlor, and proved to be the wife of General G. W. Smith, whom I had known about 1850, when Smith was on duty at West Point. She was a native of New London, Connecticut, and very handsome. She began her interview by presenting me a letter from her husband, who then commanded a division of the Georgia militia in the rebel army, which had just quitted Savannah, which letter began, "Dear Sherman: The fortunes of war, etc., compel me to leave my wife in Savannah, and I beg for her your courteous protection," etc., etc. I inquired where she lived and if anybody was troubling her. She said she was boarding with a lady whose husband had, in like manner with her own, gone off with Hardee's army; that a part of the house had been taken for the use of Major-General Ward of Kentucky; that her landlady was approaching her confinement and was nervous at the noise which the younger staff-officers made at night, etc. I explained to her that I could give but little personal attention to such matters and referred her to General Slocum, whose troops occupied the city. I afterward visited her house and saw, personally, that she had no reason to complain. Shortly afterward Mr. Hardee, a merchant of Savannah, came to me and presented a letter from his brother, the general, to the same effect, alleging that his brother was a civilian, had never taken up arms, and asked of me protection for his family, his cotton, etc. To him I gave the general assurance that no harm was designed to any of the people of Savannah who would remain quiet and peaceable, but that I could give him no guarantee as to his cotton, for over it I had no absolute control;

184

and yet still later I received a note from the wife of General A. P. Stewart (who commanded a corps in Hood's army), asking me to come to see her. This I did and found her to be a native of Cincinnati, Ohio, wanting protection, and who was naturally anxious about the fate of her husband, known to be with General Hood, in Tennessee, retreating before General Thomas. I remember that I was able to assure her that he had not been killed or captured, up to that date, and think that I advised her, instead of attempting to go in pursuit of her husband, to go to Cincinnati, to her uncle, Judge Storer, there to await the issue of events.

Before I had reached Savannah and during our stay there the rebel officers and newspapers represented the conduct of the men of our army as simply infamous; that we respected neither age nor sex; that we burned every thing we came across—barns, stables, cotton-gins, and even dwelling-houses; that we ravished the women and killed the men and perpetrated all manner of outrages on the inhabitants. Therefore it struck me as strange that Generals Hardee and Smith should commit their families to our custody and even bespeak our personal care and attention. These officers knew well that these reports were exaggerated in the extreme and yet tacitly assented to these false publications, to arouse the drooping energies of the people of the South.

As the division of Major-General John W. Geary, of the Twentieth Corps, was the first to enter Savannah, that officer was appointed to command the place, or to act as a sort of governor. He very soon established a good police, maintained admirable order, and I doubt if Savannah, either before or since, has had a better government than during our stay. The guard-mountings and parades, as well as the greater reviews, became the daily resorts of the ladies, to hear the music of our excellent bands; schools were opened, and the churches every Sunday were well filled with most devout and respectful congregations; stores were reopened, and markets for provisions, meat, wood, etc., were established, so that each family, regardless of race, color, or opinion, could procure all the necessaries and even luxuries of life, provided they had money. Of course, many families were actually destitute of this, and to these were issued stores from our own stock of supplies. I remember to have given to Dr. Arnold, the mayor, an order for the contents of a large warehouse of rice, which he confided to a committee of gentlemen, who went North to Boston, and soon returned with one or more cargoes of flour, hams, sugar, coffee, etc., for gratuitous distribution, which relieved the most pressing wants until the revival of trade and business enabled the people to provide for themselves.

Dearest Ellen,

This is Christmas Day and I hope truly and really that you and the little ones may enjoy it in the full knowledge that I am all safe after our long march. I am at this moment in an elegant chamber of the house of a gentleman named Green. The house is elegant and splendidly furnished with pictures and statuary. My bed room has a bath and dressing room attached which look out of proportion to my poor baggage. My clothing is good yet and I can even afford a white shirt. It would amuse you to see the Negroes. They flock to me, old and young; they pray and shout and mix up my name with that of Moses and Simon and other scriptural ones as well as "Abham Linkum," the Great Messiah of "Dis Jubilee."

There are many fine families in this city, but when I ask for old and familiar names, it marks the sad havoc of war—the Goodwins, Teffts, Cuylers, Habershams, Laws, etc., etc., all gone or in poverty, and yet the girls remain, bright and haughty and proud as ever. There seems no end but utter annihilation that will satisfy their hate of the "sneaking Yankee" and "ruthless invader." They no longer call my army "cowardly Yanks" but have tried to arouse the sympathy of the civilized world by stories of the cruel barbarities of my army. The next step in the progress will be "For God's sake spare us! We must surrender!" When that end is reached we begin to see daylight, but although I have come right through the heart of Georgia, they talk as defiant as ever. I think Thomas's whipping at Nashville, coupled with my march, will take some conceit out of them.

I have no doubt you hear enough about "Sherman" and are sick of the name, and the interest the public takes in my whereabouts leaves me no subject to write about. Charley and Dayton promise to write details. All I can do is to make hasty scrawls assuring you of my health and eternal affection.

W. T. Sherman

Dearest Ellen,

The Steamer Fulton *arrived at Hilton Head yesterday bringing my mails to December 24th. I got a letter from your father at Washington, Hugh in Kentucky and John Sherman, all alluding to the death of our baby, but I got nothing from you or the girls at school. I also found in the N. Y. Herald of the 22nd a full obituary and notice of funeral ceremonies from which I see you are up at South Bend. I have written you twice to Lancaster and to Minnie at Notre Dame, so you will know that I am safe again for a few days, and the Northern papers seem so full of speculations about me and my army that I suppose you are sick of seeing the name. The last letter I got from you at Kingston made me fear for our baby but I had hoped that the little fellow would weather the ailment, but it seems he too is lost to us, and gone to join Willy. I cannot say that I grieve for him as I did Willy, for he was but a mere ideal, whereas Willy was incorporated with us, and seemed to be designed to perpetuate our memories. But amid the scenes of death and desolation through which I daily pass I cannot but become callous to death. It is so common, so familiar, that it no longer impresses me as of old. You on the contrary, surrounded alone by life and youth, cannot take things so philosophically but are stayed by the religious faith of a better and higher life elsewhere. I should like to have seen the baby of which all spoke so well, but I seem doomed to pass my life away so that even my children will be strangers. I did hope for some rest but all lean on me so. Grant, the President, the army, and even the world now looks to me to strike hard and decisive blows that I cannot draw out quietly as I would and seek rest. After having participated in severing the Confederacy down the Mississippi, I have again cut it in twain and have planned and executed a campaign which judges pronounce will be famous among the grand deeds of the world. I can hardly realize it for really it was easy, but like one who has walked a narrow plank, I look back and wonder if I really did it; but here I am in the proud city of Savannah, with an elegant mansion at my command, surrounded by a confident, brave and victorious army that looks to me as its head. Negroes and whites flock to me and gaze at me as some wonderful being, and letters from great men pour in with words of flattery and praise, but still I do more than ever crave for peace and quiet, and would gladly drop all these and gather you and my little ones in some quiet place where I could be at ease. People here talk as though the war was drawing to a close, but I know better. There remains yet a large class of southern men who will not have peace, and they still have the power to do much mischief. Thomas's success in Tennessee incurs to my advantage, as his operations there are a part of my plan. I know you have written to me, and I shall expect a big handfull by the next New York steamer. It will not be long before I sally forth again on another dangerous and important quixotic venture. Love to all.*

Yours ever,
Sherman

Savannah, Georgia
January 2nd, 1865

Dearest Ellen,

I am about to send a steamer to General Grant with dispatches and propose to send Charley if I can find him, but as usual he is out of the way and cannot be found. I have written you and the children several times and the newspapers keep you well advised of my whereabouts. I am now in a magnificent mansion living like a gentleman, but soon will be off for South Carolina and then look out for breakers. You may count on me being here till the 15th. I have not yet had one word from you since you knew of my having reached the coast and only know of the death of our little boy by the New York papers of December 22nd, but was in a measure prepared for it by your letter received at Kingston. I suppose you feel his loss far more than I do because I never saw him, but all the children seemed to be so attached to him that you may be so grieved at his death you cannot write to me. I knew by the same issue that you are now at South Bend in Mr. Colfax's house. It must be very cold up there. It is really cold here, though the sun shines warm and the trees bear green leaves. Of course, no snow, but ice formed in the gutters and on the ponds. General Barnard got here last night from General Grant with dispatches which I have answered, and the clerks are copying my letters and as soon as finished I will send a flat steamer to Port Royal where a sea steamer will go to City Point and thence this letter will be sent you. I enclose a check for $800. I drew pay for November and December and kept $300 and send you the balance. It is good for you that I keep in the woods where my expenses are small and you get the lion's share of pay. I see that the state of Ohio talks of making me a present of a home, etc. For myself I would accept nothing but for you and the children I would be willing, especially if such a present were accompanied, as in Farragut's place, with bonds enough to give interest to pay taxes on property. I have received from high sources highest praise and yesterday, New Years, was toasted, etc., with allusions to Hannibal, Caesar, etc., etc., but in reply I turned all into a good joke by saying that Hannibal and Caesar were small potatoes as they had never read the New York Herald, *or had a photograph taken. But of course I feel a just pride in the confidence of my army, and the singular friendship of General Grant, who is almost childlike in his love for me. It does seem that time has brought out all my old friends, Grant, Thomas, Sheridan, etc. All sorts of people send me presents, and I hope they don't slight you or the girls. I want little in that way, but I think you can stand a good deal. Thus far success has crowned my boldest conceptions and I am going to try others quite as quixotic. It may be that [in] spite of my fears I may come out all right. Love to all.*

Yours ever,
[W. T. Sherman]

188

NOTE ON BACK—

Dearest Ellen,

I have written several times to you and to the children. Yesterday I got your letter of December 23rd and realize the despair and anguish through which you have passed in the pain and sickness of the little baby I never saw. All spoke of him as so bright and fair that I had hoped he would be spared to us to fill the great void in our hearts left by Willy, but it is otherwise decreed and we must submit. I have seen death in such quantity and is such forms that it no longer startles me, but with you it is different and 'tis well that like the Spaniards you realize the fact that our little baby has passed from the troubles of life to a better existence. I sent Charley off a few days ago to carry to General Grant and to Washington some important dispatches but told him he must not go farther than Washington, as by the time he returns I will be off again on another raid. It is pretty hard on me that I am compelled to make these blows which are necessarily trying to me, but it seems devolved on me and cannot be avoided. If the honors proferred and tendered me from all quarters are of any value they will accrue to you and the children. John writes that I am in everybody's mouth and that even he is known as my brother, and that all the Sherman's are now feted as relatives of me. Surely you and the children will not be overlooked by those who profess to honor me. I do not think that in the several grand epochs of this war, my name will have a prominent part, and not least among them will be the determination I took at Atlanta to destroy that place and march on this city, whilst Thomas, my Lieutenant, should dispose of Hood. The idea, the execution and strategy are all good and will in time be understood. I don't know that you comprehend the magnitude of the thing, but you can see the importance attached to it in England, where the critics stand ready to turn against any American general who makes a mistake or fails in its execution. In my case they had time to commit themselves to the conclusion that if I succeeded I would be a great general, but if I failed I would be set down a fool. My success is already assured so that I will be forced to sustain the title. I am told that were I to go North I would be feted and petted, but as I have no intention of going, you must sustain the honor of the family. I know exactly what amount of merit attaches to my own conduct, and what will survive the clamor of time. The quiet preparation I made before the Atlanta campaign, the rapid movement on Resaca, the crossing the Chattahoochee without loss in the face of a skillful general with a good army, the movement on Jonesboro, whereby Atlanta fell, and the resolution I made to divide my army, with one part to take Savannah and the other to meet Hood in Tennessee, are all clearly mine, and will survive us both in history. I don't know that you can understand the merit of the latter, but it will stand me in years to come and will be more appreciated in Europe than in America. I warrant your father will find parallels in the history of the

Greeks and Persians, but none on our Continent. For his sake I am glad of the success that has attended me, and I know he will feel more pride in my success than you or I do. Oh that Willy were living! How his eyes would brighten and his bosom swell with honest pride if he could hear and understand these things. I may be mistaken, but I don't think Tommy so entirely identifies himself in my fortunes. He is a fine, manly boy, and it may be as he develops he will realize our fondest expectations, but I cannot but think that he takes less interest in me than Willy showed from the hour of his birth. It may be I gave the latter more of my personal attention at the time when the mind began to develop. You will doubtless read all the details of our march and stay in Savannah in the papers whose spies infest our camps [in] spite of all I can do, but I could tell you thousands of little incidents which would more interest you. The women here are, as at Memphis, disposed to usurp my time more from curiosity than business. They had been told of my burning and killing till they expected the veriest monster, but their eyes were opened when Hardee, G. W. Smith and McLaws, the three chief officers of the Rebel army, fled across the Savannah River, consigning their families to my special care. There are some very elegant people here, whom I knew in better days and who do not seem ashamed to call on the "vandal chief." They regard us just as the Romans did the Goths and the parallel is not unjust. Many of my stalwart men with red beards and huge frames look like giants, and it is wonderful how smooth all things move for they all seem to feel implicit faith in me, not because I am strong or bold, but because they think I know everything. It seems impossible for us to go anywhere without being where I have been before. My former life from 1840 to 1846 seems providential and every bit of knowledge thus acquired is returned ten fold. Should it so happen that I should approach Charleston on that very ground where I used to hunt with Tom Poyas and Mr. Quash and ride by moonlight to save day time it would be even more strange than here where I was only a visitor. Colonel Kilburn arrived here from Louisville yesterday and begged me to remember him to you. I continue to receive letters, most flattering, from all my old friends and enclose you two, one from General Hitchcock and one from Professor Mahan. Such men do not flatter and are judges of what they write. [. . .] Tell Minnie and Lizzie that I will write them again before starting out and I will send Tommy some papers that he will value as part of the history of the campaign. My report is nearly done, but will be general, short and uninteresting. I hope you are as comfortable as you expected. I sent you a check for $800 from here and $1100 from Atlanta which you should acknowledge.

Yours,

W. T. Sherman

On the 2d of January, 1865, General J. G. Barnard, United States Engineers, arrived direct from General Grant's headquarters, bearing the following letter, in the general's own handwriting, which, with my answer, is here given:

HEADQUARTERS ARMIES OF THE UNITED STATES, }
CITY POINT, VIRGINIA, *December* 27, 1864. }

Major-General W. T. SHERMAN, *commanding Military Division of the Mississippi.*

GENERAL: Before writing you definite instructions for the next campaign, I wanted to receive your answer to my letter written from Washington. Your confidence in being able to march up and join this army pleases me, and I believe it can be done. The effect of such a campaign will be to disorganize the South, and prevent the organization of new armies from their broken fragments. Hood is now retreating, with his army broken and demoralized. His loss in men has probably not been far from twenty thousand, besides deserters. If time is given, the fragments may be collected together and many of the deserters reassembled. If we can, we should act to prevent this. Your spare army, as it were, moving as proposed, will do it.

In addition to holding Savannah, it looks to me that an intrenched camp ought to be held on the railroad between Savannah and Charleston. Your movement toward Branchville will probably enable Foster to reach this with his own force. This will give us a position in the South from which we can threaten the interior without marching over long, narrow causeways, easily defended, as we have heretofore been compelled to do. Could not such a camp be established about Pocotaligo or Coosawhatchie?

I have thought that, Hood being so completely wiped out for present harm, I might bring A. J. Smith here, with fourteen to fifteen thousand men. With this increase I could hold my lines, and move out with a greater force than Lee has. It would compel Lee to retain all his present force in the defenses of Richmond or abandon them entirely. This latter contingency is probably the only danger to the easy success of your expedition. In the event you should meet Lee's army, you would be compelled to beat it or find the sea-coast. Of course, I shall not let Lee's army escape if I can help it, and will not let it go without following to the best of my ability.

Without waiting further directions, then, you may make your preparations to start on your northern expedition without delay. Break up the railroads in South and North Carolina, and join the armies operating against Richmond as soon as you can. I will leave out all suggestions about the route you should take, knowing that your information, gained daily in the course of events, will be better than any that can be obtained now.

It may not be possible for you to march to the rear of Petersburg; but, failing in this, you could strike either of the sea-coast ports in North Carolina held by us. From there you could take shipping. It would be decidedly preferable, however, if you could march the whole distance.

From the best information I have, you will find no difficulty in supplying your army until you cross the Roanoke. From there here is but a few days' march, and supplies could be collected south of the river to bring you through. I shall establish communication with you there, by steamboat and gunboat. By this means your wants can be partially supplied. I shall hope to hear from you soon, and to hear your plan, and about the time of starting.

Please instruct Foster to hold on to all the property in Savannah, and especially the cotton. Do not turn it over to citizens or Treasury agents, without orders of the War Department.

Very respectfully, your obedient servant,

U. S. Grant, *Lieutenant-General.*

Headquarters Military Division of the Mississippi, }
in the Field, Savannah, Georgia, *January 2, 1865.* }

Lieutenant-General U. S. Grant, *City Point.*

General: I have received, by the hands of General Barnard, your note of 26th and letter of 27th December.

I herewith inclose to you a copy of a *projet* which I have this morning, in strict confidence, discussed with my immediate commanders.

I shall need, however, larger supplies of stores, especially grain. I will inclose to you, with this, letters from General Easton, quartermaster, and Colonel Beckwith, commissary of subsistence, setting forth what will be required, and trust you will forward them to Washington with your sanction, so that the necessary steps may be taken at once to enable me to carry out this plan on time.

I wrote you very fully on the 24th, and have nothing to add. Every thing here is quiet, and if I can get the necessary supplies in our wagons, shall be ready to start at the time indicated in my *projet* (January 15th). But, until those supplies are in hand, I can do nothing; after they are, I shall be ready to move with great rapidity.

I have heard of the affair at Cape Fear. It has turned out as you will remember I expected.

I have furnished General Easton a copy of the dispatch from the Secretary of

War. He will retain possession of all cotton here, and ship it as fast as vessels can be had to New York.

I shall immediately send the Seventeenth Corps over to Port Royal, by boats, to be furnished by Admiral Dahlgren and General Foster (without interfering with General Easton's vessels), to make a lodgment on the railroad at Pocotaligo.

General Barnard will remain with me a few days, and I send this by a staff-officer, who can return on one of the vessels of the supply-fleet. I suppose that, now that General Butler has got through with them, you can spare them to us.

My report of recent operations is nearly ready, and will be sent you in a day or two, as soon as some further subordinate reports come in.

I am, with great respect, very truly, your friend,

W. T. SHERMAN, *Major-General.*

PROJET FOR JANUARY.

1. Right wing to move men and artillery by transports to head of Broad River and Beaufort; reestablish Port Royal Ferry, and mass the wing at or in the neighborhood of Pocotaligo.

Left wing and cavalry to work slowly across the causeway toward Hardeeville, to open a road by which wagons can reach their corps about Broad River; also, by a rapid movement of the left, to secure Sister's Ferry, and Augusta road out to Robertsville.

In the mean time, all guns, shot, shell, cotton, etc., to be moved to a safe place, easy to guard, and provisions and wagons got ready for another *swath*, aiming to have our army in hand about the head of Broad River, say Pocotaligo, Robertsville, and Coosawhatchie, by the 15th January.

2. The whole army to move with loaded wagons by the roads leading in the direction of Columbia, which afford the best chance of forage and provisions. Howard to be at Pocotaligo by the 15th January, and Slocum to be at Robertsville, and Kilpatrick at or near Coosawhatchie about the same date. General Foster's troops to occupy Savannah, and gunboats to protect the rivers as soon as Howard gets Pocotaligo.

W. T. SHERMAN, *Major-General.*

On the 11th of January there arrived at Savannah a revenue-cutter, having on board Simeon Draper, Esq., of New York City, the Hon. E. M. Stanton, Secretary of War, Quartermaster-General Meigs, Adjutant-General Townsend, and a retinue of civilians, who had come down from the North to regulate the civil affairs of Savannah.

I saw a good deal of the secretary socially, during the time of his visit to Savannah. He kept his quarters on the revenue-cutter with Simeon Draper, Esq., which cutter lay at a wharf in the river, but he came very often to my quarters at Mr. Green's house. Though appearing robust and strong, he complained a good deal of internal pains, which he said threatened his life and would compel him soon to quit public office. He professed to have come from Washington purposely for rest and recreation, and he spoke unreservedly of the bickerings and jealousies at the national capital; of the interminable quarrels of the State Governors about their quotas and more particularly of the financial troubles that threatened the very existence of the Government itself. He said that the price of every thing had so risen in comparison with the depreciated money, that there was danger of national bankruptcy, and he appealed to me, as a soldier and patriot, to hurry up matters so as to bring the war to a close.

He left for Port Royal about the 15th of January, and promised to go North without delay, so as to hurry back to me the supplies I had called for, as indispensable for the prosecution of the next stage of the campaign. I was quite impatient to get off myself, for a city-life had become dull and tame, and we were all anxious to get into the pine-woods again, free from the importunities of rebel women asking for protection, and of the civilians from the North who were coming to Savannah for cotton and all sorts of profit.

Savannah, Georgia
January 15th, 1865

Dearest Ellen,

I have all your letters up to the 4th as also yours to Charley which I have read in his absence, so that I am now well advised of all matters. It may be some days yet before I dive again beneath the surface to turn up again in some mysterious place. I have a clear perception of the move, but take it for granted that Lee will not let me walk over the track without making me sustain some loss. Of course, my course will be north. I will feign on Augusta and Charleston, avoid both and make for Columbia, Fayetteville and Newbern, North Carolina. Don't breathe, for the walls have ears and foreknowledge published by some mischievous fool might cost many lives. We have lived long enough for men to thank me for keeping my own counsels, and keeping away from armies those pests of neswpaper men. If I have attained any fame it is pure and unalloyed by the taint of parasitic flattery and the result is to you and the children more agreeable, for it will go to your and their benefit more than all the surface flattery of all the newspaper men of the country. Mr. Stanton has been here and is cured of that Negro nonsense which arises not from a loss of the Negro but a desire to dodge service. Mr. Chase and others have written to me to modify my opinions, but you know I cannot, for if I attempt the part of a hypocrite it would break out at each sentence. I want soldiers made of the best bone and muscle in the land, and won't attempt military feats with doubtful materials. I have said that slavery is dead and the Negro free, and want him treated as free and not hunted and badgered to make a soldier of, when his family is left back on the plantations. I am right and won't change. The papers of the 11th are just in and I see Butler is out. That is another of the incubi of the army. We want and must have professional soldiers, young and vigorous. Mr. Stanton was delighted at my men and the tone which pervades the army. He enjoyed a good story, which is true, told by one of my old Fifteenth Corps men. After we reached the coast we were out of bread, and it took some days for us to get boats up. A foraging party was out and got a boat and pulled down the Ogeechee to Ossabaw and met a steamer coming up. They hailed her and got answer that it was the Nemeha, and had Major-General Foster on board; the soldiers answered "Oh Hell, we've got twenty-seven Major-Generals up at camp. What we want is hard tack." The soldiers manifest to me the most thorough affection and a wonderful confidence. They haven't found out yet where I have not been. Every place we go, they hear I lived there once, and the usual exclamation is, the "old man" must be "omnipresent" as well as "omnipotent." I was telling some officers the other day if events should carry us to Charleston I would have advantage because I know the ground, etc., etc. They laughed heartily at my innocence, for they knew I had been everywhere. But really my long sojourn in this quarter of the world from 1840 to 1846 was and is providential to me.

I have read most of the current discourses about me, those you sent inclusive; but take more interest in the London Spectator, *the same that reviewed my Knoxville campaign. He is surely a critic, for he catches the real points well. The* Times *utterly overstates the cases and the Dublin papers are too fulsome. Our American papers are shallow. They don't look below the surface. I receive letters from all the great men, so full of real respect that I cannot disregard them, yet I dread the elevation to which they have got me. A single mistake or accident, my pile, though well founded, would tumble; but I base my hopes on fair fame on the opinion of my own army and my associates.*

I know nothing as yet of the project to present us a farm or house. I would personally prefer land cleared and improved as property but won't think of it till asked, or I will say nothing if you conduct the whole matter, as I cannot expect ever to have a local habitation. I would rather have such a property settled on the children or entailed on the survivor of the name. For myself individually I should hardly accept. I sent you a check for $1100 from Atlanta and $800 since my arrival here. I can hardly expect any more for two months as I will surely be off in the course of this week, and you will hear of me only

195

through Richmond for two months. You have got used to it now and will not be concerned, though I think the chances of getting killed on this trip about even. If South Carolina lets me pass across without desperate fighting her fame is gone forever. Charley is still absent North, but I look for him hourly. He should not go beyond Washington or be there more than one day. He will have written and telegraphed you. No doubt you will see several persons who have seen me here and the newspapers complete the picture. Savannah would be an agreeable place to me less burdened with the care of armies, women, cotton, Negroes and all the disturbing elements of this war. I would not be surprised if I would involve our government with England. I have taken all the cotton as prize of war, 30,000 bales, equal to thirteen millions of dollars, much of which is claimed by English merchants. I disregard their Consular Certificates on the ground that this cotton has been notoriously employed to buy cartridges and arms and piratical ships, and was collected here for that very purpose. Our own merchants are equally culpable. They buy cotton in advance and take the chance of capture and then [make] claims. I am glad Tommy is now fairly established at school. I will resist his being a priest. Of course I should regret such a choice and ask that no influence be [used?] to produce that result. Let him have a fair manly education, and his own instincts will lead him right. I don't care how strict he may be in religion, but don't want him a priest, but he is too young for even the thought. As to myself, don't distress yourself. I am as good as the average and must take my chances, and exposed as I have been and still am, you may rest assured I have given death a fair study and fear it but little. I fear somewhat your mind will settle into the "Religio Melancholia" which be assured is not of divine inspiration, but rather a morbid state not natural or healthful. [letter breaks off here]

On January 19th, I made the first general orders for the move. It was to me manifest that the soldiers and people of the South entertained an undue fear of our Western men, and, like children, they had invented such ghostlike stories of our prowess in Georgia, that they were scared by their own inventions. Still, this was a power, and I intended to utilize it. Having accomplished all that seemed necessary, on the 21st of January, with my entire headquarters, officers, clerks, orderlies, etc., with wagons and horses, I embarked in a steamer for Beaufort, South Carolina.